The Information Retrieval Series

Series Editor

W. Bruce Croft

Maristella Agosti

Editor

Information Access through Search Engines and Digital Libraries

Foreword by W. Bruce Croft

With 18 Tables and 39 Figures

 Springer

Editor

Maristella Agosti
Department of Information Engineering
University of Padua
Via Gradenigo 6/a
35131 Padova, Italy
E-mail: maristella.agosti@unipd.it

ISBN: 978-3-540-75133-5   e-ISBN: 978-3-540-75134-2

Library of Congress Control Number: 2007937241

ACM Codes: H.3, I.7, J.5

Cover Design: KünkelLopka, Heidelberg

Printed on acid-free paper

9 8 7 6 5 4 3 2 1

springer.com

Foreword

The Information Management Systems group at the University of Padua, led by Maristella Agosti, has been a major contributor to information retrieval and digital libraries for nearly twenty years. This group has produced some of Italy's best-known IR researchers, whose work spans a broad range of topics, as the papers in this book demonstrate. One of the goals of the IR book series is to highlight the work of academic research centers in our field, in order to balance the perception that everyone in IR works for a search engine company. One of the best aspects of our field is that, as academic researchers, we can work with new graduate students and collaborate with companies to ensure that our research has direct impact on systems that people use every day. The Padua group is typical in this respect, and has been involved in a series of collaborations and major European projects over the years. I hope this volume inspires graduate students to pursue research in IR, and I encourage other research groups to contribute their own collections of papers.

Amherst, Massachusetts. July 2007.   *W. Bruce Croft*

Preface

The Information Management Systems (IMS) Research Group was formed in the Department of Information Engineering (formerly Department of Electronics and Computer Science) of the University of Padua, Italy, in 1987 when the department was established. The group activities are concerned with the design, modeling and implementation of advanced information retrieval tools – such as search engines – and digital library systems.

The main aims of the IMS research group are:

- to contribute to the advancement of basic and applied research in the area of the management of digital information in its diverse and multiform materializations, by participating in national and European research projects, together with serving on editorial boards of international journals and program committees of international and European conferences and initiatives,
- to provide a good environment to facilitate the acquisition of knowledge of information management foundations to graduate and undergraduate students, and actively organize workshops and summers schools devoted to the transfer of competence to young researchers and particularly PhD students, and
- to make possible the transfer of results and expertise to industry and public organizations of the region surrounding Padua, but also at the national and European level.

The IMS research on Information Retrieval addresses theoretical methods and experimental approaches for the efficient and effective gathering, indexing, organization and retrieval of all and only the multimedia data that are relevant to users' information needs from large document collections. Specific research efforts have been directed to solve crucial aspects of retrieval of information from the Web and to design and implement effective search engines.

The IMS research on Digital Libraries addresses methods, systems, and tools to build and make available effective and distributed digital library management systems to end users. What makes Digital Libraries different from the Web is the rigorous and sophisticated organisation of heterogeneous multimedia data, and the need to support distributed, fast and easy access to those data.

Through its long-standing tradition in information retrieval, and more recently in digital libraries, the group has gained a strong reputation at the national and European level, and it has good relationships with many outstanding researchers worldwide.

The papers in this book report the original research results built on the past work of the group which open up new directions and new areas of possible fruitful cooperation in the context of new research projects.

In the initial paper, *Information Access using the Guide of User Requirements*, Agosti presents an interpretation of the evolution of events in the information retrieval area. Focusing mainly on the last twenty years, the paper pays particular attention to the system which needs to be envisaged and designed to support the end user in accessing relevant and interesting information. The end user is considered the guide of the researcher, since he prompts the researcher to conceive and invent solutions of real use for the user himself.

Crestani's paper, *From Linking Text to Linking Crimes: Information Retrieval, But Not As You Know It*, proves that information retrieval techniques that have been used for a long time to identify links between textual items for the automatic construction of hypertexts and electronic books are proving of great value in different application areas. Crestani presents an approach to automatic linking of textual items that is used to prioritise criminal suspects in a police investigation. Crimes are linked to each other and to suspects in a conceptual model that closely resembles the one used to design hypertexts. A free-text description of an unsolved crime is compared to previous offence descriptions where the offender is known. By linking the descriptions, inferences about likely suspects can be made. Language Modeling is adapted to produce a Bayesian model which assigns a probability to each suspect. The model presented in this paper could be easily extended to take account of additional crime and suspect linking data, such as geographical location of crimes or suspect social networks. This would enable large networks of investigative information automatically constructed from police archives to be browsed.

Melucci's paper, *Modeling Retrieval and Navigation in Context*, addresses the topic of *context* in information retrieval; in fact current information retrieval systems are designed and implemented to retrieve all and only the documents relevant to the information need expressed by the user without considering the context in which the user is when asking for information. But what is relevant to one user in one place at one time may no longer be relevant to another user, in another place or at another time. This means that an information retrieval system should be context-aware. In practice classical systems, such as search engines, are unaware of such a highly dynamic search environment and contextual features are not captured at indexing-time, nor are they exploited at retrieval-time. Melucci's paper describes a model for navigation and search in context, that is, the navigation and search which adapts the retrieval results according to what the end user does during interaction. As hypertext is the main information retrieval tool for navigating information spaces, so the paper illustrates how the model can be applied when automatic links are built for document collections or electronic books, although the model is more general and can be applied in the future to different domains.

In the following paper, *Two Algorithms for Probabilistic Stemming*, Melucci and Orio face a central topic of information retrieval, that of the *stemming* which is performed to allow words, which are formulated with morphological variants, to group up with each other, indicating a similar meaning. Most stemming algorithms reduce word forms to an approximation of a common morphological root, called "stem", so that a relevant document can be retrieved even if the morphology of their own words is different from the one of the words of a given query. Two probabilistic stemming algorithms are presented and the main conclusion of the reported research is that a stemmer can be built for many European languages without much linguistic knowledge and with simple probabilistic models. This scientific conclusion has been confirmed by various experiments carried out using different standard test collections and it opens up interesting possibilities in a European and international setting where the collections of documents that an information retrieval tool has to manage are most of the time multilingual.

The paper by Di Nunzio, *Automated Text Categorization: The Two-Dimensional Probabilistic Model*, presents the *Two-Dimensional Probabilistic Model (2DPM)*, which is a retrieval model able to represent documents on a two-dimensional space. The model has proved to be a valid visualization tool for understanding the relationships between categories of textual documents, and for helping users to visually audit the classifier and identify suspicious training data. In addition, the model has the advantage of needing neither a reduction of the vocabulary of terms to reduce the complexity of the problem nor smoothing of probabilities to avoid zero probabilities during calculations. The paper shows that it is possible to address the modeling in information retrieval from a probabilistic point of view, using an approach that can be a little obscure to the end user, since it is an approach that operates server-side and makes the system, which is implemented making use of it, like a black box to the user; nevertheless, it can be used as a tool for better presenting the retrieved documents to the final user. The graphical representation of the groups of documents that are retrieved by the system can be further applied to the representation of documents that are given as output to users of information retrieval and digital library systems supporting them with graphical interfaces that give directions and help in the selection of documents of interest from among the many retrieved by the system.

The next paper, *Analysis of Web Link Analysis Algorithms: The Mathematics of Ranking* by Pretto, addresses relevant aspects of the algorithms that have been designed to enhance the performance of Web search engines by exploiting the topological structure of the digraph associated with the Web. Link analysis algorithms are now also used in many other fields, sometimes far removed from that of Web searching. In many of their applications, their *ranking* capabilities are of prime importance; from here the need arises to perform a mathematical analysis of these algorithms from the perspective of the *rank* they induce on the nodes of the digraphs on which they work. Pretto's paper investigates the main theoretical results for the questions that arise when ranking is under investigation and some novel extensions are presented.

In *Digital Annotations: a Formal Model and its Applications* Ferro focuses on the rich and elusive concept of *annotation*. Even though the concept of annotation is familiar to us, it turns out to be particularly elusive when it comes to being explicitly and formally defined, mainly because it is a far more complex and multifaceted concept than one might imagine at a first glance. There are different viewpoints about annotation, which are often considered as separated, and this situation prevents us from exploiting synergies and complementarities among the different approaches, and makes it more difficult to determine what the differences between annotations and other concepts are, and what the advantages or disadvantages of using annotations are, even when they seem so similar to other concepts. The paper discusses different perspectives and presents a formal model that formalizes the main concepts concerning annotations and defines the relationships between annotations and annotated information resources. In addition, this formal model constitutes the necessary tool that can be used to design and implement search algorithms that can make use of annotations to enhance retrieval capabilities from multimedia distributed collections of digital content.

In *Music Indexing and Retrieval for Multimedia Digital Libraries* Orio addresses the topic of multimedia retrieval based on content with a focus on *music information retrieval*. Starting from the consideration that users of multimedia digital libraries have different levels of knowledge and expertise – and this is particularly true for music, where the level of music education may vary remarkably among users, who may range from casual listeners to performers and composers – untrained users may not be able to use bibliographic values or take advantage of metadata when searching for music, the consequence is that the access to music digital libraries should really be content-based. The main idea underlying content-based access and retrieval is that a document can be described by a set of features that are directly computed from its content. This approach is the basis for most of the methodologies for information retrieval, where the content of a textual document is automatically processed and used for indexing and retrieval. Even if multimedia data require specific methodologies for content extraction, the core information retrieval techniques developed for text may be extended to other media. The paper presents a novel methodology based on approximate indexing of music documents. The basic idea is to merge the positive effects of document indexing in terms of efficiency and scalability, with the positive effects of approximate matching in terms of robustness to local mismatches. The methodology has been tested with encouraging results for future developments and applications.

The paper *A Statistical and Graphical Methodology for Comparing Bilingual to Monolingual Cross-Language Information Retrieval* by Crivellari Di Nunzio and Ferro is a collaborative study of cross-lingual *Information Retrieval Systems (IRSs)* and on a deep analysis of performance comparison between systems which perform monolingual tasks, i.e. querying and finding documents in one language, with respect to those which perform bilingual tasks, i.e. querying in one language and finding documents in another language. The study aims at improving the way of comparing bilingual and monolingual retrieval and strives to provide better methods and tools for assessing the performances. Another aspect of the work is that it can help the organizers of an evaluation forum during the topic generation process; in particular, the study of the hardness of a topic can be carried out with the goal of refining those topics which have been misinterpreted by systems. The authors propose a twofold methodology which exploits both thorough statistical analyses and graphical tools: the former will provide *MultiLingual Information Access (MLIA)* researchers with quantitative and more sophisticated analysis techniques, while the latter will allow for a more qualitative comparison and an easier presentation of the results. Concrete examples about how the proposed methodology can be applied by studying the monolingual and bilingual tasks of the *Cross-Language Evaluation Forum (CLEF)* 2005 and 2006 campaigns are provided.

As the reader can appreciate in reading the book, all the papers contribute towards the development of the area of *information access* to digital contents and give insights to future possible enhancements of information management systems.

I would like to thank Alexander Cormack, whose revisions have undoubtedly added to the quality of the work presented in this volume.

Finally, I would like to acknowledge the faculty and students that over the years have cooperated with the IMS group and that have collaborated in its achievements.

Padua, August 2007   *Maristella Agosti*

Contents

Contributing Authors

Maristella Agosti is full professor in computer science, with a main focus on databases, digital libraries and information retrieval, at the Faculty of Humanities and at the Department of Information Engineering of the University of Padua, Italy. She is one of the founding members and the coordinator of the Information Management Systems research group of the department. She coordinates a number of national and international research projects, and she has been the organizer of national and international conferences. She is member of the Editorial Board of Information Processing & Management (Pergamon Press) and of the International Journal on Digital Libraries (Springer-Verlag). She has been active in research since 1975.

Fabio Crestani is a full professor at the Faculty of Informatics of the University of Lugano (Università della Svizzera Italiana) since 2007. Previously he was a Professor at the University of Strathclyde in Glasgow, a research fellow at the International Computer Science Institute in Berkeley and at the University of Glasgow. During 1992-97 he was Assistant Professor at the University of Padua, Italy, and was one of the initial members of the Information Management Systems research group. Crestani has been active in research in Information Retrieval, Text Mining, and Digital Libraries since 1990. His current main research interests lie in the modeling of the uncertainty, imprecision and vagueness of information access in unstructured or semi-structured documents.

Franco Crivellari is associate professor in computer science, with a main focus on databases, object oriented languages, and information retrieval, at the Faculty of Psychology and at the Department of Information Engineering of the University of Padua, Italy. He is member and one of the founding members of the Information Management Systems research group of the department. He has been active in research since 1975.

Giorgio Maria Di Nunzio is assistant professor in computer science, with a main focus on multimedia information retrieval, at the Faculty of Humanities and at the Department of Information Engineering of the University of Padua,

Italy. He has participated in a number of national and international projects. He participated in the CLEF evaluation campaign, for which he is currently working on the infrastructure. His current research interests are in probabilistic models for automated text categorization and information retrieval, and visual data mining.

Nicola Ferro is assistant professor in computer science, with a main focus on digital libraries and multilingual information access and retrieval, at the Faculty of Statistics and at the Department of Information Engineering of the University of Padua, Italy. He has participated in a number of national and international projects. He is currently working on digital library models and architectures including multilingual aspects within the DELOS Network, and in the CLEF evaluation campaign, for which he is currently working on the evaluation infrastructure. His current research interests are in formal models and architectures for annotations and multimedia digital archives.

Massimo Melucci received his PhD on Computer Science in 1996. He is associate professor in Computer Science at the Faculty of Statistics and at the Department of Information Engineering of the University of Padua, Italy, where he works on information retrieval and digital libraries. He is currently in the Steering Committee of the Symposium on String Processing and Information Retrieval and in that of the Conference on Discovery Science. He is member of the Editorial Board of the Journal of Information Retrieval (Kluwer).

Nicola Orio has a PhD in Computer Engineering. He is assistant professor of Computer Science, with a main focus on multimedia information retrieval, at the Faculty of Humanities and at the Department of Information Engineering of the University of Padua, Italy. His current research interests are in multimedia digital libraries and in music identification and retrieval, these activities are developed through the collaboration in a number of national and international projects. He participated in the CLEF and MIREX evaluation campaigns, and in multilingual and music information retrieval, respectively.

Luca Pretto was awarded a degree in electronic engineering (1999) and a PhD in computer engineering (2003), both from the University of Padua, Italy. He is currently a lecturer of database systems for the Faculty of Engineering and a post-doc researcher in computer science at the Department of Information Engineering at the University of Padua, where he is a member of the Information Management Systems research group. His main research interests are in link analysis and Web algorithmics.

Information Access using the Guide of User Requirements

Maristella Agosti

Department of Information Engineering – University of Padua
Via Gradenigo, 6/b – 35131 Padua – Italy
agosti@dei.unipd.it

Abstract. This study presents an interpretation of the evolution of the events in the information retrieval area. Focusing mainly on the last twenty years, the study pays particular attention to the system which needs to be envisaged and designed to support the end user in accessing relevant and interesting information. The end user can be considered the guide of the researcher, prompting him to conceive and invent solutions of real use for the user himself.

Key words: information retrieval, information access, information retrieval process, user information need, information retrieval model, user's requirements, system-oriented information retrieval

1 Introduction

The term *information retrieval* identifies the activities that a person – the *user* – has to conduct to choose, from a collection of documents, those that can be of interest to him to satisfy a specific and contingent information need. It follows that the aim of the area of information retrieval is to help and support the user in choosing, among the available documents, those that, with higher probability are more suitable to satisfy his information need. Figure 1 sketches the situation: the user has the possibility of choosing the documents of interest to him from an available collection, but he needs to have a tool that can help him in choosing the subset of documents which are of of interest for him without needing to invest a lot of time in inspecting all the documents of the collection.

Figure 1 also shows the three main actors and aspects that information retrieval needs to address:

- user,
- collection of documents,
- retrieval, which means a function or model used in retrieving and accessing information.

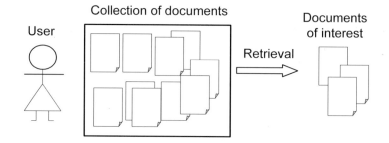

Fig. 1: Information retrieval aim

Where the user is the central actor of the situation, the collection of documents is the source from which information can be extracted in the hope it is of interest to the user, and retrieval is the function that transforms a user information need into a set of documents that are supposed to satisfy the user information need. The retrieval process begins with the user analysing his information need and trying to transform it in such a way that it becomes applicable to the collection of documents through a function that is able to produce as output the subset of documents that mostly satisfy the user information need.

When the collection of documents reaches a size that makes a manual inspection of the documents prohibitive, the construction and management of the collection together with the application of the retrieval function are managed in an automatic way through an information retrieval system. This means that an information retrieval system models and implements the retrieval process from the user input – i.e. it often takes the shape of a user *query* – to the production of an output that is constituted by a subset of collection documents most likely of interest to the user.

The approach to the modeling of the information retrieval process has dramatically changed over the years, mostly in a positive and evolutionary way, with the final aim of passing from an information retrieval approach towards an information access one where the real user is the focus of interest. This paper critically analyzes the evolution of the modeling of the information retrieval process, mainly in the last twenty years, relating the general analysis to the analysis of activities and experiences that have been conducted in the context of the Information Management Systems (IMS) Research Group of the Department of Information Engineering of the University of Padua, which started its activities twenty years ago. The approach used in this analysis is coherent with the one that has been named *system-oriented information retrieval* by Ingwersen and Järvelin in [24]. The term "system-oriented information retrieval" approach is intended to mean the approach of designing and developing models and systems of information retrieval that concentrate on the side of a *system* which has to be conceived and designed to support the user in the access to the information. This approach is a sort of *system-side* approach and is in contrast to a *user-oriented* one.

The main focus of paper is on Sect. 2, which presents an interpretation of the evolution of the events in the information retrieval area using a system-oriented approach; attention is mostly focused on the last twenty years. Section 3 draws some final conclusions.

2 The Evolution of System-Oriented Information Retrieval

Early Days

In the early days of computer science, the common approach to information retrieval was to consider the specific type of documents constituting the collection and to manage and design the system and applications around it. The attention of the system designer was concentrated on the type of documents, mostly because the available technology limited the possibilities of representation and management of different types of documents in a single system; the only documents which could be considered were only textual and written in a single language. In addition to this, the form, that is the external appearance of the documents, was taken into account, so a system was designed to describe or to manage one specific type of textual document at a time; these included, for example, catalogue, bibliographic, and full-text documents. The consequence was that it was more efficient and effective to concentrate on one single type of document at a time and to build a system able to manage abstracts of documents [27], bibliographic documents [13], or full-text documents [64]. Sometimes the specific subject area of the documents, together with their external form, was also considered an aspect to take into consideration when designing a system; therefore, a system was designed for textual documents that were materialized in a specific form and that were all related to a specific subject area. Two significative examples are the medical area, where the Medical Literature Analysis and Retrieval System (MEDLARS) was built with the prime purpose of producing the *Index Medicus* and other recurring bibliographies [26][1], and the legal area, where the LEXIS system was designed to provide a service specifically devoted to the manipulation of legal information [64, p. 46].

1977-1986: The Last Decade of Centralized Systems

The attention of the system designer was prevalently focused on the textual collection of documents more than the user and the specific function or model to implement in the system. Still in the decade from 1977 to 1986 systems

---

[1] Reprinted in [34, pp. 223–246].

were only able to manage single type of document, and the systems were named in accordance with the specific type of documents that collections were designed to manage in a specialized way. But by the end of that decade the relational database management systems started to be generally available and it became possible to manage, in a single application, both structured and unstructured – textual – documents. At the same time, the application of distributed systems started to be considered, thus opening the way to the study of distributed systems also in the area of the management of unstructured information [6]. The possibility of introducing special-purpose hardware was also under study worldwide; in fact, a sector of research and development was flourishing with the aim of producing special-purpose hardware devices to be introduced in conventional computer systems to improve system capabilities for the management of numerical and non-numerical applications; in [1] the introduction of special-purpose hardware in the range of information management systems is examined and discussed.

As well, it was in those years that a new generation of library automation systems started to be designed with the purpose of enabling the retrieval of a combination of different types of data: structured catalogue data together with unstructured data representing the contents of the catalogued documents. This new type of library automation systems also supports the interactive retrieval of information through textual data – this interaction is made possible through the component known as *Online Public Access Catalogue (OPAC)* [23].

1987-1996: Towards a User-Oriented Decentralized Environment

By the end of the previous decade, probably in part due to the rapid introduction and evolution of personal computer systems and telecommunications, the attention of information management system researchers started to move from the collection of documents towards the user and the retrieval model, with the focus on the invention of models better able to support user-system interaction. So, at the beginning of that decade, researchers took new directions, trying to support the users with new types of retrieval models or with a combination of different models. Some significant examples of the attempt to open new directions towards new types of retrieval models are the work of van Rijsbergen, reported in [36] and in [35], where a model based on non-classical logic was proposed, the work of Croft [17] which proposed new approaches to intelligent information retrieval, and a collaborative work of many researchers [15] where distributed expert-systems were dealt with. A new type of system able to carry out an effective combination of multiple searches based on different retrieval models is proposed by Croft and Thompson [19], and the method of combining different information retrieval approaches has proved to be really effective over the years and through different ways of implementing solutions as reported in [18].

It is in this scientific context that the Information Management Systems Research Group was formed at the University of Padua in 1987. The group was joined by scientists formerly working with the School of Engineering, the School of Statistics and the School of Psychology. The background of the members of the group was in information retrieval, database management, and library automation systems – these last can be considered the "ancestors" of present-day *digital library systems*. The background topics of interest can be appreciated looking at the left-side of Fig. 2, which represents the range of the research interests and the topics dealt with by the group starting from 1987 up to now.

Naturally, at the beginning of its activities the group was tempted to continue to address the same research areas that were previously dealt with by its components. However, also partly due to the flourishing scientific context of those years, the group made use of the possibility of synergically applying the competence of the members, and immediately started to propose new ideas and, in particular, a new approach to information retrieval based on the linking of documents and of descriptive objects based on the hypertext paradigm [2]. The study of hypertext methods was at the basis of a new sort of *network-based* and *associative information retrieval* entitled EXPLICIT. Associative information retrieval methods are those retrieval methods which have been

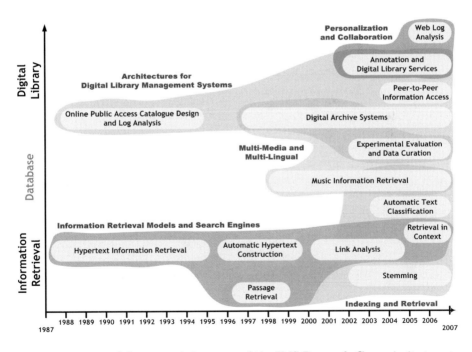

Fig. 2: The range of the research interests of the IMS Research Group in its twenty years of existence

proposed and experimented since the early days of information retrieval [20, 30]. They seek to expand query formulation by adding to an initial query some new terms related to the terms of the initial query, and similarly expand the retrieved document set using terms related to the already used terms; [32] makes use of associative information retrieval methods and shows that the difficulty encountered in applying associative retrieval methods resides in the identification of related terms and documents which would improve retrieval operations, and this is one of the research topic that still remains to be fully solved.

The EXPLICIT model was based on a two-level architecture initially proposed in [10] and refined in [5]. The two-level architecture holds the two main parts of the informative resource managed by an information retrieval tool: on the one hand the collection of content objects (e.g. a single collection of documents, different collections of different types of digital content objects), and on the other the term structure, which is a schema of concepts that can be composed of either one single indexing structure or some cooperative content representation structures such as those depicted in Fig. 3, in a sort of a "semantic network". The system manages this network to retrieve information of use for the final user, but also to present the representation of the contents of the collections to the user, who can use them for browsing and becoming acquainted with the information richness of the managed collections.

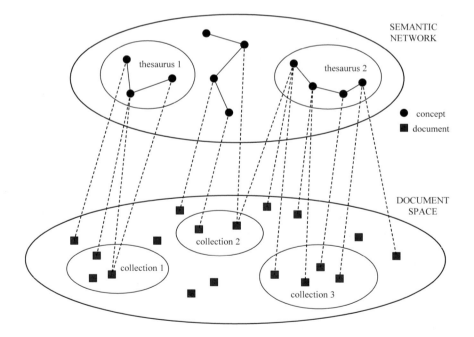

Fig. 3: The EXPLICIT architecture and model

The model was presented in [4] where the prototype developed to validate the model in a personal computing environment was also introduced; in the prototype the schema of concepts was made available to the end user as a frame of reference in the query formulation process. As shown in Fig. 3, the EXPLICIT model supports the concurrent use of different schemas of concepts to satisfy the information needs of different categories of users; the schemas of objects can be a term structure derived from the automatic indexing process, together with a classification system and/or a thesaurus.

In those years other hypertext network-based models were introduced, opening an area of information retrieval that was named *hypertext informa-tion retrieval*. Most of hypertext information retrieval models represent, as one layer, the document network and, as another, a concept network. Links relate concept nodes and document nodes together. The users, who make use of systems based on those models, can browse both the concept network and the document network, and move back and forth between the two informative structures. An important characteristic of hypertext information retrieval models is the capacity of integrating different information access approaches: browsing, navigation, and retrieval. The book by Agosti and Smeaton [14] is a reference for the different models that have been proposed in the area.

Having as a basis hypertext information retrieval models, a new area started to emerge, that of the *automatic construction* or *authoring* of hypertexts to be used for information retrieval purposes. Many proposals were suggested as reported in Crestani's chapter of this book, and the IMS research group has contributed to those results.

Together with the work on the automatic hypertext construction, the group was also continuing its activities in library automation, participating in the design and development of the first academic OPAC made available through Internet access in Italy [11].

1997-2006: The Overwhelming Amount of Digital Documents

During this decade it became clear that the most relevant aspect is the continuous growth of diverse collections of documents in digital form, so major efforts are tackling different aspects related to the growing of digital collections. The problem is dealt with through proposals of new retrieval models able to manage the Web collection of documents [12], large-scale evaluation efforts [21], and multimedia content retrieval.

In relation to models able to manage Web documents, it is worth noting that the different hypertext information retrieval models that have been proposed in the previous decade are precursors of Web retrieval techniques employing link information [24], such as the proposal by Marchiori, which suggested exploiting the hyperlink structure of the Web to try to enhance the performance of Web search engines in [28] and the PageRank algorithm proposed by Brin and Page [16]. Based on these new techniques different search engines were designed and made available to the general public.

A different way of approaching the problem is to consider that the number and size of Web collections and databases storing unstructured textual data that are made available to the final user present high degrees of heterogeneity at the level of content and language. Such a situation can be dealt with by extracting and managing specific and relevant pieces of data from larger data objects. The study of this possibility is named *passage retrieval* [31], which is the identification and extraction of fragments from large or short heterogeneous full-text documents; passages are chunks of contiguous text belonging to a larger text, usually sentences or sequences of sentences identified by punctuation marks, such as full stops or semi-colons. A probabilistic method that models the document language to identify relevant passages has been proposed by Melucci and is presented in [29].

In this period large-scale evaluation campaigns for information retrieval were launched. *Text REtrieval Conference (TREC)* has been the precursor for large-scale efforts [22, 37], TREC has been followed up by Cross-Language Evaluation Forum mainly for European multilingual-efforts [7] and by *NII-NACSIS Test Collection for IR Systems (NTCIR)* mainly for Asian languages [25]. All these international evaluation campaigns have shown their validity over the decade, because the retrieval effectiveness of the retrieval systems has steadily grown over the years also in part due to the stimulus provided by those efforts.

Multimedia retrieval is the other relevant area that researchers started to face in a systematic way and for different media during the decade. The complexity of the management of collections of multimedia digital documents can be faced in particular for information retrieval purposes, but also from a general architectural point of view, that is, the area of digital libraries and digital library systems. The many European research groups participating in the DELOS Network of Excellence on Digital Libraries, in the Information Society Technologies (IST) Program of the European Commission[2], have greatly contributed to the development of the area, obtaining significant results. A European forum that has greatly contributed to the growth in attention and has given the research community a systematic appointment over the year has been *European Conference on Research and Advanced Technology for Digital Libraries (ECDL)*, which was inspired starting from 1996 by Costantino Thanos, who is also the coordinator of the DELOS Network of Excellence. The IMS research group has actively participated in the research regarding multimedia and digital libraries; most of the chapters of this book refer on pertinent research results.

From 2007 on

The new decade that starts this year is opening up new exciting challenges, in particular for multimedia search engines which are not yet available and for

---

[2] DELOS Web site at the URL: http://www.delos.info/

which much remains to be done to make them available. The IMS research group is participating in the *Search in Audio-visual content using Peer-to-peer Information Retrieval* (SAPIR) project[3] an EU IST FP6 research project, which will contribute to making multimedia search engines available.

Another area where the IMS group has actively operated, but which still has many topics which require the attention of researchers, is that of digital library systems both on the side of architectures and on the contents, so we can look forward to many exciting topics to be dealt with the next decade.

3 Conclusions

At this point the reader might ask himself why the title of this study is *Information Access using the Guide of User Requirements*. In fact, the user has been mentioned many times, when addressing the problem of the retrieval of information, but *user requirements* have never been explicitly dealt with.

The title derives from the consideration that the research activities of the IMS group have been mostly guided by the users that have cooperated over the years with the members of the group. The research proposals and solutions that have been conducted by the group have been derived from a common initial phase of requirements analysis and design that has always been conducted together with the end users of the specific system or tool that was under investigation. Just some of the examples are: the design of the EXPLICIT model together with experts of legal documents, the design of the DUO OPAC together with the librarians and the users of the University of Padua, the feasibility study of the *Digital Archive of Venetian Music (ADMV)* project aimed to build an effective digital library which users can fully access to retrieve bibliographic records, digitalized scores, and high quality sound of Venetian music which is presented in [3] and conducted together with experts of Italian national institutions, and more recently the *Imaginum Patavinae Scientiae Archivum (IPSA)* system together with national experts of illuminated manuscripts [8, 17].

This means that the guide of the IMS research group has always been the user, who must be the focus of the attention of the researchers who want to propose new information access solutions.

References

1. Agosti, M.: Special Purpose Hardware and Effective Information Processing. Information Technology: Research and Development **3**(1), 3–14 (1984)
2. Agosti, M.: Is Hypertext a New Model of Information Retrieval? In: Proceedings of the 12th International Online Information Meeting, Vol. I, pp. 57–62. Learned Information, Oxford (1988)

---

[3] http://www.sapir.eu/

3. Agosti, M., Bombi, F., Melucci, M., Mian, G.A.: Towards a digital library for the Venetian music of the eighteenth century. In: M. Deegan, J. Anderson, H. Short (eds.) DRH98: Selected Papers from Digital Resources for the Humanities 1998, pp. 1–15. Office for Humanities Communication, Publication 12, London (2000)

4. Agosti, M., Colotti, R., Gradenigo, G.: A two-level hypertext retrieval model for legal data. In: E.A. Fox (ed.) Proc. 14th Annual International ACM SIGIR Conference on Research and Development in Information Retrieval (SIGIR 1991), pp. 316–325. ACM Press, New York, USA, Chicago, USA (1991)

5. Agosti, M., Crestani, F., Gradenigo, G., Mattiello, P.: An approach for the conceptual modelling of IR auxiliary data. In: Ninth Annual IEEE International Conference on Computers and Communications, pp. 500–505. Scottsdale, Arizona (1990)

6. Agosti, M., Dalla Libera, F., Johnson, R.G.: The Use of Distributed Data Bases in Libraries. In: R.D. Parslow (ed.) BCS '81: Information Technology for the Eighties, pp. 559–570 (1981)

7. Agosti, M., Di Nunzio, G.M., Ferro, N., Peters, C.: CLEF: Ongoing Activities and Plans for the Future. In: N. Kando (ed.) Proc. 6th NTCIR Workshop Meeting on Evaluation of Information Access Technologies: Information Retrieval, Question Answering and Cross-Lingual Information Access, pp. 493–504. National Institute of Informatics, Tokyo, Japan (2007)

8. Agosti, M., Ferro, N., Orio, N.: Annotating Illuminated Manuscripts: an Effective Tool for Research and Education. In: M. Marlino, T. Sumner, F. Shipman (eds.) Proc. 5th ACM/IEEE-CS Joint Conference on Digital Libraries (JCDL 2005), pp. 121–130. ACM Press, New York, USA (2005)

9. Agosti, M., Ferro, N., Orio, N.: Graph-based Automatic Suggestion of Relationships among Images of Illuminated Manuscripts. In: H.M. Haddad, K.M. Liebrock, R. Chbeir, M.J. Palakal, S. Ossowski, K. Yetongnoon, R.L. Wainwright, C. Nicolle (eds.) Proc. 21st ACM Symposium on Applied Computing (SAC 2006), pp. 1063–1067. ACM Press, New York, USA (2006)

10. Agosti, M., Gradenigo, G., Mattiello, P.: The hypertext as an effective information retrieval tool for the final user. In: A.A. Martino (ed.) Pre-proceedings of the 3rd International Conference on Logics, Informatics and Law, Vol. I, pp. 1–19 (1989)

11. Agosti, M., Masotti, M.: Design of an OPAC Database to Permit Different Subject Searching Accesses in a Multi-disciplines Universities Library Catalogue Database. In: N.J. Belkin, P. Ingwersen, A. Mark Pejtersen, E.A. Fox (eds.) Proc. 15th Annual International ACM SIGIR Conference on Research and Development in Information Retrieval (SIGIR 1992), pp. 245–255. ACM Press, New York, USA (1992)

12. Agosti, M., Melucci, M.: Information Retrieval on the Web. In: M. Agosti, F. Crestani, G. Pasi (eds.) Lectures on Information Retrieval: Third European Summer-School (ESSIR 2000), pp. 242–285. Springer, Berlin/Heidelberg (2001)

13. Agosti, M., Ronchi, M.E.: DOC-5 - The Bibliographic Information Retrieval System in CINECA Library Automation Project. In: Proceedings of ECODU-29 Conference, pp. 20–31. Berlin, Germany (1980)

14. Agosti, M., Smeaton, A.F. (eds.): Information Retrieval and Hypertext. Kluwer Academic Publishers, Boston, USA (1996)

15. Belkin, N.J., Borgman, C.L., Brooks, H.M., Bylander, T., Croft, W.B., Daniels, P.J., Deerwester, S.C., Fox, E.A., Ingwersen, P., Rada, R.: Distributed

Expert-Based Information Systems: An Interdisciplinary Approach. Information Processing & Management **23**(5), 395–409 (1987)

16. Brin, S., Page, L.: The anatomy of a large scale hypertextual Web search engine. In: Proceedings of the World Wide Web Conference (1998)

17. Croft, W.B.: Approaches to Intelligent Information Retrieval. Information Processing & Management **23**(4), 249–254 (1987)

18. Croft, W.B.: Combining Approaches to Information Retrieval. In: W.B. Croft (ed.) Advances in Information Retrieval: Recent Research from the Center for Intelligent Information Retrieval, pp. 1–36. Kluwer Academic Publishers, Norwell (MA), USA (2000)

19. Croft, W.B., Thompson, R.H.: I3R: a New Approach to the Design of Document Retrieval Systems. Journal of the American Society for Information Science **38**(6), 389–404 (1987)

20. Doyle, L.B.: Information Retrieval and Processing. Melville, Los Angeles (1975)

21. Harman, D.: Evaluation Issues in Information Retrieval, introductory paper to the Special Issue on: Evaluation Issues in Information Retrieval. Information Processing & Management **28**(4), 439–440 (1992)

22. Harman, D.: Overview of the First Text REtrieval Conference (TREC-1). In: D.K. Harman (ed.) The First Text REtrieval Conference (TREC-1). National Institute of Standards and Technology (NIST), Special Pubblication 500-207, Whasington, USA. http://trec.nist.gov/pubs/trec1/papers/01.txt [last visited 2007, March 23] (1992)

23. Hildreth, C.R.: Online public access catalog. In: M.E. Williams (ed.) Annual Review of Information Science and Technology (ARIST), Vol. 20, pp. 233–285 (1985)

24. Ingwersen, P., Järvelin, K.: The Turn. Springer, The Netherlands (2005)

25. Kishida, K., Chen, K.H., Lee, S., Kuriyama, D., Kando, N., Chen, H.H., Myaeng, S.H.: Overview of CLIR Task at the Fifth NTCIR Workshop. In: N. Kando, M. Takaku (eds.) Proc. of the Fifth NTCIR Workshop Meeting on Evaluation of Information Access Technologies: Information Retrieval, Question Answering and Cross-Lingual Information Access. http://research.nii.ac.jp/ntcir/workshop/OnlineProceedings5/data/CLIR/NTCIR5-OV-CLIR-KishidaK.pdf [last visited 2007, March 23] (2005)

26. Lancaster, F.W.: MEDLARS: Report on the evaluation of its operating efficiency. American Documentation **20**, 119–142 (1969)

27. Luhn, H.P.: The Automatic Creation of Literature Abstracts. IBM Journal of Research and Development **2**(2), 159–165 (1958)

28. Marchiori, M.: The Quest for Correct Information on the Web: Hyper Search Engines. Computer Networks and ISDN Systems **29**(8–1), 1225–1235 (1997)

29. Melucci, M.: Passage Retrieval: A Probabilistic Technique. Information Processing & Management **34**(1), 43–68 (1998)

30. Salton, G.: Associative document retrieval techniques using bibliographic information. Journal of the ACM **10**, 440–457 (1963)

31. Salton, G., Allan, J., Buckley, C.: Approaches to Passage Retrieval in Full Text Information Systems. In: R. Korfhage, E. Rasmussen, P. Willett (eds.) Proc. 16th Annual International ACM SIGIR Conference on Research and Development in Information Retrieval (SIGIR 1993), pp. 49–58. ACM Press, New York, USA (1993)

32. Salton, G., Buckley, C.: On the use of spreading activation methods in automatic information retrieval. In: Y. Chiaramella (ed.) Proc. 11th Annual International ACM SIGIR Conference on Research and Development in Information Retrieval (SIGIR 1988), pp. 147–159. ACM Press, New York, USA (1988)
33. Salton, G., McGill, M.J.: Introduction to modern information retrieval. McGraw-Hill, New York, NY, USA (1983)
34. Sparck Jones, K., Willett, P. (eds.): Readings in Information Retrieval. Morgan Kaufmann, San Francisco, CA, USA (1997)
35. van Rijsbergen, C.J.: A New Theoretical Framework for Information Retrieval. In: Proc. 9th Annual International ACM SIGIR Conference on Research and Development in Information Retrieval (SIGIR 1986), pp. 194–200. ACM Press, New York, USA (1986)
36. van Rijsbergen, C.J.: A Non-Classical Logic for Information Retrieval. The Computer Journal **29**(6), 481–485 (1986)
37. Voorhees, E., Harman, D. (eds.): TREC: Experiment and Evaluation in Information Retrieval. The MIT Press, Cambridge, MA, USA (2005)

From Linking Text to Linking Crimes: Information Retrieval, But Not As You Know It

Fabio Crestani

Faculty of Informatics – University of Lugano (USI)
Via G. Buffi 13 – CH-6904 Lugano – Switzerland
fabio.crestani@unisi.ch

Abstract. Information retrieval techniques have been used for a long time to identify links between textual items for the automatic construction of hypertexts and electronic books where sought information can be accessed by browsing. While research work in this area has been steadily decreasing in recent years, some of the techniques developed in that context are proving very valuable in a number of new application areas. In this paper we present an approach to automatic linking of textual items that is used to prioritise criminal suspects in a police investigation. A free-text description of an unsolved crime is compared to previous offence descriptions where the offender is known. By linking the descriptions, inferences about likely suspects can be made. Language Modeling is adapted to produce a Bayesian model which assigns a probability to each suspect. An empirical study showed that the linking of free text descriptions of burglaries enables prioritisation of offenders. The model presented in this paper could be easily extended to take account of additional crime and suspect linking data, such as geographical location of crimes or suspect social networks. This would enable large networks of investigative information automatically constructed from police archives to be browsed.

Key words: text mining, language modeling, crime suspect prioritisation

1 Not Your Standard Information Retrieval

Information Retrieval (IR) has been created with the purpose of enabling a user to access information relevant to the user information need expressed in a query, where the information is contained in large archives of textual data. A variety of indexing and retrieval models have been developed with this purpose in mind. This is the conventional face of IR. However, a number of researchers soon realised that such models and techniques can also be used for other purposes. IR indexing models can be used to automatically link textual items to create large network structures that users can navigate to find relevant information by browsing. Accessing information by browsing is an approach able to tackle one of the main problems of IR that is related to the frequent inability of the user to describe in a query what he is looking for. In fact, it is a well know problem of IR that users do not often know what they are looking for, but they can easily recognise it when they see it. Accessing information by browsing has also become very popular with the advent of the World Wide Web which has provided a paradigm and several tools (Web browsers) to facilitate users' browsing.

The group lead by Maristella Agosti at the University of Padua was one of the first to explore this unconventional use of IR techniques. Since the late eighties the group has experimented with the use of IR indexing techniques for the automatic construction of hypertexts [2]. Large network structures were built from document collections that could be browsed according to a conceptual model that would help the user avoid getting 'lost in hyperspace'. This approach was followed by a number of other researchers developing different techniques and tools for the automatic construction of hypertexts not just from document collections, but also from single or multiple books or from multimedia document collections (hypermedia).

With these network structures becoming larger and larger, it has become more and more difficult for a user to access information contained in it solely by browsing. While some attempts have been made to build techniques and tools to help the user in this task by suggesting directions for the browsing (see for example [15]), the research area directly related to the automatic construction of hypertext has been steadily losing momentum.

In this paper we review some of this work and show that the same paradigm of accessing information by browsing automatically constructed network structures of textual items can be used for other very useful purposes. This is still IR, but not as you know it.

This paper is structured as follows. In Sect. 2 we present some background work. This is related to linking textual items in document collections and books. We show how this task can be designed using a conceptual model and implemented using a variety of IR techniques. We also show a successful example of this work in the Hyper-TextBook project. Section 3 shows how a very similar approach can be used to link crimes using their textual descriptions. Crimes can be linked to each other and to suspects in a conceptual model that closely resembles the one used to design hypertexts. The implementation of such a model can be carried out using IR techniques similar to those used to build hypertexts. The section describes some work aimed at finding the best IR model for this task. We also show how this work can be successfully implemented into a prototype criminal investigation analysis system. The paper concludes with Sect. 4 describing some further work currently being carried out.

2 Linking Text

Linking textual items, be they news items, scientific articles or pages of a textbook, requires a number of steps. It is widely accepted that building a hypertext requires at least three phases:

Design phase: modeling and design of the target hypertext, or in other words, devising what kind of hypertext the author wants to produce given the task and the users.

Authoring phase: the actual transformation of the initial single document or collection of documents into a hypertext.

Publishing phase: making the hypertext available to the users using some specific hypertextual format, and presentation and browsing tool.

The design phase can be greatly facilitated if one follows a conceptual model of the target hypertexts. This not only helps in the authoring phase in providing a conceptual reference architecture, but also helps the user navigating the published hypertexts, as the conceptual model provides a frame of reference for the browsing. In Sect. 2.1 we will present a conceptual model that has been a constant reference for much of the work on automatic construction of hypertexts carried out at the University of Padua.

The authoring phase can range from a completely manual to a completely automatic process. Initially, it was common to manually author a hypertext, but as the collection of textual items grows larger (e.g. a thick book) or consists of multimedia documents, a completely manual authoring become tedious and expensive. It is therefore important to have a set of techniques for the automatic or semi-automatic authoring of hypertexts. In addition, we also need techniques for the automatic updating of hypertexts in order to insert, modify, and cancel part of it over time. In this article we are concerned with the use of IR techniques for the automatic construction of hypertexts, and Sect. 2.2 reports a brief survey of past and current work in this direction.

Finally, the publishing phase makes the hypertext available to users. With the advent of the World Wide Web a universal format for authoring hypertexts (HTML) and a large number of tools for browsing hypertexts written in that format have become available and greatly facilitated a fully automatic publishing task. In Sect. 2.3 we briefly describe an example of a hypertext that was automatically authored using IR techniques following the conceptual model presented and published in HTML format.

2.1 A Conceptual Model

One of the first results of research in the automatic construction of hypertexts is the recognition of the need of a conceptual modeling tool [2]. Notice that here we use the term "conceptual model" in a loose sense, considering it a reference model, rather than a formal modeling tool as these tools are intended in the Artificial Intelligence and Databases areas.

Different conceptual models have been proposed in the past, and the earliest ones date back to the late eighties [23, 40]. Most of these models employ different types of data structure at the higher abstraction levels to describe the informative content of the document collection placed on the lowest level of abstraction. It is well accepted that the most effective hypertext models for IR are based on a two-level architecture [1, 11, 27]. In most of our work we adopted the two-level EXPLICIT model [1] as our reference model for the design of the conceptual structure of automatically built hypertexts. The model is based on two types of entity: data and auxiliary data. Data are the elementary objects of interest of the final user. Data are indexed and retrieved, and can consist of multimedia documents or fragments. Auxiliary data are the objects which describe the semantic content of data. They are the result of an indexing process, for example index terms or other extracted information. Thus, the main elements of the EXPLICIT model are *nodes* and *links*, where links are used to express semantic relations between data and auxiliary data nodes. Figure 1 gives a schematic diagram of the conceptual model and depicts the relation between nodes and links.

This model is very flexible and allows for many different implementations. In one implementation of the EXPLICIT model, i.e. the Hyper-TextBook project (see later), nodes at the lower level represent pages (P) of a book. The user can access related pages starting from any page by means of automatically constructed links. The page containing the Table of Contents has been used as the entry point to the first page of a chapter. The Table of Contents can be used whenever the user gets lost during hypertext navigation. Nodes at the upper level of abstraction model Subject Index Term Nodes (T) representing concepts or topics dealt in pages.

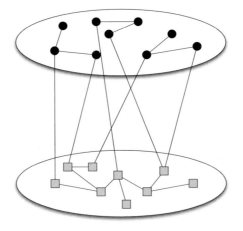

Fig. 1: The EXPLICIT conceptual model of hypertexts

There are four different types of links: PT, TP, PP, and TT. PT and TP links represent relations between a page and terms and a term and pages. A page is linked to terms describing the page content. In the case of a hypertextbook, a sub-set of TP links are already available; these are the links identified by the author in the Subject Index. Statistical techniques are used to determine new PT and additional TP links in combination with the available TP links. Links are ranked according to statistical values measuring the representation power of each link. The higher the value, the more the two nodes are estimated to be semantically close. PP links relate a page to other pages. Structural PP links, such as "next", "previous" or "go to the Table of Contents" links are easily detectable, while statistical techniques help exploit the "semantic similarity" between pages estimated to be semantically close, namely pages addressing the same topics. Finally, TT links relate a term to other terms. Links between terms are meant to provide the user with the "semantic association" functionality of the EXPLICIT model, aiming at making clear and explicit the semantics of a term. Statistically determined links relate semantically similar terms, that is, terms estimated to address the same topics. These links are constructed using a similarity measure computed on the basis of the distribution of terms within pages (term-term occurrence, or term co-occurrence). The higher the similarity measure, the more the two terms are assumed to be semantically close.

2.2 Automatic Construction of Hypertext Using Information Retrieval Techniques

Automatic authoring has been addressed by researchers since the early days of hypertexts. It is well recognised that automatic authoring of hypertext has several advantages over manual authoring:

- it is faster and involves less expensive human intervention than manual authoring;
- it assures a higher consistency of segments and links detection than manual authoring;
- it assures a higher completeness of segments and links detection than manual authoring.

Although it is easy to recognise that a general purpose automatic technique for the authoring of hypertexts is not an achievable goal, when we focus on a particular typology of documents and hypertexts then it is possible to design an appropriate automatic technique. In this paper we focus on the use of IR techniques for the automatic authoring of hyper-textbooks. The reason why we chose to use IR techniques lies in the fact that IR is concerned with methods and techniques for content-based access to information. Since the most difficult part of the automatic authoring of a hypertext is the building of links that connect semantically related documents or document fragments, it is natural to use the results of many years of IR research and make full use of existing IR techniques for that purpose. In fact, it is easy to recognise that IR techniques have always dealt with the construction of relationships (or links) dependent on the mutual relevance of the objects to relate [5]. The use of IR techniques for automatic authoring is particularly useful in the case of authoring a large hypertext made up of a large number of quite small and highly related pieces of text.

A complete survey of the use of IR techniques for the automatic construction and authoring of hypertext is reported in [5]. Here we only report the most significant work related to the objectives of this paper.

One of the earliest works in the field of the automatic transformation of text into hypertext was performed by Furuta et al. In [24] the design and implementation of a technique for converting a regularly and consistently structured document into a hypertext is presented. Regularly and consistently structured documents are those having a well-identified and fixed structure, such as bibliographic cards or manual pages. The methodology is based on the reasonable assumption that there is a close relationship between the physical components of a document and hypertext nodes.

In [34], Robertson et al. showed how to discover content links using standard IR techniques. However, the establishing of these links is addressed as a semi-automatic task: an authoring toolkit aids a human editor in the identification of possible links, but it is a human decision to accept them or not and embed them in the hypertext. This is a consequence of their view that it is not possible to convert text to hypertexts without human intervention. We agree that this is the case for a general conversion methodology that aims to be valid for any kind of document and usage task. However, we believe that for very specific documents and for very specific tasks a completely automatic transformation methodology can be designed and implemented.

In [33] Rada addresses the combination of structural links and content links. The author was the first to distinguish between first-order and second-order hypertext. First-order hypertexts use only structural links based on the document mark-up (explicit links). Structural links are, for example, links connecting outline headings, citations, cross-references, or indices. In second-order hypertexts, links are not explicitly put in the text by the author, but are detected using some automatic procedures (implicit links). The use of first and second order links in the same hypertext enables it to reflect both the structural schema of the source documents and an alternative schema, reflecting the way index terms are distributed across the documents. In the cited paper, second-order links were set up between index terms using co-occurrence data. The technique is based on the use of a threshold on the co-occurrence data to set up or not links between index terms.

Another interesting approach is reported in [37], where Smeaton and Morrissey address the problem of the automatic construction of a hypertext from a text using techniques from IR that are dynamically guided by an overall measure of how good the resulting hypertext is. The novelty of this approach is in the selective creation of links based on a measure of the hypertext compactness that controls the adding of a new link in relation to its influence on the overall hypertext topology [10, 36]. What remains to be discussed is the relevance of the hypertext topology to the hypertext effectiveness. As the authors highlighted, some very compact hypertexts may result in the user being disoriented because of too many links. Nevertheless, in a hypertext with a large number of links the user can be aided in the browsing by providing more information about links, such as information about link types.

Botafogo et al. address the problem of identifying aggregates within existing hypertexts mostly by analysing link patterns [9, 10]. The aggregate identification method can be used as a guideline to design algorithms for the automatic construction of hypertexts. The authors also address a well-known problem within hypertext called "user disorientation". User disorientation comes from the high number of links we need to follow to get interesting nodes. A high number of links sometimes indicates a too complex hypertext structure. A hierarchical structure is often the most natural organisation of information. Hypertext authors often start to create hypertexts in a hierarchical way, but this guideline is often lost because of the intrinsic network nature of cross-referenced documents. The authors propose an improvement of authoring techniques through the identification of specific hypertext substructures, such as clusters or hierarchies, and the definition of metrics called "compactness" and "stratum". These tools are aimed to help authors in writing hypertexts, and then to solve the user disorientation problem. The main conclusion of their work is that a designer needs some guidelines to keep hypertext construction in control especially whenever scaling up is required. This is essential if automatic construction processes have to be performed.

In [39] Tebbutt presents a different approach to automatically constructed hypertext links. The main characteristics of this approach is the use of domain experts of the source document collection from which the hypertext has been constructed. The fact that the involved subjects were experts of the domain and trained in using the source document collection enables an interesting interpretation of the results. Positive results are: (i) navigating links is useful when the user's information need is ill-defined and cannot directly be mapped onto a query, and (ii) the speed of finding information in the document collection can increase if good links are available for browsing. However, Tebbutt's study showed that similarity-based inter-document links may be confusing, and that link browsing effectiveness decreases with the domain expertise of the user. It is nevertheless recognised that the adherence to a conceptual model in the design and implementation of a hypertext might reduce the risk of user disorientation.

In [20, 21] Egan et al. report on a very influential project, called "SuperBook", aiming at constructing a hypertext system to support users to find information more quickly and precisely than with conventional paper-based books. The most important contribution of this work is the identification of some of the most effective semi-automatic strategies to be used for the design and implementation of such systems.

Finally we should not forget the extensive work carried out at the University of Padua on the automatic construction of hypertexts using IR techniques. The work started with the presentation of a full methodology for the automatic constructions of hypertext that closely followed the EXPLICIT model [2]. This methodology was implemented in a tool, TACHIR, which with small modifications was used to build hypertexts from document collections [4], textbooks [14, 18], and entire libraries of textbooks [28].

This brief survey shows how many researchers have used IR in an unconventional way to aid information access by automatically building network structures that can be browsed by the user. Many of the concepts presented here and some techniques (in particular those developed at the University of Padua) are at the foundation of the work presented in the second part of this paper, in Sect. 3. But first we will present the results of a project that reached the highest development of the experience in automatics construction of hypertext at the University of Padua.

2.3 The Hyper-TextBook Project

In 1997 we started working on a project that was a spin off of previous work on the automatic construction of hypertexts [2,3]. In our previous work we developed and tested a prototype tool using large collections of small documents (e.g, bibliographic references, newspaper articles) and the prototype worked well in that context. It was when we started working on small collections of large and very large documents (e.g., journal articles, books) that we realised that our methodology and tool needed to be modified to take into consideration the different characteristics of these new documents: the Hyper-TextBook project was born.

The *Hyper-TextBook project* was carried out during 1997-2002 at the University of Padua. The objective of the project was to develop a methodology to enhance the paper-based version of a textbook by the automatic insertion of semantic links. Effectively, the Hyper-TextBook project aimed at developing a tool for the automatic construction of hyper-textbooks from textbooks. The work was based on the requirement of preservation of the features of the paper version. The already available text-based features were to be enhanced, not removed by the implementation of hypertext capabilities since the readers of the textbook have long been familiar with the physical page-based organisation [26]. In particular:

1. The book pages are the unit of reference for our hyper-textbook. The user can browse the book sequentially, going from one page to the next or to the previous one.
2. The relevance relationships from Subject Index terms to pages have to be preserved because the Subject Index is the set of terms the author used

to index the textbook, and therefore it is the most important structure for browsing.

3. The Table of Contents has to be preserved and augmented, since it is one of the most used features of the paper textbook [20].

The first point, in particular, needs to be explained. The main reason why we decided to remain faithful to the original textbook pages in structuring the hyper-textbook is related to our assumptions about the use of textbooks. We assume users will employ textbooks mostly for referencing and for recalling information they have already seen. In such a case we need a structuring of the book that will be consistent across formats (paper, on screen, printed), platforms (small laptop screen, large desktop screen, personal data assistant screen) and that will make it easy for users to exchange pointers to information. The most obvious choice of structure is the one that the textbook already has: the original textbook pages, so we tried to enhance this structure, rather than upset it.

To enhance the textbook we developed a methodology to: (1) author the pages through the insertion of structural and semantic links to other pages or relevant data, and (2) add new semantic links from the Subject Index to the pages and vice versa, and between the Subject Index terms.

We will not present the full details of the methodology in this paper; these have been reported in a number of papers (see for example [14, 16–18]). We only present the results of the work by showing how a user could browse a specific hyper-textbook built by following this methodology to find relevant information. We will return to this way of accessing information by browsing later when we will present how this is carried out in the iMOV project (Sect. 3.4) and the similarities will be readily apparent.

Figures 2 to 4 report an example of the use of a hyper-textbook built from a popular IR textbook [11]. The full version of the hyper-textbook can be found in the accompanying CD-ROM [7].

In Fig. 2 the user is at the first page of the third chapter, which deals with automatic classification. He has reached this page via the table of contents. He is now interested in exploring the main concepts of automatic classification and therefore asks to see what are the main concepts that are linked to this page.

Figure 3 shows the main concepts related to automatic classification and also shows which pages are the most similar in content to the page the user is looking at (p. 36). Notice the presence of a bar of variable length close to each concept and each page. The bar expresses graphically the relevance of some concepts to the current page and the similarity of the page with other pages. The user decides to select the concept of numerical taxonomy, to see which pages of the book deal with this topic.

In Fig. 4 the user sees concepts that are closely related to topic of numerical taxonomy and also sees the pages dealing with that topic. He could then move directly to p. 61 which is indicated to be the page most relevant to the topic

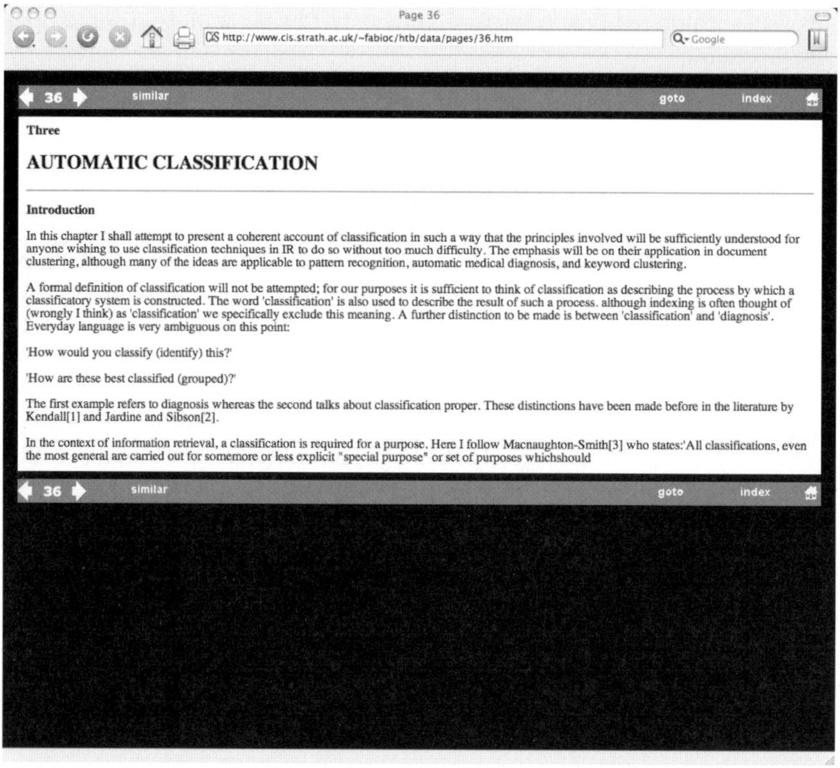

Fig. 2: The Hyper-TextBook: p. 36, a page on automatic classification

of numerical taxonomy or he could further explore related concepts to find other information relevant to his current needs.

A user and task based evaluation of the usability and effectiveness of hyper-textbooks was carried out. A detailed presentation of the results of the evaluation are reported in [14, 19]. The evaluation compared finding information necessary to complete a few tasks in different versions of the same textbooks: a paper version (the actual printed book), a flat file version (the searchable PDF of the book) and the hyper-textbook version. The evaluation showed that users were more effective, in terms of finding the information faster and with less effort, with the hyper-textbook than with the other two forms of the same book. It also showed that the larger the book and the more complex the task, the better the hyper-textbook performed in comparison with other versions. We believe we can generalise this result to say that automatically constructed browsable information structures, built using IR techniques, can be effective in helping a user to find relevant information hidden in the nodes of the structure.

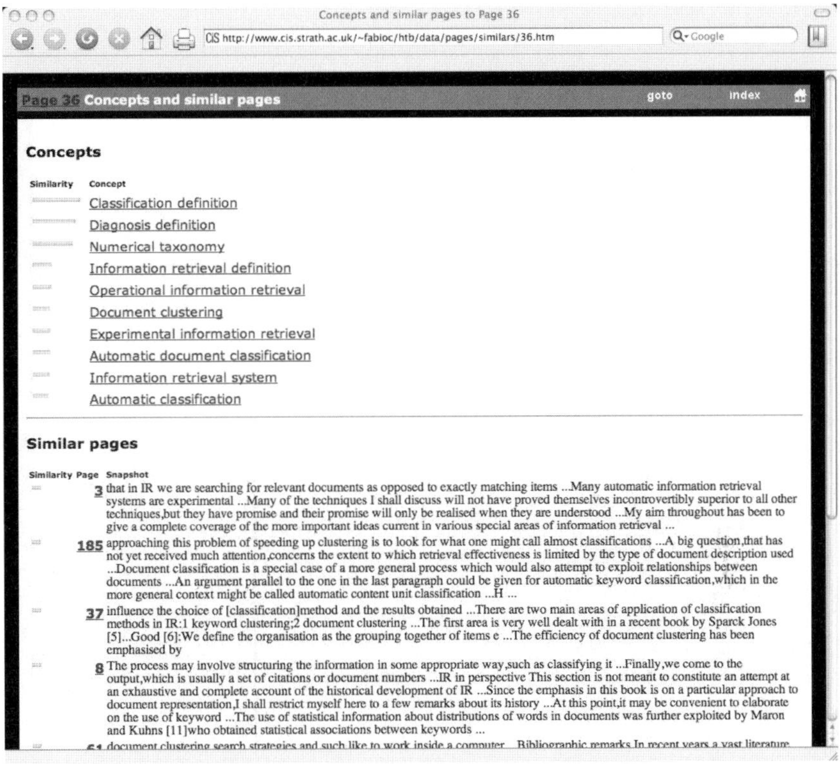

Fig. 3: The Hyper-TextBook: concepts and pages related to p. 36

3 Linking Crimes

The lessons learned from linking text to build hypertexts that enable a user to find relevant information by browsing can also be applied to a number of other areas that would seem far from IR. One area that we recently targeted in collaboration with the Centre for Investigative Psychology of the University of Liverpool is text mining of police archives. Police archives contain a huge amount of information related to the description of crimes, persons that have been stopped and searched, criminal cases that have been brought to court and that were solved or that remain unsolved. The largest part of this information is free text and can be mined for many different purposes with techniques that originated from IR. In the context of our work we are concerned with:

Linking crimes to suspects: this is often referred to as 'suspect prioritisation', as only a court case can eventually really link with certainty a crime to an offender.

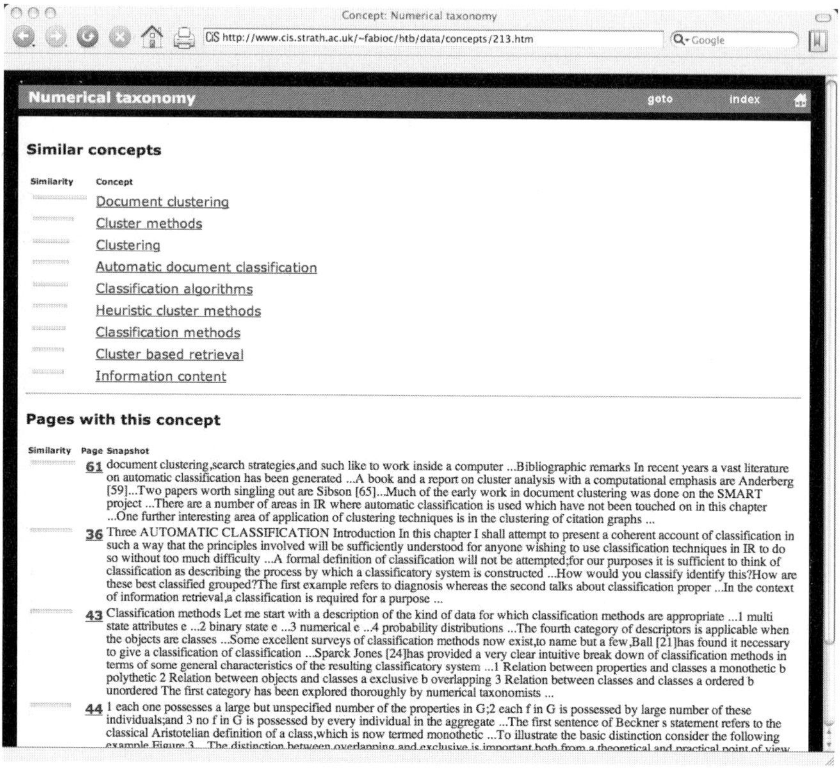

Fig. 4: the Hyper-TextBook: concepts and pages related to the concept of numerical taxonomy

Linking crimes with other crimes: for crimes that have been committed by the same offender or that are likely to have been committed by the same suspect.

Linking suspects/offenders: for crimes committed by more that one person or for other reasons (e.g. selling/handling stolen goods, hiding, helping, etc.).

In [12] Canter asserts that since the earliest criminological studies it has been clear that criminals have characteristics that distinguish them from the general population. There have also been attempts to demonstrate that certain classes of crime are typically committed by people who have similar characteristics. It has also been claimed that criminals exhibit a 'style' in the crime they commit. This is better described as a pattern of behaviour, typical of any set of crimes, that relates directly to subsets of characteristics of offenders. This process of making inferences about significant features of an offender on the basis of the kinds of people who commit crimes in that style has often been called 'offender profiling'. In general such 'profiles' are drawn from the subjective judgement and experience of experts. In a few studies most notably the Canter and FritzonÕs study of arson [13] it has been demonstrated that there are empirically sound relationships between, inter alia, the age, psychiatric background and personal relationships of offenders and dominant features of the crime, such as the nature of the target and whether there was more than one linked incident. However, in the work presented in the rest of this paper we are mostly concerned with the more well established theory that when offenders commit the same type of offence they are likely to do it in a similar manner [12]. In other words, offenders show some degree of consistency of behavioural style across crimes. The police use this fact to prioritise suspects for an unsolved crime by comparing the way the crime was committed, known as Modus Operandi (MO), with previously solved crimes. However, given the enormous human effort required to look through and compare the descriptions of many previous crimes, such a strategy is usually reserved only for the most serious crimes such as murder and rape. Nevertheless, the police do record both free text and structured descriptions of offender behaviour for volume crimes such as burglaries, vandalism and street robbery in large textual archives that could be mined to extract very valuable linking information.

Similar to the way the MO can be used to prioritise suspects, it can also be used to group together and link different crimes, solved or unsolved, as exhibiting similar characteristics that might suggest they have been committed by the same person. However, it is important to notice that there might be many different ways to link crimes, not just by the description of the act, but also by its geographical location or time in which it was committed and that sometime there is no clear reasons why two crimes are eventually linked, as they might simply be crimes of opportunity.

Finally, the linking of suspects with each other or with convicted criminals is a recent area of research that makes use of social networks constructed from relational information extracted from the same police archives. It can be used to discover gangs and important relations between criminals and suspects.

The analogy between the linking of crimes and the linking of text described in Sect. 2 should now be clear. Suspects, convicted criminals, solved and unsolved crimes can be linked in a large hypertext that can be browsed by police analysts and criminologists to discover important information useful for prioritising and apprehending suspects related to unsolved crimes. Section 3.1 describes the conceptual model behind such network structures. Section 3.2, the core of this part of the paper, presents a model that has been used to link suspects to crimes, that is, to prioritise suspects in relation to unsolved crimes based on the MO. Section 3.3, presents an evaluation of the model and an analysis of the results. Finally, Sect. 3.4 presents the context in which this work is carried out and shows how the results could be fruitfully used by the police in an implemented system.

3.1 A Conceptual Model

In order to be able to access information by browsing automatically built networks of textual items extracted from police archives we need to design the networks following a conceptual model. We decided to use the EXPLICIT model which can be easily adapted to model our situation. In fact, nodes on the upper layer can be used to model suspects or convicted criminals, while nodes on the lower level can be used to model crimes. Thus, the model enables the representation of relationships between crimes and suspects/offenders, between individual crimes, and between individual suspects. These relationships need to be inferred from the textual items found in police archives, hence the necessity to use IR techniques to attempt to find and quantify these relationships.

The document used to describe a crime may take many forms. For example, it could be a witness statement from the victim of an assault, recorded by police officers during an interview. The descriptions are usually short (fewer than 40 words) and are grammatically informal with sentences often having no subject or main verb. There are a few typographical errors since there appears to be no spell checking, and punctuation is also informal. For these reasons, Natural Language Processing would be inappropriate. Here are two examples of descriptions of burglaries of average length:

> By suspect breaking in through ground floor window using jemmy, conducting untidy search and making off with quantity of cigarettes.

> By suspect posing as a council official inorder to gain entry to the premises then attempt to steal property.

We can see from these examples that certain terms such as jemmy, (a short crowbar) cigarettes, posing, and council official give information about the MO employed by the burglar. It is worth noting also that these documents hardly ever contain negative information e.g. 'suspect did not use the front door', so the presence of a term will indicate it relates to something that happened.

However, for there to be a similarity between descriptions of crimes by a common offender, we need to make the following assumptions:

- When an offender commits a number of similar crimes he roughly follows the same MO.
- The offender's MO is observable either directly from eyewitnesses or indirectly from the evidence left behind.
- The police record the evidence faithfully in written form so the resultant document can be seen as being about the MO.

The first two assumptions are rooted in psychology [8]. The third assumption rests on police procedure. They have a standard way of writing up descriptions of crimes either when taking a statement or providing their own summary for a crime database. However, the descriptions are so short that there might not be sufficient information in them to enable us to find meaningful similarities (similarities that reflect an MO). This is an important aspect that we will need to investigate.

3.2 Linking Crimes Descriptions

Our work exploits the fact that we have a number of offenders who commit a particular class of crime within a particular police district. We have one or more offences believed to be committed by each offender and a document associated with each offence. We wish to measure the similarity of an unsolved offence of a particular class with each set of offences linked to an offender to prioritise which offenders should be investigated.

Unlike the archetypal IR problem we do not have a user-generated query. Thus the concept of relevance is not useful here. Instead we define the concept of correspondence: a document is said to correspond to an offender if it describes an offence believed to have been committed by that offender. Correspondence is thus a Boolean attribute. Note that a document may correspond to more than one offender. To test any model we would want to define and calculate a measure of effectiveness from solved crimes to determine if the model did indeed help identify the offender. Such a measure of effectiveness must link correspondence with ranking functions extracted from term vectors derived from descriptions of crimes. In this section we present a study aimed at finding if meaningful and reliable similarities between descriptions of crimes can be obtained from police archives.

Processing the Text

In order to obtain term vectors from descriptions of crimes we need to process them using IR indexing techniques. Two approaches to indexing the documents were taken:

1. The text was tokenised into individual words and these were stemmed using Porter's stemming algorithm [14].
2. The words were stemmed using a purpose-built stemmer and tokeniser which use WordNet [29].

The second of these requires more explanation. WordNet provides sets of synonyms of nouns, verbs, adjectives and adverbs. We did not actually use the synonym information itself but rather utilised other files used to index the synonym sets. For each part of speech there is a list of entries, most of which are a single word, but many comprise more than one word such as 'public house' or 'dispose of'. The tokeniser searches for possible multiword tokens in the text for both the WordNet noun and verb sets. Since plurals and various parts of verbs would occur in the text, a stemmer would have to be sensitive to the requirement to look up words in the index file. Stemmers such as Porter will often mutilate the words and combine related words rather than different forms of the same word. Thus a stemmer was constructed using the list of irregular nouns and verbs also provided by WordNet. The motivation for constructing this tokenised text was driven by a different part of the project where other forms of analysis are performed on the text descriptions. It was worth seeing what the effect of the new tokeniser would be on the performance of the system.

In each case, stopwords from a list of 571 were removed [11]. Thus for the Porter stemmer, 'front door' would appear as two tokens and, using the WordNet approach, as a single token. For Porter, 'broke in' would be reduced to 'broke' since 'in' is a stopword. Using WordNet, it would be 'stemmed' to break and recognised as a single token. It is worth noting that given that the descriptions were short, very few tokens appeared more than once in a document.

Linking Crimes Using The Vector Space Model

The Vector Space Model defines ranking functions which take as parameters both the query and a document [42]. Since these are some of the simplest and well tried IR techniques that have proved very effective for the automatic construction of hypertexts, we tried to see if these models could be used to address the problem. As we noted above we do not have a user query. Nevertheless, a query can be generated by using the principle of relevance feedback or query by example. This query can then be used to rank the documents (crime descriptions) in the collection.

When a user submits a query to a typical IR system it will return a list of documents ranked in order. The user's search can then be refined by marking which of the documents are relevant or not and constructing a new query which is submitted to the system. Rocchio [35] defines a method for doing this for the Cosine Correlation model although it can be readily generalised. To specify the problem generally, suppose we have a ranking function $r : Q \times D \to \mathcal{R}$. Let there be two disjoint subsets of the document collection $D_r \subset D$ and $D_n \subset D$ representing the set of relevant and non-relevant documents. We seek to find an optimal query q', for which:

$$max_{q'}(\frac{1}{\mid D_r \mid} \sum_{d \in D_r} r(q', d) - \frac{1}{\mid D_n \mid} \sum_{d \in D_r} r(q', d)) \tag{1}$$

Such a query will seek to separate the documents deemed relevant and non-relevant. Although Rocchio proposes that q' should be used to modify the existing query q, it could be used as a query in its own right, which is what we attempted. It is worth noting that this query may be seen as a way of capturing the common features of the offence set corresponding to the offender.

For the crime data, we can generate a query linked to a particular offender by using subsets of documents which correspond and do not correspond to an offender. This generated query can be used to retrieve documents from the collection minus the ones used to construct the query. It should be noted that the set D_n will often be much larger than D_r because usually we would expect to have a large number of solved crimes believed not to have been committed by that offender.

We selected three well-known vector ranking functions: cosine correlation, coordination level and pivoted normalisation (as defined in [22]). Rocchio already provides query generation for Cosine Correlation. Adapting Rocchio's formula for the other two is straightforward. Measuring effectiveness using precision and recall showed some correlation between offender identifier and the description and were certainly better than random, but not nearly precise enough to be of any practical use. At 10% recall, precision was only 14%, implying that correspondence would occur 1 in 7 times. For higher levels of recall the precision was lower still.

One explanation for the inaccuracy is that correspondence is fundamentally different from relevance in that the former is rival. A document may be relevant to any number of queries, but an offence will only correspond to a small number (usually 1) of suspects and the model fails to capture this attribute. Furthermore, there is no way to readily incorporate other information into the model such as location of the offence or even how prolific the suspect is. Another problem is that the ranking functions provide only an ordinal measure, which means the ranking value gives no clue as to how much confidence should be attached to the prediction. It may be that a document contains no useful information to identify the suspect and there is no way of knowing this. Thus we now propose a model based on probability which obviates these problems.

Linking Crimes Using Language Modeling

Probabilistic Language Models were originally used in speech recognition, but in the last 10 years unigram language models (ones which ignore word order) have been adapted to construct ranking functions [25,38]. Here we summarise the case for using them in IR.

We assume that each document in the collection was created by its own language model, a random process which emits terms from a predefined vocabulary with given probabilities for each term. For a given query, q, we can then calculate the probability that such a language model, associated with document d, could generate this query:

$$P(q \mid d) = \prod_{t \in q} p_d(t)^{c(t,q)} \qquad (2)$$

where t is a term, $p_d(t)$ is the probability that the language model will emit term t and $c(t, q)$ is the number of occurrences of t in q. The argument here is that a higher probability that the query will be generated will imply a higher probability that q describes information addressed by d.

We actually want to estimate the probability that each document is relevant to a query in order to rank the documents. If we assume that the user constructed the query q with the intention of finding a unique relevant document in the collection, then by using Bayes' theorem we can derive the probability that d is that very document. This becomes the ranking function.

$$P(d \mid q) = \frac{P(d) \cdot P(q \mid d)}{P(q)} \qquad (3)$$

Here, $P(d)$ is the prior probability of the document being relevant to any query. In the absence of other information this is assumed to be the same for all documents. $P(q)$ is the probability that the query would be constructed, but since it is the same in all cases it can be treated as a constant.

Given that the only known output of the language model is the document d, the maximum likelihood estimator for $p_d(t)$ will be:

$$p_d(t) = tf_d(t) \qquad (4)$$

where $tf_d(t)$ is simply the term frequency of that term in document d. However, this leads to the Zero Probability Problem (ZPP) [31]. If the query contains a term which is not in the document, then the probability that the language model will emit that term is zero and thus the probability of the query being generated is also zero. The solution is to use smoothing and estimate the language model using both the document and information about the whole collection several approaches exist. One example of smoothing, Jelinek-Mercer smoothing, is given here. This was found to be the most effective method for our data:

$$p_d(t) = (1 - \lambda) \cdot tf_d(t) + \lambda \cdot tf_c(t) \qquad (5)$$

where $tf_c(t)$ is the term frequency in the whole collection and λ is the smoothing parameter. A value around 0.3-0.5 was found empirically to work best.

We assume that two descriptions containing many of the same terms will imply similar behaviour. So, for example, if the terms 'smash', 'window' and 'cd' appear in the description of a burglary, this is likely to imply the mode of entry and what was taken. Thus we use the Language Modeling approach to derive a ranking function for suspects. The description of the unsolved crime is deemed to be the query. Language models are estimated not for each solved crime but for each set of solved crimes that has a common offender. Note that where there are two or more offenders, the same crime description may appear in more than one set. For brevity we shall say that each model corresponds to one offender, although strictly speaking, it models the behaviour of one offender when committing one type of crime. Using Bayes' theorem from above and replacing in equation 3 q with u (unsolved crime) and d with o (offender) we have:

$$P(o \mid u) = \frac{P(o) \cdot P(u \mid o)}{P(u)} \qquad (6)$$

We can interpret $P(u \mid o)$ as the probability that o committed crime u, given there was only one offender; this is used to prioritise the suspects. It is the posterior probability of having observed the crime description. $P(o \mid u)$ is the probability that o would commit a crime such as u and is calculated from the language model. $P(u)$ is the probability that a crime such as this could have been committed by anybody. It can be eliminated from the calculation. $P(o)$ is the probability that the offender would commit any crime of this type. This is the prior probability and needs to be considered in more detail.

The simplest way to estimate the prior is to assume that all suspects are equally likely to offend and this we term the *naïve prior*. However, since it is known that some criminals have a greater propensity to offend than others, the prior can be based on the past frequency of offending. This we refer to as the *Casablanca prior* since, if we know nothing else, we assume that the most likely offender is the one with the most previous offences (as in 'round up the usual suspects'). We also can conceive of an intelligence-based prior, the *statistical prior*, where probabilities are based on timely knowledge about which offenders are believed to be active based on police intelligence or intuition [30], although we currently have no sufficient data to validate this approach.

3.3 Evaluation

For any system based on this model to be used by police analysts, it would be necessary to establish that there was some relation between the suspect prioritisation and who the actual offenders were. Here we can partition the solved crimes into a training set of 'solved' crimes and a test set of crimes deemed 'unsolved' for the purpose of the experiment. If we use the analogy with IR that a crime u is 'relevant' to o if o is the offender or one of the offenders, then precision and recall measures can show the effectiveness of the prioritisation and in particular that it is better than picking the names of suspects out of a hat.

Given a query, for the first n retrieved documents in the ranked list, *precision* is the proportion of retrieved documents that are relevant and *recall* is the proportion of all relevant documents which have been retrieved. As n increases, recall rises and precision tends to fall.

Assessing Suspect Likelihood

In traditional IR applications, the probabilities generated by Language Modeling are never actually used other than ordinally to rank documents. This is firstly because a user will browse through a list of retrieved documents until he finds one of interest and so the actual probabilities are not that useful. Secondly, the probabilities are only meaningful where there is a unique relevant document in the entire collection, which is rare. For this reason, the ranking function used is usually the log probability and the actual values of $P(d)$ and $P(q)$ are ignored since they become constant terms. We argue this is different for suspect prioritisation.

Probabilities can be useful as a measure of suspect likelihood. Firstly, if the police are investigating a number of crimes of one type with limited resources, they may be inclined to put those resources into crimes where a clear front runner emerges. Ranking alone cannot tell us this. Secondly, the existence of a single offender for a given crime is not unreasonable. Indeed, when two or more criminals act together, they usually take on the behaviour of the dominant member of the group and so this would be the one identified.

However, the probabilities cannot be taken at face value. The models will often overestimate the probability of the prime suspect, so that a probability of 0.99 will in reality be closer to 0.6. Nevertheless, even an imperfect measure of likelihood would be an improvement over simple ranking.

An inspection of the actual descriptions of crimes shows that some are very specific about what happened and others contain little more than a vague description of the crime. Even in this case the model will still prioritise suspects, but the probabilities of the highly ranked suspects would be little more than the ones ranked low and the user could conclude that the system was not revealing much.

When assessing the effectiveness of an IR model, it is usual for the precision and recall metrics to be calculated for each query and then the mean taken over all queries. Here, we take a different approach so that we can compare prioritising the suspects, on the one hand, merely by the ordering imposed by the ranking function and, on the other hand, by taking account of the actual probabilities. We define entire precision and entire recall thus: for each possible combination of unsolved crime and suspect we calculate some ranking metric and then calculate the precision and recall over the set of pairs. In the context of suspect prioritisation this has a natural interpretation. Assume that there are a number of unsolved crimes to be cleared up. We proceed successfully to investigate each suspect by going down the list of all suspects for all crimes. Thus, if there were m crimes, each suspect would appear m times in this list. If we are using the probabilities in a purely ordinal way, we would first investigate all the highest ranked suspects for each crime, then and only then all the second highest ranked suspects and so on. If we are using the actual probabilities, we first investigate the pair of suspect and crime with the highest probability, then the second highest pair and so on. Therefore we may well investigate suspects 1, 2 and 3 for crime A before suspect 1 of crime B if the probabilities of the former were higher. Precision in this context means the proportion of those suspects investigated that turned out to be the offenders (note that one suspect investigated for 2 crimes counts as 2). Recall is the proportion of the crimes that have been solved. As we go down the list we will solve more crimes (recall increases) and would expect to get a diminishing yield of offenders (precision falls).

If the actual probabilities tell us something useful about suspect likelihood, then entire precision will be higher for a given level of recall measures. The analysis below supports this.

Results and Analysis

Table 1 summarises the eight crime sets taken from the police database. Only serial solved offenders were considered (two or more offences) and this restriction meant that for some crime types (excluded here) there were not enough data points to make analysis meaningful.

For each crime set, the offences were partitioned into a training set to estimate the language models and a test set to evaluate the model. The training consisted of n offences randomly selected per offender where n was set to 1 for all but two of the sets. For these larger data sets n was set to 2 for shoplifting and 4 for burglary. The remaining offences not used for training formed the test set. In cases where n was greater than 1, it was necessary to ensure that only offenders with at least $n + 1$ were considered suspects. The random partitioning into sets does create a source of variability and thus for all statistics, 100 runs were performed, each with its own random partition, and the mean was taken.

Since precision and recall will vary depending how far down the list we consider the suspects, a common convention is to draw precision and recall graphs where precision is interpolated at various levels of recall. The convention here is the one recommended in [11].

Each set was analysed using naïve and Casablanca priors; both simple ranking and actual probabilities were considered. The Casablanca prior calculation is based on the propensity to offend in the test set (since this is unbiased). Figures 5 and 6 show the precision/recall graph for naïve prior for criminal damage and assault. Note that actual probabilities outperform simple rankings and also that prioritisation is more effective for criminal damage than assault. The graphs show a downward slope; this phenomenon is repeated for all the other crime sets, which for reasons of space cannot be shown. If the

Table 1: Summary of crime data analysed

Set No.	Crime Type	No. Crimes	No. Offenders
1	Theft from Vehicles	155	51
2	Other Theft	83	28
3	Shoplifting	803	294
4	Assault	436	205
5	Criminal Damage	255	82
6	Criminal Damage to Vehicles	37	17
7	Burglary	854	227
8	Street Robbery	138	62

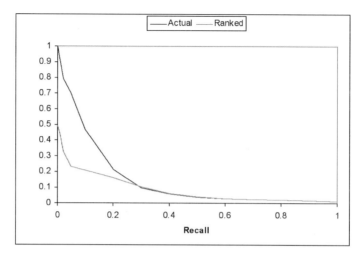

Fig. 5: Precision and Recall Graph for Criminal Damage using Naïve Prior

model were to find no behavioural similarities in the crimes then the graphs would run flat roughly parallel and close to the x-axis which is clearly not the case here.

An alternative measure which captures precision and recall at different points is average precision which is, loosely speaking, the area under the graph. Table 2 gives values for all datasets. Note that a higher value implies more effective prioritisation.

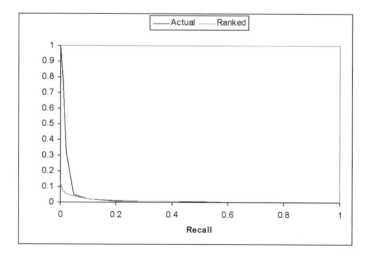

Fig. 6: Precision and Recall Graph for Assault using Naïve Prior

Table 2: Entire Average Precision

Set No.	Naïve Prior		Casablanca Prior	
	Actual	Ranked	Actual	Ranked
1	0.211	0.138	0.322	0.214
2	0.253	0.174	0.285	0.213
3	0.023	0.015	0.028	0.021
4	0.024	0.011	0.025	0.012
5	0.137	0.083	0.173	0.112
6	0.585	0.508	0.625	0.533
7	0.116	0.066	0.150	0.100
8	0.124	0.086	0.141	0.101

It is a mathematical fact that the Casablanca prior will give no worse results than the naïve prior given the way it was constructed from data. Table 2 shows that it is always better, but by varying degrees. It is also worth noting that actual probabilities outperform simple ranking in 8 out of 8 cases, although simple ranking always outperforms random prioritisation. Using the sign test we can conclude with greater than 99.5% confidence that actual probabilities give more information than simple ranking which in turn is better than random.

It appears from these statistics that prioritisation works better for some types of crime than others. Possible explanations are that for some types of offence behaviour is more characteristic of a particular offender or the behaviour is more observable and thus more readily recorded. An example here is damage to motor vehicles where different offenders appear to damage vehicles in their own peculiar way and the nature of the damage is observable and thus recorded.

The data sets which appear to perform poorly over all (shoplifting and assault) actually do quite well at low levels of recall implying that there will be a small number of cases when the model will find a link and identify the offender. Table 3 gives precision statistics for these low levels of recall for actual probabilities (Casablanca prior). This corresponds to where suspects are given very high actual probabilities and are thus the ones most likely to be the offenders. We still see that prioritisation works better for some data sets than others.

The results clearly show that the use of Language Modeling can be effective for prioritisation of suspects and does so by linking offenders' behaviour expressed by terms from the natural language descriptions. This not only validates this approach but also shows more generally that behavioural aspects can be used to help in the investigation of volume crimes where details are stored as free text. The links between crimes by a common offender appear stronger in some datasets than in others. It is not possible from the small number of data sets here to conclude that this is an intrinsic property of the offence, but there is some reason to believe that some offences give rise to more offender-specific behavioural information than others.

Table 3: Precision at Low Recall

Set No.	Recall			
	0.01	0.02	0.05	0.1
1	0.999	0.983	0.933	0.888
2	1.000	0.988	0.863	0.658
3	0.750	0.208	0.069	0.039
4	0.798	0.398	0.054	0.021
5	0.933	0.850	0.803	0.630
6	1.000	1.000	0.919	0.740
7	1.000	0.948	0.640	0.358
8	1.000	1.000	0.557	0.261

The use of Bayes' theorem means that other information can be introduced into the prior. This makes the model extensible so that other information can be included. For example, it would be possible to construct a prior based on geographical locations of the crime and the offender's base.

We have shown that actual probabilities give more information than simple ranking since they imply suspect likelihood. Thus we have extended the use of Language Modeling more generally. It is an open question whether the actual probability can be used in traditional IR as a measure of relevance likelihood.

3.4 From Investigative Psychology to Terms Vectors: The iMOV Project

The work we presented in the previous section has been carried out in the context of the iMOV project. The EPSRC project iMOV aims at building an interactive MO visualisation system integrating geographical information for suspect prioritisation and investigation management. The project is a collaboration between the Department of Computer and Information Sciences of the University of Strathclyde[1] and the Department of Psychology of the University of Liverpool in UK.

The project is still at its early stages since it started in late 2006 but, as the work reported in the previous section shows, we are making good progress toward finding the best IR techniques to be used for linking crimes to suspects [6].

The iMOV project was preceded by a feasibility study that was funded by the London Metropolitan Police and carried out by the Kelvin Institute in Glasgow, in collaboration with the Department of Computer and Information Sciences of the University of Strathclyde and the Department of Psychology of

---

[1] Fabio Crestani was a Professor of Computer Science at the University of Strathclyde from March 2000 to December 2006 and is still the principal investigator of the project for that university.

the University of Liverpool in UK. In that study, named iOPS, state of the art techniques for linking crimes and suspects were employed to find, among other things, relations between crimes and suspects. The study also made use of geographical information related to offender behaviour which was displayed on a graphical user interface. The prototype system thus enabled a police analyst to browse information extracted from police archives to help investigate new crimes. Figures 7 to 10 show an example of the use of the prototype.

Figure 7 shows crimes of a specific type (for example burglary) committed in a selected geographical area. The analyst can position the mouse over each crime and see its description.

Given a new crime, the analyst can specify some keywords that he believes characterise the MO of the offender. The system highlights crimes that exhibit similar MOs. The crimes, displayed as small crosses, are grouped in geographical clusters. In Fig. 8 the analyst has selected one of these clusters.

Once a cluster is selected, the analyst can ask for suspects living in the selected geographical area to be displayed. The suspects houses or assumed bases of operation are displayed as small squares. The analyst can position the mouse over any of the squares and see the data relative to the suspect. In addition, the analyst can select one or more crimes and ask the system to prioritise suspects related to these crimes. Figure 8 shows such a case[2].

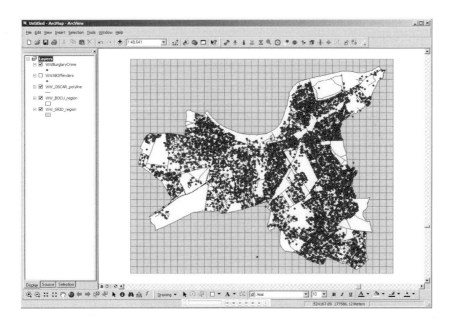

Fig. 7: Crimes committed in a specific geographical area

---

[2] The data displayed in the example are, obviously, fictitious.

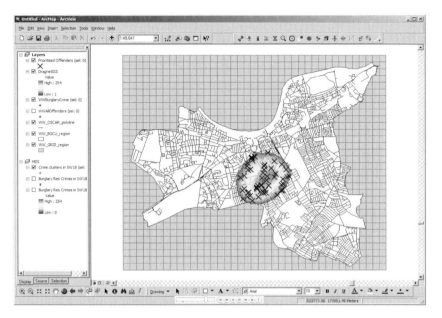

Fig. 8: A cluster of crimes exhibiting similar MOs

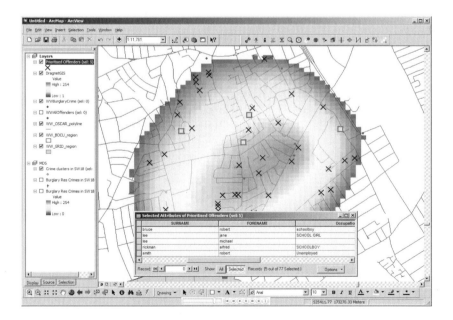

Fig. 9: Suspect prioritisation

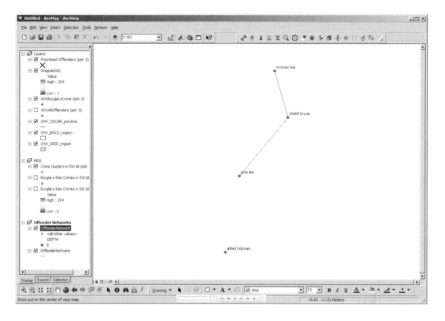

Fig. 10: Visualisation of social relationship between suspects

Once one suspect is selected, the analyst can request to have other suspects related to the selected one to be displayed. Figure 10 shows the known social network related to the selected suspect.

This brief example shows how it is possible to browse a large network of information related to crimes and suspects that has been automatically constructed using IR (or related) techniques and that follows a clear conceptual model.

In iMOV we intend to move forward from the result of iOPS by using more advanced techniques for linking crime and suspects, such as the one presented in this paper.

4 Conclusions

In this paper we have presented how a conceptual model and a set of IR techniques that have been used for automatically building hypertexts can be extended also to other tasks, such as linking crimes. This is an unconventional but still useful application of these techniques. In this context we have presented how language modeling can be used for suspect prioritisation and we have shown how actual probabilities can be used as measure of suspect prioritisation likelihood. This work is part of the iMOV project in which the model presented here will be extended to include additional available information in police archives that can be used to improve suspect prioritisation, like the geographical location of crimes and the suspect's base or the suspect's social network.

Acknowledgements

This work is partially supported by the UK EPSRC (Engineering and Physical Sciences Research Council) under the grant EP/D040639/1.
    A large part of the theoretical and experimental work reported in Sect. 3 was carried out by Dr. Richard Bache at the Department of Computer and Information Sciences of the University of Strathclyde, Glasgow, UK.

References

1. Agosti, M., Colotti, R., Gradenigo, G.: A two-level hypertext retrieval model for legal data. In: E.A. Fox (ed.) Proc. 14th Annual International ACM SIGIR Conference on Research and Development in Information Retrieval (SIGIR 1991), pp. 316–325. ACM Press, New York, USA, Chicago, USA (1991)
2. Agosti, M., Crestani, F.: A methodology for the automatic construction of a Hypertext for Information Retrieval. In: Proceedings of the ACM Symposium on Applied Computing, pp. 745–753. Indianapolis, USA (1993)
3. Agosti, M., Crestani, F., Melucci, M.: Automatic authoring and construction of hypertext for Information Retrieval. ACM Multimedia Systems $3(1)$, 15–24 (1995)
4. Agosti, M., Crestani, F., Melucci, M.: Design and implementation of a tool for the automatic construction of hypertexts for Information Retrieval. Information Processing and Management $32(4)$, 459–476 (1996)
5. Agosti, M., Crestani, F., Melucci, M.: On the use of Information Retrieval techniques for the automatic construction of hypertexts. Information Processing and Management $33(2)$, 133–144 (1997)
6. Bache, R., Crestani, F., Canter, D., Youngs, D.: Application of language models to suspect prioritisation and suspect likelihood in serial crimes. In: International Workshop on Computer Forensics. Manchester, UK (2007)
7. Belew, R.: Finding Out About: A Cognitive Perspective on Search Engines Technology and the WWW. Cambridge University Press, Cambridge, UK (2000)
8. Bennell, C., Canter, D.: Linking commercial burglaries by modus operandi: test using regression and ROC analysis. Science and Justice $42(3)$ (2002)
9. Botafogo, R.: Cluster analysis for hypertext systems. In: R. Korfhage, E.M. Rasmussen, P. Willett (eds.) Proc. 16th Annual International ACM SIGIR Conference on Research and Development in Information Retrieval (SIGIR 1993), pp.116–125. ACM Press, New York, USA, Pittsburgh, PA, USA (1993)
10. Botafogo, R., Rivlin, E., Shneiderman, B.: Structural analysis of hypertextx: identifying hierarchies and useful metrics. ACM Transactions on Information Systems $10(2)$, 142–180 (1992)
11. Bruza, P., van der Weide, T.: Stratified hypermedia structures for information disclosure. The Computer Journal $35(3)$, 208–220 (1992)

12. Canter, D.: Offender profiling and criminal differentiation. Journal of Legal and Criminological Psychology **5**, 23–46 (2000)

13. Canter, D., Fritzon, K.: Differentiating arsonists: a model of firesetting actions and characteristics. Legal and criminal psychology **3**, 73–96 (1998)

14. Crestani, F., Landoni, M., Melucci, M.: Appearance and functionality of electronic books. International Journal of Digital Libraries **6**(2), 192–209 (2006)

15. Crestani, F., Lee, P.: Searching the web by constrained spreading activation. Information Processing and Management **36**(4), 585–605 (2000)

16. Crestani, F., Melucci, M.: A case study of automatic authoring: from a textbook to a hyper-textbook. Data and Knowledge Engineering **27**(1), 1–30 (1998)

17. Crestani, F., Melucci, M.: A methodology for the enhancement of a hypertext version of a textbook by the automatic insertion of links in the subject index. In: Proceedings of the IEEE ADL'98 Conference, pp. 157–166. Santa Barbara, CA, USA (1998)

18. Crestani, F., Melucci, M.: Automatic construction of hypertexts for self-referencing: the hyper-textbook project. Information Systems **28**(7), 769–790 (2003)

19. Crestani, F., Ntioudis, S.: User centred evaluation of an automatically constructed hyper-textbook. Journal of Educational Multimedia and Hypermedia **11**(1), 3–19 (2002)

20. Egan, D., Remde, J., Gomez, L., Landauer, T., Eberhardt, J., Lochbaum, C.: Formative design-evaluation of SuperBook. ACM Transactions on Information Systems **7**(1), 30–57 (1989)

21. Egan, D., Remde, J., Landauer, T., Lochbaum, C., Gomez, L.: Acquiring information in books and superbooks. Machine Mediated Learning **3**, 259–277 (1989)

22. Fang, H., Tao, T., Cheng-Xiang, Z.: A formal study of information retrieval heuristics. In: M. Sanderson, K. Järvelin, J. Allan, P. Bruza (eds.) Proc. 27th Annual International ACM SIGIR Conference on Research and Development in Information Retrieval (SIGIR 2004), pp. 49–56. ACM Press, New York, USA, Sheffield, UK (2004)

23. Frisse, M.: Searching for information in a medical handbook. Communications of the ACM **31**(7), 880–886 (1988)

24. Furuta, R., Plaisant, C., Shneiderman, B.: Automatically transforming regularly structured linear documents into hypertext. Electronic Publishing **2**(4), 211–229 (1989)

25. Lafferty, J., Cheng-Xiang, Z.: Probabilistic relevance models based on document and language generation. In: W.B. Croft, J. Lafferty (eds.) Language modelling for information retrieval. Kluwer Academic Publisher, Dodrecht, The Netherlands (2003)

26. Landoni, M.: The Visual Book system: a study of the use of the visual rhetoric in the design of electronic books. PhD Thesis, Department of Information Science, University of Strathclyde, Glasgow, Scotland, UK (1997)

27. Mayfield, J.: Two-level models of hypertext. In: C. Nicholas, J. Mayfield (eds.) Intelligent Hypertexts: advanced techniques for the World Wide Web, Lecture Notes in Computer Science, pp. 91–108. Springer Verlag, Berlin, Germany (1997)

28. Melucci, M.: Making digital libraries effective: automatic generation of link for similarity search across hyper-textbooks. Journal of the American Society for Information Science and Technology **55**(5), 414–430 (2004)

29. Miller, G.A.: WordNet: An on-line lexical database. International Journal of Lexicography **3**(4), 235–312 (1990)
30. Oatley, G., Ewart, B.: Crime analysis software: pins in maps, clustering and bayes net prediction. Expert Systems with Applications **25**(4), 569–588 (2003)
31. Ponte, J., Croft, W.B.: A language modelling approach to information retrieval. In: Proc. 21st Annual International ACM SIGIR Conference on Research and Development in Information Retrieval (SIGIR 1998), pp. 275–281. ACM Press, New York, USA Melbourne, Australia (1998)
32. Porter, M.: An algorithm for suffix stripping. Program **14**(3), 130–137 (1980)
33. Rada, R.: Converting a textbook to hypertext. ACM Transactions on Information Systems **10**(3), 294–315 (1992)
34. Robertson, J., Merkus, E., Ginige, A.: The hypermedia authoring research toolkit (HART). In: Proceedings of the ACM European Conference on Hypermedia Technology, pp. 177–185. Edinburgh, Scotland, UK (1994)
35. Salton, G., McGill, M.: The SMART retrieval system - experiments in automatic document retrieval. Prentice Hall Inc., Englewood Cliffs, USA (1983)
36. Smeaton, A.: Building hypertext under the influence of topology metrics. In: Proceedings of the IWHD Conference. Montpellier, France (1995)
37. Smeaton, A., Morrissey, P.: Experiments on the automatic construction of hypertext from text. Tech. Rep. CA-0295, School of Computer Application, Dublin, Ireland (1995)
38. Sparck Jones, K., Robertson, S.E., Hiemstra, D., Zaragoza, H.: Language modelling and relevance. In: W.B. Croft, J. Lafferty (eds.) Language modelling for information retrieval. Kluwer Academic Publisher, Dodrecht, The Netherlands (2003)
39. Tebbutt, J.: User evaluation of automatically generated semantic hypertext links in a heavily used procedural manual. Information Processing and Management **35**(1), 1–18 (1999)
40. Thompson, R.: The design and implementation of an intelligent interface for Information Retrieval. Technical report, Computer and Information Science Department, University of Massachusetts, Amherst, MA. USA (1989)
41. van Rijsbergen, C.J.: Information Retrieval, second edn. Butterworths, London, UK (1979)
42. Wong, S., Ziarko, W., Raghavan, V., Wong, P.: On modelling of information retrieval concepts in vector spaces. ACM Transactions on Information Systems **12**(2), 299–321 (1987)

Modeling Retrieval and Navigation in Context

Massimo Melucci

Department of Information Engineering – University of Padua
Via Gradenigo, 6/b – 35131 Padua – Italy
melo@dei.unipd.it

Abstract. There is a growing realization that context can constrain Information Retrieval thereby reducing the complexity of a retrieval system. At this aim, a system has to retrieve documents by considering time, place, interaction, task, and many other factors that are implicit in the user environment. Instead of resorting to heuristics, a principled approach to Information Retrieval in Context may help understand how to design these systems. In this chapter, a principled approach to context-aware navigation and retrieval is presented.

Key words: vector spaces, information retrieval in context, personalization, implicit feedback, Vector Space Model

1 Introduction

An Information Retrieval (IR) system is designed and implemented with the view to searching all and only the documents relevant to any information need of any user, at any moment and in any place. What is relevant to one user in one place at one time may no longer be relevant to another user, in another place or at another time. The features characterizing users, time, places, or anything emerging from user-system interaction form a notion which is usually called context. In principle an IR system should be context-aware. In practice classical systems such as search engines are unaware of such a highly dynamic search environment and contextual features are not captured at indexing-time, nor are they exploited at retrieval-time.

It is during interaction that context can be observed and measured. As interaction takes the form of navigation and query-based search in the information space, an approach to modeling navigation would comprise the way context affects navigation and search. For this reason, this chapter describes a model for navigation and search in context, that is, the navigation and search which adapt the retrieval results according to what the end user does during interaction. As hypertext is the main information retrieval tool for navigating information spaces, this chapter illustrates how the model can be applied when automatic links are built for document collections or electronic books, although the model is more general and can be applied to different domains.

One approach to retrieving information in context is to inject space, histories, profiles, sensors data, clocks and calendars into indexing or retrieval algorithms. This approach does not usually operate at model-level since the most common models lack a formal representation of context. Indeed, IR models were defined by ignoring the multiplicity of the users, of the information needs, of the locations, of the times and of the histories. The probabilistic model for IR might provide the constructs for modeling context, and the probability of relevance can be updated through Bayes' Theorem when context features are modeled as random events. This type of probability revision mechanism is the core of Relevance Feedback (RF), which incorporates interaction in a more or less formal way and captures some contextual features through query modification [11]. The Vector Space Model (VSM) provides the constructs for implementing RF too [12], yet RF remains an application of the VSM. It is our belief that context should be incorporated at model level and should not only be an application, since IR is intrinsically and naturally context-dependent.

The material illustrated in this chapter is based on the theory developed in [6] for modeling and discovering context – here, the main concepts and the implications for search and navigation across hypertext are illustrated after introducing the main ideas underlying the model. A vector is generated by a basis just as an informative object or an information need is generated in a context. Every basis vector refers to a distinct dimension of context, such as time, space, word meaning or topic. In this way, a document may be represented in a subspace spanned by basis vectors which represent a topic derived from term, query or document clusters, or which represent the genre, e.g. introductory level or advanced level. As a consequence, a different basis would generate a different vector in the same way as a different context would generate different information needs or informative objects.

This chapter also presents the function for ranking objects in context originally introduced in [7]. Let us consider an object vector and let a basis be a representation of a context. The problem is to measure to what extent the vector has been generated by the basis which represents a context. Such a measure can be defined, since the basis spans a subspace. The ranking function is basically a distance measure between the document vector and the subspace. Even though ranking is still based on the inner product between vectors, the basic difference is that the distance depends on the basis, i.e. on the dimensions of context and ultimately on context itself. Finally, different bases can arise and as a result ranking can change, since an informative object can be produced by different contexts.

The chapter is structured as follows. The idea of employing the notion of basis is outlined in Sect. 2, while the ranking function is illustrated in Sect. 3.

How context can be formalized is illustrated in Sect. 4, while Sect. 5 illustrates the way the model describes navigation in context. Some related research is reported in Sect. 6.

2 Modeling Context

The idea of using bases for modeling context is based on this parallel: an object vector is generated by a basis just as an informative object is generated within a context. Therefore, a basis generates a vector subspace; this subspace includes all the vectors generated by a basis and the subspace can be considered as the representation of a context. One can visually think of a context as a plane in a three-dimensional space and all the vectors lying in the plane represent objects placed in the same context. As one vector spans a ray passing through the origin, the ray is an equivalent representation of the object – it is worth noting that a ray is a one-dimensional subspace of the vector space; as a consequence, subspaces and not only vectors are a representation of objects. As infinite planes include a ray, the fact that one object belongs to a myriad of contexts can simultaneously be represented.

The features characterizing users, time, places, or anything emerging from user-system interaction form a notion which can be referred to as context. Since context is an ambiguous concept, the following definitions used in this chapter are provided:

- Variable: refers to either an entity of the context, for example, user, task, topic, or document, or a relationship between entities, for example, relevance or aboutness.
- Dimension: refers to a property of an entity, for example, user behavior, task difficulty, topic clarity, document genre, or relevance.
- Factor: refers to a value of a property, for example, browsing, complex search task, hard topic, relevant, non-relevant, or mathematical document.

These definitions are sufficiently precise for describing in this section a framework that can be used in algorithms automated by IR systems to support searching in context. Through their interaction behavior users can define their own interaction context that may be representative of contextual influence from the task or other constraints on them. For example, many short document display times may be indicative of a user attempting a time-constrained task. When some evidence is gathered from context, implicit relevance feedback (IRF) can be performed for expanding queries, reordering retrieval results, or re-searching. Implicit feedback algorithms utilize interaction between searchers and search systems to learn more about users' needs and interests than expressed in query statements alone. This additional information can be used to formulate improved queries or directly improve retrieval performance. The framework described is based on Linear Algebra concepts which gives an algebraic representation of vectors, operators and subspaces. Once some variables and dimensions of context are selected from the domain for which a context-aware IR tool is designed, the methodology presented in this chapter can be summarized as follows:

1. for each dimension of context a set of orthogonal vectors is defined – each orthogonal vector of such a set models one factor of the dimension of context;
2. a basis is built for representing a context by selecting one or more factors from each dimension – in this way, a context is modeled by a set of possible contextual factors and one factor refers to one dimension;
3. an informative object is matched against a context by computing a function of the distance between the vector and the subspace spanned by the basis – the closer the vector to the subspace, the more the object is "in the context".

To support the description of the framework let us begin with an example. In Fig. 1 we show how the framework represents a document seen from two points of view given by two dimensions. There are two sets of axes – one set of rays is spanned by the vectors $E = \{\mathbf{e}_1, \mathbf{e}_2, \mathbf{e}_3\}$, while the other set is spanned by the vectors $U = \{\mathbf{u}_1, \mathbf{u}_2, \mathbf{u}_3\}$; for example, $\mathbf{e}_1$ spans $L(\{\mathbf{e}_1\})$, namely, $L(\{\mathbf{e}_1\})$ is the subspace of the vectors which are obtained by multiplying $\mathbf{e}_1$ by a scalar. A set of coordinates describes a dimension of context; for example, the dimension of context spanned by E may be "document genre". A ray depicts a one-dimensional subspace, e.g. $L(\{\mathbf{u}_i\})$. As a subspace (e.g. a ray) is spanned by a vector, e.g. $\mathbf{u}_i$, the vector describes a value (contextual factor) of this dimension – for example, if the dimension is document genre, $\mathbf{u}_1$ may refer to "introductory" while $\mathbf{u}_2$ may refer to "advanced". In this way, a mathematical representation of contextual factors and dimensions is provided.

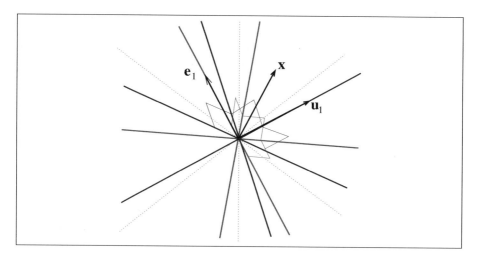

Fig. 1: A vector is generated by infinite dimensions

The mathematical properties of vectors and subspaces can be exploited for representing the properties of contextual factors and dimensions.

In general, factors of distinct dimensions are mutually independent [1]. This means that a contextual factor cannot be described by a vector which is derived by linearly combining the vectors of other factors. In particular, the rays, namely, the vectors corresponding to a given dimension of context are mutually orthogonal for signifying that the values taken by the dimension are mutually exclusive. Orthogonality implies that the inner product between the vectors spanning the rays is null, thus measuring the event that a mutual exclusion relationship exists between the contextual factors represented – for example, "introductory" excludes "advanced" and viceversa. The way orthogonality can be used as a measure of mutual exclusion is introduced in [16].

Figure 1 depicts how many distinct dimensions co-exist in the same space. This superposition of dimensions can naturally be represented by the infinite sets of coordinates which can be defined in the vector space. In the figure, E superposes U. Both E and U can "generate" the same vector $\mathbf{x}$. The myriad of dimensions model a document or a query from different points of view and each perspective corresponds to a dimension of context. Mathematically, a vector $\mathbf{x}$ is generated by the contextual factors $\{\mathbf{u}_1, \mathbf{u}_2\}$ as $\mathbf{x} = p_1^2\mathbf{u}_1 + p_2^2\mathbf{u}_2$ where $\mathbf{u}_1 \perp \mathbf{u}_2$, $p_1^2 + p_2^2 = 1$ and $p_i^2 \geq 0$. At the same time, $\mathbf{x} = q_1^2\mathbf{e}_1 + q_2^2\mathbf{e}_2$ where $\mathbf{e}_1 \perp \mathbf{e}_2$, $q_1^2 + q_2^2 = 1$ and $q_i^2 \geq 0$ [2].

Let us consider a set of vectors $B = \{\mathbf{b}_1, \ldots, \mathbf{b}_k\}$ where $\mathbf{b}_i$ represents a contextual factor of a dimension of context – as the $\mathbf{b}_i$'s can be of different dimensions, they are independent and not necessarily mutually orthogonal. One projector can be computed from each vector. A projector is an operator that maps a vector to another vector which belongs to a given subspace. A projector is a symmetric and idempotent operator, that is, $\mathbf{B}_i^\top = \mathbf{B}_i$ and $\mathbf{B}_i^2 = \mathbf{B}_i$ – the projectors onto the subspaces $L(\{\mathbf{b}_i\})$'s are defined as $\mathbf{b}_i \cdot \mathbf{b}_i^\top$. If $L(\{\mathbf{b}_i\})$ is the ray containing $\mathbf{b}_i$, then the projection of $\mathbf{y}$ onto $L(\{\mathbf{b}_i\})$ is $\mathbf{B}_i \cdot \mathbf{y}$. If $\mathbf{b}_i, \mathbf{b}_j$ refer to the same dimension, $\mathbf{B}_i \cdot \mathbf{B}_j = 0$ when $i \neq j$ thus defining the notion of projector orthogonality. In general, two projectors $\mathbf{B}_i$ and $\mathbf{B}_j$ are oblique and non-commutative, that is, $\mathbf{B}_i \cdot \mathbf{B}_j \neq 0$ and $\mathbf{B}_i \cdot \mathbf{B}_j \neq \mathbf{B}_j \cdot \mathbf{B}_i$. As there is a one-to-one correspondence between a subspace spanned by a set of vectors and its projector, a projector can be taken as the algebraic operator for a contextual factor and a linear combination of projectors is a mathematical operator which refers to a mixture of contextual factors.

Indeed, a contextual factor is a sort of atomic notion that cannot be decomposed into simpler notions. But, more complex notions can be built by combining contextual factors. Mathematically, the most natural combination which can represent a context is the linear combination. Thus, the operator

---

[1] A set of vectors are mutually independent if no vector is a linear combination of the others.

[2] An explanation of these expressions is given in [8].

adopted in this chapter is a linear function of projectors formulated by using a predefined set of coefficients which measure the weight of each dimension of context. Therefore, the operator is

$$\mathbf{C}_B = w_1 \mathbf{B}_1 + \cdots + w_k \mathbf{B}_k \tag{1}$$

where the w_i's are non-negative coefficients such that $w_1 + \cdots + w_k = 1$ and the $\mathbf{B}_i$'s are the projectors onto the subspaces $L(\{\mathbf{b}_i\})$'s. $\mathbf{C}_B$ is called *context matrix* or *context operator* in this chapter, since it describes the context described by B.

The linear combination of some basis vectors well reflects the idea that an object is generated by a *mixture* of dimensions of context, i.e. a context influences the materialization of the object by combining different dimensions. The elements of $\mathbf{p}$ are the coefficients that linearly combine the basis vector for generating $\mathbf{x}$. The p_i's are a measure of the degree to which the respective basis vector $\mathbf{b}_i$'s are chosen for generating $\mathbf{x}$. For example, a document is materialized by combining different meanings or different aspects, such as informative content, space, time, or search history. Alternatively, the basis vectors can describe different meanings given to keywords, while each basis vector corresponds to a keyword – in this way two physically equivalent documents or queries can have different meaning because their constituent keywords correspond to different basis vectors.

3 Retrieval in Context

If the objects are described by the $\mathbf{y}$'s, ranking in context reorders the vectors by the averaged distance between them and the subspaces $L(\{\mathbf{b}_i\})$'s which describe the contextual factors. Therefore, if $\mathbf{y}$ and $\mathbf{C}_B$ are the object vector and the context operator, the ranking function is

$$\mathbf{y}^\top \cdot \mathbf{C}_B \cdot \mathbf{y} \ .$$

From Equation 1, the function becomes

$$\mathbf{y}^\top \cdot \mathbf{C}_B \cdot \mathbf{y} = w_1 \mathbf{y}^\top \cdot \mathbf{B}_1 \cdot \mathbf{y} + \cdots + w_k \mathbf{y}^\top \cdot \mathbf{B}_k \cdot \mathbf{y}.$$

As $\mathbf{B}_i = \mathbf{b}_i \cdot \mathbf{b}_i^\top$, it follows that

$$\begin{aligned}
\mathbf{y}^\top \cdot \mathbf{B}_i \cdot \mathbf{y} &= \mathbf{y}^\top \cdot \mathbf{b}_i \cdot \mathbf{b}_i^\top \cdot \mathbf{y} \\
&= (\mathbf{b}_i^\top \cdot \mathbf{y})^\top \cdot \mathbf{b}_i^\top \cdot \mathbf{y} \\
&= (\mathbf{b}_i^\top \cdot \mathbf{y})^2,
\end{aligned}$$

and therefore

$$\mathbf{y}^\top \cdot \mathbf{C}_B \cdot \mathbf{y} = w_1 (\mathbf{y}^\top \cdot \mathbf{b}_1)^2 + \cdots + w_k (\mathbf{y}^\top \cdot \mathbf{b}_k)^2 \tag{2}$$

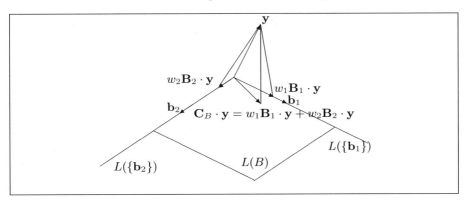

Fig. 2: A geometric representation of the ranking function

A pictorial description of the ranking function is illustrated in Fig. 2. The vector $\mathbf{B}_1 \cdot \mathbf{y}$ is the projection of $\mathbf{y}$ to the subspace (i.e. ray) spanned by $\mathbf{b}_1$ and is scaled by w_1. If $w_1\mathbf{B}_1 \cdot \mathbf{y}$ is summed to $w_2\mathbf{B}_2 \cdot \mathbf{y}$, one obtains a vector which belongs to $L(B)$, namely, the two-dimensional subspace spanned by B – this vector is expressed by $\mathbf{C}_B \cdot \mathbf{y}$. Equation 2 illustrates the degree to which the object represented by $\mathbf{y}$ is close to the contextual factors of B; this degree is a weighted average of the size of the projections of $\mathbf{y}$ to the $L(\{\mathbf{b}_i\})$'s.

4 How to Formalize a Context

The basis that generated an informative object vector, namely, $\mathbf{x}$ or $\mathbf{y}$ is often unknown. Therefore, these vectors are only what one observes; for example, when $\mathbf{y}$ is produced after indexing a document, no evidence is given about the context in which the information content was expressed by the document. The computation of the basis that generated a vector is a basic step in order to be provided with a representation of the context and for ranking objects by distance from a context – something similar happens when expressing an information need.

Let a user be a searcher accessing the system for retrieving documents relevant to his information need. The searcher may employ query descriptors for expressing the information content of the documents sought. When using a descriptor for expressing a query, the user is giving the descriptor semantics which is different from the semantics of the same descriptor used by another user or by the same user in another place, time, need – in other words, the use of a descriptor depends on context. A similar dependency on context occurs when the searcher browses documents. Therefore, context influences the selection of the descriptors, their semantics and inter-relationships. When using the VSM, descriptors are vectors, i.e. points in a vector space. According to Sect. 2, descriptors are represented by basis vectors which may change as context does. In this way a descriptor, e.g. a keyword, has as many vector representations as there are contexts.

The formalization of a (search) context as a basis might be approached in an automatic way. Let us consider some real-life examples which help us understand how such an approach would work. After a series of actions, e.g. typing a keyword, about `computers`, a context-aware system should compute a basis reflecting a computer-oriented context. However, such a context definition should be finer depending on whether the user is wanting to buy a computer or to compile a report on computer technology. For this purpose, the system should associate a (basis) vector to the typed keywords whose numerical configuration reflects the context at the finest definition possible. Similarly, when the user is searching for restaurants close to Padua and types that keyword while traveling to Venice, the basis vector configuration should include some data about Venice. As another example, when a document being sought is general, highly specific terms are unlikely to be included in the wanted documents together with general terms, since specific terms are more frequently used in technical documents. The keywords typed to query the system should be described by basis vectors whose configuration is different from that of the vectors describing the keywords of a query submitted for looking for technical documents.

If dimensions are keywords, for example, the approach should output an ordered n-tuple, namely, a vector, for every keyword. Such an assignment would however be grounded on a "theory" which drives the designer in compiling those basis vectors. IR often resorts to this sort of theory, which would be similar to the guidelines followed, for example, for building document vectors according to the VSM which dictates that the i-th element of a document vector is the weight of index term i in the document. Whereas the manual definition of basis vectors appears as "simple" for textual documents and for representing informative content only, the task is much less simple for nontextual documents or for representing other context dimensions, such as time or space. How such a theory should work for building basis vectors from context is not fully clear and is matter of future research.

Automatic approaches can leverage matrix manipulation algorithms which extract (orthogonal) sets of orthogonal vectors, like the $\mathbf{u}_i$'s, from a set of non-orthogonal vectors. In general, the idea is to

1. collect some vectors which describe objects about a dimension of context,
2. process the collected vectors for compiling a symmetric matrix, and
3. compute orthogonal matrices whose columns can be used as the vectors which correspond to the potential values of the dimension of context.

Singular Value Decomposition (SVD) may be used for extracting the candidate basis vectors from the symmetric matrices. These matrices are compiled from the data collected for describing a dimension of context. Let us suppose a set of documents is available and let each document be described as a vector; let $\{\mathbf{y}_1, \ldots, \mathbf{y}_m\}$ be these vectors. Each collected vector is defined in an

n-dimensional space of features. It may be assumed that $y_{ij} = 1$ if feature j occurs in document i, otherwise $y_{ij} = 0$ – this is the common binary weighting scheme. In the event that the dimension of context is the informative content of a document, the features are index terms. The feature co-occurrence matrix $\mathbf{S}$ can be decomposed into its eigenvectors $\mathbf{u}_1, \ldots, \mathbf{u}_k$ through SVD , that is,

$$\mathbf{S} = \mathbf{U} \cdot \mathbf{D} \cdot \mathbf{U}^{\top} \tag{3}$$

where $\mathbf{U}$ is orthonormal.

Example 1. If the document vectors are organized as the rows of the matrix

$$\begin{bmatrix} 1\,1\,0\,0 \\ 1\,0\,1\,0 \\ 0\,1\,1\,1 \\ 0\,0\,0\,1 \\ 0\,0\,1\,1 \end{bmatrix} \quad \text{then} \quad \mathbf{S} = \begin{bmatrix} 2\,1\,1\,0 \\ 1\,2\,1\,1 \\ 1\,1\,3\,2 \\ 0\,1\,2\,3 \end{bmatrix}$$

and

$$\mathbf{U} = \begin{bmatrix} -0.270500 & 0.748590 & -0.212605 & 0.566781 \\ -0.392760 & 0.369167 & 0.743279 & -0.396222 \\ -0.648776 & -0.033105 & -0.585134 & -0.485399 \\ -0.593008 & -0.549757 & 0.244854 & 0.534935 \end{bmatrix}$$

and

$$\mathbf{D} = \begin{bmatrix} 5.85041 & 0 & 0 & 0 \\ 0\ 2.44893 & 0 & 0 \\ 0 & 0\ 1.25615 & 0 \\ 0 & 0 & 0\ 0.44451 \end{bmatrix}$$

The interpretation of the eigenvectors of $\mathbf{S}$ can be the same as that given in the context of Latent Semantic Indexing, namely, the eigenvectors describe latent factors. In this chapter, the latent factors play the role of contextual factor of the dimension of context which refers to the informative content.

At the same time, another dimension of context, e.g. document genre, may be observed. Similarly, to the informative content, the genre of a document can be described by some features, such as document size, degree of logical structuring, vocabulary exhaustivity. The procedure for computing the vectors of this dimension of context is the same as that followed for computing the $\mathbf{u}_i$'s. After a set of documents have been collected and described by the features of the genre of a document, another symmetric matrix can be computed and as a result another set of eigenvectors is achieved. It is useful to note that the features describing this new dimension may have been used for describing the informative content; for example, the occurrence of the symbol log in a document can be a feature of both informative content and document genre – the occurrence of this symbol may indicate that the document is about mathematics and that the document genre is mathematical. Let us suppose that, for example, the eigenvectors describing the values of the document genre are:

$$\mathbf{E} = \begin{bmatrix} -0.45970 & 0 & 0.88807 \\ -0.62796 & -0.70711 & -0.32506 \\ -0.62796 & 0.70711 & -0.32506 \end{bmatrix}$$

The interpretation of the $\mathbf{e}_i$'s may be similar to the interpretation given to the factors of the informative content. When considering document genre, the $\mathbf{e}_i$'s may represent the distinct values of this dimension of context. When, for instance, the features are document size, degree of logical structuring, vocabulary exhaustivity, the second eigenvector is telling us that a value of the document genre can be described by a contrast between vocabulary exhaustivity and the degree of logical structuring, while document size is not important.

A context may be built by linearly combining the first eigenvector of $\mathbf{S}$ and, say, the second column of $\mathbf{E}$; if, for example, no common features existed, the linear combination would yield:

$$\mathbf{C}_B = w_1 \begin{bmatrix} -0.270500 \\ -0.392760 \\ -0.648776 \\ -0.593008 \\ 0 \\ 0 \\ 0 \end{bmatrix} \cdot \begin{bmatrix} -0.270500 \\ -0.392760 \\ -0.648776 \\ -0.593008 \\ 0 \\ 0 \\ 0 \end{bmatrix}^{\top} + w_2 \begin{bmatrix} 0 \\ 0 \\ 0 \\ 0 \\ 0 \\ -0.70711 \\ 0.70711 \end{bmatrix} \cdot \begin{bmatrix} 0 \\ 0 \\ 0 \\ 0 \\ 0 \\ -0.70711 \\ 0.70711 \end{bmatrix}^{\top}$$

Therefore, a document which has been produced in B has the following characteristics:

1. the informative content is described by all the index terms weighted according to $\mathbf{u}_1$;
2. the genre is described by vocabulary exhaustivity and degree of logical structuring, yet with opposite roles.

5 Navigation in Context

Navigation is naturally contextual. When the end user navigates the information space, he interacts with the retrieval system. During user-system interaction, the end user's information need changes because the context in which the user is immersed changes. When the system needs to effectively meet the information needs, some sort of adaptation to the evolving context needs to be set up. Techniques for adaptive retrieval and implicit relevance feedback are already available and reported in the literature – see for example, [9,11,17,19].

In this section, the vectorial framework presented in the previous section is applied to navigation to show how the notions of subspaces and the ranking function effectively model contextual retrieval.

Suppose an end user is navigating an information space implemented by a hypertext, e.g. the Web. When searching for relevant information, the end user accesses a series of information objects which are documents, index terms, concepts or any other type of object – these objects may be multimedia or multilingual when they are textual. There are two main observations from which a model based on the notion of vector subspaces can be defined for navigation in context:

- first, any object can be represented by a vector or equivalently by a ray – in general, any object can be represented by a subspace;
- second, a link placed between two objects *and* followed by the end user signifies that the two objects are in the same context.

Figure 3 depicts a navigation path across a hypertext – the horizontal series of objects and links is the navigation path from which alternative paths begin. For every object, a vector (subspace) can be defined for representing the object. It is important to note that a vector is defined in the same vector space for any type of objects, that is, every type of object has a representation in a single space. Consider a context made of a pair of objects, namely, a document and an index term represented by $\mathbf{y}_2$ and $\mathbf{y}_3$, respectively. Therefore, a subspace expressed by $\mathbf{C}_B$ can be computed for representing the context. Of course, if k vectors are used, a k-dimension subspace is computed. The weights can be used for giving more importance to some objects than to the others.

Let us examine a procedure for employing this methodology. A user is navigating an information space including objects of diverse kinds, e.g. documents, index terms and concepts. While navigating, the user sees some documents, reads them, and perhaps annotates them by placing bookmarks, comments, or

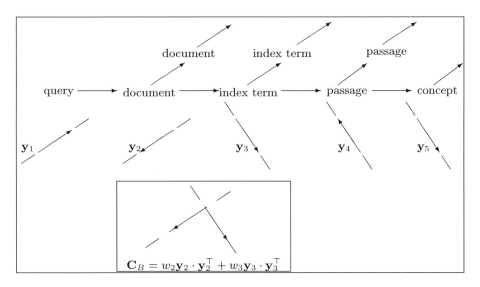

Fig. 3: A navigation path and the subspace which represents the induced context

highlights. One can suppose that k information objects have been seen, written or annotated at time t. For each information object, a vector can be generated, thus making the computation of $S^{(t)} = \{\mathbf{y}_1, \ldots, \mathbf{y}_k\}$ at time t possible. By linear combination, $\mathbf{C}_B^{(t)}$, i.e. the context operator of the subspace describing the context at time t, can be computed. Linear Algebra shows that $\mathbf{y}_i^\top \cdot \mathbf{C}_B^{(t)} \cdot \mathbf{y}_i = 1$ for $i = 1, \ldots, k$. At time $t+1$, the user can access other object $\mathbf{y}$'s after the system ranked them by $\mathbf{y}^\top \cdot \mathbf{C}_B^{(t)} \cdot \mathbf{y}$. When the newly accessed objects contribute to the description of a new context, then $\mathbf{C}_B^{(t+1)}$ can be computed and the subsequent accessed object $\mathbf{z}$'s are ranked by $\mathbf{z}^\top \cdot \mathbf{C}_B^{(t+1)} \cdot \mathbf{z}$.

6 Related Work

To fully recognize the high complexity of IR, the fact that IR is context-dependent and the interaction between the system and the environment need to be addressed. This observation dates back to some decades ago when researchers pointed out that context is the key factor affecting retrieval performance. Since then it has been recognized that context implies user-system interaction and that user models should be integrated in system models [2,5]. Recently the issue has been further investigated by calling attention to identifying "useful abstractions of contextual information" [1]. The need to look at context is currently even stronger than in the past since classical inverted file-based systems have reached their maximum effectiveness.

The VSM gives an intuitive yet formal view of indexing and retrieval – in fact it has attracted many researchers and newcomers, since it was introduced in [15] and [14]. It has proved a very effective, sound framework in retrieving documents in different languages, on different subjects, of different sizes, and of different media, thanks to a number of proposed and tested weighting schemes and applications.

The potential of vector spaces has not been fully exploited in practice, even though some attempts have been made in the past with some success. Although the notion of context was ignored, an early effort to reevaluate the VSM is reported in [18]. Two issues among many were term dependence and the role played by the term-document frequency matrix. The discussion on the assumptions and the potential is the subject of [4].

Despite its apparent simplicity, the mathematical properties of vector spaces can be leveraged to achieve further results. In particular, the idea of using a *basis* of a vector space to represent context was proposed in [6] by starting from some of the issues pointed out in [18]. In this chapter and in [6] some mathematical constructs are leveraged for addressing the issue of context and taking a step toward context-aware IR modeling. The generation of a vector performed by a basis emulates what context does in producing the informative object represented by the vector. However, the framework presented in [6] does not provide a retrieval function which ranks documents by a measure of the degree to which an object has been generated in a context.

The hypothesis that the term-document frequency matrix encloses information about the correlation among terms and among documents was cited in [13], stated in [18] and was further exploited in [3] in defining Latent Semantic Indexing (LSI). The latter is a technique based on Singular Value Decomposition (SVD) which aims to decompose the term-document co-occurrence matrix and disclose the principal components used to represent fewer independent concepts than many inter-dependent index terms. The idea of using vectors to model informative objects dates back to the VSM or the LSI for which index terms are descriptors of the semantic content and correspond to the dimensions of the space. However, the incorporation of the notion of basis is a key issue since every object can be in principle generated by a distinct basis. Such incorporation is made natural by the correspondence between basis and matrix, thus making the operations between object vectors and context matrices immediate.

A recent reconsideration of the geometry underlying IR, and indirectly of the VSM, was presented in [16]. In that book Hilbert's vector spaces are used to see documents as vectors, relevance as a linear transformation, relevance statuses as the eigenvalues of the linear transformation, and the computation of the probability of relevance of a document as the projection of the document vector onto an eigenvector of the linear operator. In other words, the size of the projection of the document vector onto an eigenvector of the operator is the probability that the document is about the relevance state represented by the corresponding eigenvalue.

Further research work is underway for investigating how the geometry of context induced by the vector spaces can support personalized retrieval and navigation. In [9, 11], a geometric and statistical framework that utilizes multiple sources of evidence present in this interaction context (e.g., display time, document retention) is illustrated to develop enhanced implicit feedback models personalized for each user and tailored for each search task. Both Web servers and rich interaction logs (and associated metadata such as relevance judgments), gathered during a longitudinal user study, are used as relevance stimuli to compare an implicit feedback algorithm developed using the framework with alternative algorithms. The findings demonstrate both the effectiveness of the framework and the potential value of incorporating multiple sources of interaction evidence when developing implicit feedback algorithms.

The proposed framework as the potential of connecting context-based retrieval to the theoretical notions of Quantum Mechanics. In [8] the use of some Quantum Mechanics concepts is explored for modeling a context-aware information retrieval system. Superposition models the production of informative objects in their own context, and models the generation of a dimension of context using other dimensions; examples of informative objects are documents and queries. Probability measures the uncertainty of the influence a dimension of context has in an informative object. Density operators models informative objects as non-orthogonal projectors, whereas projectors represent dimensions of context.

References

1. Belkin, N., Callan, J.: Context-based information access. In: Report of the Discussion Group on Context-Based Information Access of the Workshop on "Information Retrieval and Databases: Synergies and Syntheses". National Science Foundation, Washington, D.C., USA (2003). `http://www2.cs.washington.edu/nsf2003/discussionGroups.html`
2. Belkin, N., Oddy, R., Brooks, H.: ASK for Information Retrieval: Part I. Background and Theory. Journal of Documentation **38**(2), 61–71 (1982)
3. Deerwester, S., Dumais, S., Furnas, G., Landauer, T., Harshman, R.: Indexing by latent semantic analysis. Journal of the American Society for Information Science **41**(6), 391–407 (1990)
4. Dubin, D.: The most influential paper Gerard Salton never wrote. Library Trends **52**(4), 748–764 (2004)
5. Ingwersen, P.: Information Retrieval Interaction. Taylor Graham, London (1992)
6. Melucci, M.: Context modeling and discovery using vector space bases. In: Proceedings of the ACM Conference on Information and Knowledge Management (CIKM), pp. 808–815. ACM Press, Bremen, Germany (2005)
7. Melucci, M.: Ranking in context using vector spaces. In: Proceedings of the ACM Conference on Information and Knowledge Management (CIKM), pp. 477–478. ACM Press, Arlington, VA, USA (2006)
8. Melucci, M.: Exploring a mechanics for context-aware information retrieval. In: Proceedings of the AAAI Spring Symposium on Quantum Interaction. AAAI Press, Stanford, CA, USA (2007)
9. Melucci, M., White, R.: Discovering hidden contextual factors for implicit feedback. In: Proceedings of the Second Workshop on Context-based Information Retrieval. CEUR, Roskilde, Denmark (2007). Forthcoming
10. Melucci, M., White, R.: Utilizing a geometry of context for enhanced implicit feedback. In: Proceedings of the ACM Conference on Information and Knowledge Management (CIKM). ACM Press, Lisbon, Portugal (2007). Forthcoming
11. van Rijsbergen, C.: Information Retrieval, second edn. Butterworths, London (1979)
12. Rocchio, J.: The SMART Retrieval System. Prentice Hall, Englewood Cliffs, N.J., USA (1971)
13. Salton, G.: Mathematics and information retrieval. Journal of Documentation **35**(1), 1–29 (1979)
14. Salton, G.: Automatic Text Processing. Addison-Wesley (1989)
15. Salton, G., Wong, A., Yang, C.: A vector space model for automatic indexing. Communications of the ACM **18**(11), 613–620 (1975)
16. van Rijsbergen, C.: The Geometry of Information Retrieval. Cambridge University Press, UK (2004)
17. White, R., Ruthven, I., Jose, J., van Rijsbergen, C.: Evaluating implicit feedback models using searcher simulations. ACM Transactions on Information Systems **23**(3), 325–361 (2005)

18. Wong, S., Raghavan, V.: Vector space model of information retrieval – a reevaluation. In: Proceedings of the ACM International Conference on Research and Development in Information Retrieval (SIGIR), pp. 167–185. Cambridge, England (1984)
19. Zigoris, P., Zhang, Y.: Bayesian adaptive user profiling with explicit and implicit feedback. In: Proceedings of the ACM Conference on Information and Knowledge Management (CIKM), pp. 397–404 (2006)

Two Algorithms for Probabilistic Stemming

Massimo Melucci and Nicola Orio

Department of Information Engineering – University of Padua
Via Gradenigo, 6/b – 35131 Padua – Italy
{melo, orio}@dei.unipd.it

Abstract. This chapter describes two algorithms for probabilistic stemming. A probabilistic stemmer aims at detecting word stems by using a probabilistic or statistical model with no or very little knowledge about the language for which the stemmer has been built. While illustrating two probabilistic stemming models, a reflection and an analysis of the potentialities of this approach to stemming in the context of information retrieval are made.

Key words: stemming, multilingual information retrieval, statistical models, hidden Markov models

1 What is Stemming

An Information Retrieval (IR) system, which manages text resources, processes words to extract and assign content descriptive index terms to documents or queries. As we use spoken or written language naturally, words are formulated with many morphological variants, even if they refer to a common concept. Therefore, stemming has to be performed in order to allow words, which are formulated with morphological variants, to group up with each other, indicating a similar meaning. Most of the stemming algorithms reduce word forms to an approximation of a common morphological root, called "stem", so that a relevant document can be retrieved even if the morphology of their own words is different from the one of the words of a given query. It is interesting to note that a stemming algorithm is a special case of query expansion because it provides the users with a tool for expanding the set of query terms with their morphological variants.

Despite the success of query expansion, the effectiveness of stemming is a debated issue, and there are different results and outcomes on its effectiveness, as reported by [3]. If effectiveness is measured by the traditional precision and recall measures, it seems that for a language with a relatively simple morphology, like English, stemming has little influence on the overall performance, as reported by [7]. In contrast, stemming can significantly increase the retrieval effectiveness, especially precision, for short queries or for languages with a more complex morphology, like the romance languages, as shown by [9] and by [13]. Despite this debate, it is commonly accepted that the use of a stemmer is intuitive to many users who can express the query using a specific term without having to manually add all its variants that might appear in relevant documents [7]. Thus, stemming should be a feature of the user interface of an IR service, supplied for example by digital libraries.

To design a stemming algorithm, it is possible to follow a linguistic approach based on prior knowledge of the morphology of the specific language, or a statistical approach which employs some methods based on statistical principles to infer the word formation rules from a corpus of documents. The linguistic approaches are likely to be more effective because the quality of the morphological analysis has been assured by experts in the linguistic field, but the benefits that could be gained are outweighed by the time necessary to complete the morphological analysis, especially when new languages have to be added to an IR service. Furthermore, encoding all of the word formation rules for languages with a complex morphology is a demanding task and the resulting stemmers can still be imprecise; in addition it is not always feasible to consult an expert for each language. On the other hand, stemming algorithms based on statistical methods ensure no additional costs to add new languages to the system – this is an advantage that becomes crucial, especially for applications like digital libraries that are often constructed for a particular institution or nation, and are able to manage a great amount of non-English documents and, in general, documents written in many different languages. Of course, the low cost of stemmer generation provided by stemming algorithms based on statistical methods might be counterbalanced by a degradation of the quality of the morphological analysis and, consequently, the retrieval effectiveness.

The research reported in this chapter has originated from the study and the experimentation of two probabilistic stemming algorithms originally introduced in [1, 11] and described in Sects. 2 and 3. In this chapter, a summary and review is provided by highlighting common problems and solutions especially regarding the probabilistic issues of the two methods. Both approaches are instances of affix removal-based stemming and in particular that of suffix stripping – suffix stripping stemming, which splits a word and considers the prefix as the stem, is described in [4] and adopted by most stemmers currently in use by IR, like those reported by [10, 12], and [14].

The chapter is structured as follows. The algorithms are presented in Sect. 2 and in Sect. 3, while their experimental evaluation is reported in Sect. 4. Some conclusions are drawn in Sect. 5.

2 A Mutual Reinforcement-Based Model for Stemming

First, an intuitive description of the algorithm is provided by introducing the concept of mutual reinforcement for stemming. Then, a mathematical description is provided in terms of the probabilistic model.

2.1 The Underlying Intuition of Applying Mutual Reinforcement to Stemming

Given a collection of words, we can look at a collection of sub-strings obtained by splitting each word into two parts: the prefix is the first part of the word, and the suffix is the second part. Each prefix or suffix is a node of a graph where each link corresponds to the word obtained by concatenating the linked prefix and suffix. We introduced the notion of mutual reinforcement between stems and derivations in order to identify the optimal prefixes and suffixes. An optimal prefix corresponds to a stem and an optimal suffix corresponds to a derivation. The rationale to use mutual reinforcement was based on the idea that stems are prefixes which are completed at a high frequency rate by the derivations; derivations, in turn, are suffixes which complete, at a high frequency rate, the stems – in graphical terms, derivations tend to be linked to stems, and viceversa, thus forming communities in the graph. Thus the mutual reinforcement relationship is a kind of *coupled frequent usage* of prefixes and suffixes that are used to form words. It is important to note that a high frequency of prefixes or suffixes is not a necessary condition nor is it a sufficient condition employed in discovering stems and derivations – very frequently used prefixes are very likely to be stems, but they are discarded if they are not followed by very frequently used suffixes.

The method used to discover the communities of stems and derivations, which are coupled together by mutual reinforcement, is based not only on a computation of the sub-string frequency, as in [6] or [5], but also on link analysis algorithms which have proved to be effective in Web retrieval.

2.2 The Probabilistic Model of Mutual Reinforcement for Stemming

The main thrust of this section is to take a step forward from the graph-based stemming algorithm just described and to introduce a probabilistic framework which models the mutual reinforcement between stems and derivations. The idea here is to consider stemming as the inverse of an agent which generates words by concatenating prefixes and suffixes. The section then shows how the estimation of the probabilities of the model relates to the notion of mutual reinforcement and to the discovery of the communities of stems and derivations.

Given a finite collection W of words, let U be the set of non-empty substrings generated after splitting each word $w \in W$ into all the possible positions. If w has n characters, it is split at $n - 1$ possible positions. U is the set of sub-strings from which the stemmer will be built. From now on, we assume that words are divided into two parts only. If x, y are the prefix and the suffix of word w respectively, then we obtain that $w = xy$. For example, if $W = \{\mathsf{abc}, \mathsf{cd}\}$, then $U = \{\mathsf{a}, \mathsf{bc}, \mathsf{ab}, \mathsf{c}, \mathsf{d}\}$. The event space is the set of pairs of sub-strings of U built from W, that is:

$$\Omega = \{(x, y) \in U \times U : \exists w \in W, w = xy\}$$

The stemming algorithm based on the notion of mutual reinforcement works as an agent that has to guess the pair $\omega^* \in \Omega$ of sub-strings of U, i.e. a prefix and a suffix of a word of W, that is, the most probable pair of sub-strings that the agent has chosen to generate w. As the agent exploits some knowledge about the language, the most probable pair will be formed by the stem and the derivation, i.e. the suffix that completes the word. Therefore, a stemmer has to compute the expression

$$\omega^* = \arg\max_{\omega} \Pr(\omega \mid w)$$

to find the "right" split, i.e. the most probable prefix and suffix that generate w. Therefore, $\Pr(\omega \mid w)$ has to be computed in order to select the most probable split. Using the Bayes' theorem,

$$\Pr(\omega \mid w) = \frac{\Pr(w \mid \omega)\Pr(\omega)}{\Pr(w)} \ .$$

Note that $\Pr(w \mid \omega) = 1$, because ω yields w only, then $\Pr(\omega \mid w) = \Pr(\omega) \,/\, \Pr(w)$. Because the denominator does not influence the ranking of the possible split of w, we have the stemmer compute

$$\omega^* = \arg\max_{\omega} \Pr(\omega)$$

In other words, the "right" split, i.e. the right pair prefix-suffix is the most probable split ω^* of w.

At this point, it is worth noting that the probability of the pair $\omega_i = (x_i, y_i)$ can be expressed in two equivalent ways:

$$\Pr(x_i, y_i) = \Pr(y_i \mid x_i)\Pr(x_i)$$

and

$$\Pr(x_i, y_i) = \Pr(x_i \mid y_i)\Pr(y_i)$$

The probability that the hypothetical agent has chosen x_i as prefix and y_i as suffix to generate w, depends on the product of two probabilities – the probability $\Pr(x_i)$ of choosing x_i as prefix and the probability $\Pr(y_i \mid x_i)$ of choosing y_i as the suffix to complete w. Equivalently, $\Pr(x_i, y_i)$ depends on the probability $\Pr(y_i)$ of choosing y_i as suffix to complete a word, and the probability $\Pr(x_i \mid y_i)$ of having chosen x_i as the prefix.

Whereas the conditional probability $\Pr(y_i \mid x_i)$ can be seen as a "bridge" to complete w, the probability $\Pr(x_i)$ represents the probability of the first step of word generation. The latter probability is a sort of "pivot" probability, which significantly affects the computation of $\Pr(x_i, y_i)$. Then we consider $\Pr(x_i)$ as the most crucial step of estimation and we concentrate on these "pivot" probabilities.

Given the a-priori probability $\Pr(y_i \mid x_i)$, the stemmer looks for $\Pr(x_i)$ that maximizes $\Pr(x_i, y_i)$, i.e. the highest probability that $\omega_i = (x_i, y_i)$ generates w. In other words, the stemmer has to compute

$$\arg \max_{i=1,\ldots,n-1} \Pr(y_i \mid x_i) \Pr(x_i)$$

which is an equivalent expression of $\omega^* = \arg\max_i \Pr(\omega_i)$. The problem is how to estimate these probabilities. Whereas the conditional probabilities can be estimated using the distribution of prefixes and suffixes over the words, the estimation of the probability $\Pr(x_i)$ becomes crucial because it represents the corner stone of word generation.

At first sight, it would seem that the maximization of $\Pr(x_i)$ is sufficient to maximize $\Pr(x_i, y_i)$ using some maximum likelihood criterion, given $\Pr(y_i \mid x_i)$. However, the maximization of $\Pr(x_i)$ is tightly coupled with the maximization of $\Pr(y_i)$. In order to estimate $\Pr(x_i)$ and $\Pr(y_i)$, we introduce the following notion of mutual reinforcement in stemming.

Stems are prefixes that are completed by derivations, and derivations are suffixes that in turn complete stems.

If a collection of words is observed, a prefix is completed by diverse suffixes, and a suffix completes diverse prefixes. The mutual relationship emphasizes that stems are more likely to be completed by derivations, and derivations are more likely to complete stems. This means that if both the probability of the fact that a prefix will be completed by a suffix is high and the probability of the fact that *the* suffix will complete *the* prefix is high, then the corresponding split is likely to be the right one.

Let us formalize the notion of mutual reinforcement in stemming. It is a fact that $\Pr(x_i) = \sum_{j=1}^{|Y|} \Pr(x_i, y_j)$ and that $\Pr(y_j) = \sum_{i=1}^{|X|} \Pr(x_i, y_j)$, where $|Y|$ is the total number of suffixes and $|X|$ is the total number of prefixes. Note that the $\Pr(x_i, y_i)$s are unknown and therefore have to be estimated. The maximum likelihood estimator would be $1 \,/\, |U|$, as you can test after computing $\Pr(x_i, y_j) = \Pr(y_j \mid x_i) \Pr(x_i) = \frac{1}{|X_i|} \frac{|X_i|}{|U|}$, where $|X_i|$ is the number of words with prefix x_i. We exploit the fact that $\Pr(x_i, y_j) = \Pr(y_j \mid x_i) \Pr(x_i)$ and that $\Pr(x_i, y_j) = \Pr(x_i \mid y_j) \Pr(y_j)$. Thus, we have the mutual relationship

$$\Pr(x_i) = \sum_{j=1}^{|Y|} \Pr(x_i \mid y_j) \Pr(y_j) \qquad\qquad i = 1, \ldots, |X| \qquad (1)$$

N: number of substrings extracted from all the words in W
K: the number of iterations
$\mathbf{1}$: the vector $(1, ..., 1) \in \mathcal{R}^N$
$\mathbf{s}^{(k)}$: suffix score vector at step k
$\mathbf{p}^{(k)}$: prefix score vector at step k
$a_{ji} = \Pr(x_i \mid y_j)$
$b_{ij} = \Pr(y_j \mid x_i)$
$\mathbf{p}^{(0)} = 1/N$
for $k = 1, ..., K$ **do**
    for $j = 1, ..., N$ **do**
      $s_j^{(k)} = \sum_{i=1}^{N} p_i^{(k-1)} \times b_{ij}$
    end for
    for $i = 1, ..., N$ **do**
      $p_i^{(k)} = \sum_{j=1}^{N} s_j^{(k)} \times a_{ji}$
    end for
    normalize $\mathbf{p}^{(k)}$ and $\mathbf{s}^{(k)}$ so that $\mathbf{p}^{(k)'}\mathbf{1} = \mathbf{s}^{(k)'}\mathbf{1} = 1$
end for

Fig. 1: Compute suffix scores and prefix scores from z

and

$$\Pr(y_j) = \sum_{i=1}^{|X|} \Pr(y_j \mid x_i) \Pr(x_i) \qquad j = 1, \ldots, |Y| \qquad (2)$$

The mutual relationship is given by the fact that $\Pr(x_i)$ is an average mean of the $\Pr(y_j)$s, and at the same time $\Pr(y_j)$ is an average mean of the $\Pr(x_i)$s. Given this relationship, $\Pr(x_i)$ is directly proportional to both $\Pr(x_i \mid y_j)$ and $\Pr(y_j)$, i.e. the higher the probability that x_i is chosen as stem, the higher the probability that its potential suffixes are derivations and that x_i is completed by its potential suffixes. Similarly, the higher the probability that y_i is chosen, the higher the probability that its potential prefixes are stems and that y_i completes its prefixes. Equations 1 and 2 highlight that a circular relationship between $\Pr(x_i)$ and $\Pr(y_j)$ exists. To resolve this circularity, the following algorithm is proposed.

The algorithm that computes prefix and suffix scores is illustrated in Fig. 1 using pseudo-code. It is easy to see that the algorithm is an application of Hyper-linked Induced Topic Search (HITS) algorithm [8].

3 A HMM-Based Stemming Algorithm

One of the methods proposed for stemming is based on Hidden Markov Models (HMMs). Also in this case an intuitive description of the approach is given, followed by a short introduction to HMMs; the interested reader can find comprehensive descriptions of HMMs in [15] for applications to automatic speech recognition, and in [2] for applications to biological sequence analysis. Finally, the implementation of the complete description is described formally.

3.1 The Intuition Behind HMM-based Stemmers

The simplest way to describe a word, at least for the languages that are based on an alphabet, is to consider it as a sequence of letters. As is common practice in string processing, it can be assumed that sequences are generated by a finite-state automaton which, at each time unit, performs a state transition and emits a letter until it reaches a final state. Given that different languages correspond to different sets of sequences of letters, it can be considered that each language is associated with a given automaton. For the sake of simplicity, we assume the existence of an ideal finite-state automaton for a language that consists of hundreds of thousands of word variants.

As discussed in Sect. 2.1, for the aims of stemming each word can be considered as the concatenation of a prefix and a suffix. Thus, it is natural to consider that also the automaton that generates words in a given language is divided in two parts, one that generates prefixes and the other that generates suffixes. In particular, the set of states can be partitioned in two subsets, a prefix-set and a suffix-set. Such a partition imposes a number of restrictions on the possible initial and final states and on the transitions between states of the two sets:

1. initial states belong only to the prefix-set – i.e. a word always starts with a prefix;
2. transitions are not allowed from states of the suffix-set to states of the prefix-set – a word can only be a concatenation of a prefix and a suffix;
3. final states belong to both sets – i.e. a prefix can have a number of different inflections, but it may also have an inflection without any other suffix.

It is important to note that these restrictions imply that words are the concatenation of a stem, the prefix, and a single derivation, the suffix. The presence of a suffix is not mandatory, because final states belong to both sets. These considerations apply to many Indoeuropean languages, but do not take into account word compounding that is typical of the German language. Figure 2 represents a general finite-state automaton that fulfills the proposed constraints.

If the automaton is completely observable, the identification of the prefix and of the suffix of a given word is a straightforward task. Given the proposed constraints, there could be at most one transition from the prefix-set to the suffix-set. A direct inspection of when this transition is performed allows us to find the correct split exactly. Unfortunately, a finite-state automaton that generates all the words in a given language, correctly split in prefixes and suffixes, is very complex to build, and its design would require a deep analysis of the morphology of each language, which is in contrast with the aims of the proposed approach. A number of simplifying assumptions have to be made

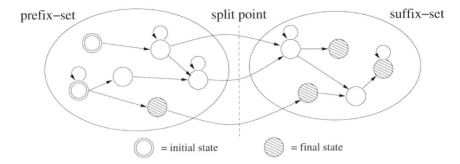

Fig. 2: Graphical representation of a finite-state automaton partitioned in a prefix and a suffix set

in order to solve the problem, with the introduction of stochastic finite-state automata as a tool for stemming.

The first assumption is that stochastic automata can generate any sequence of letters, even the ones that do not correspond to an actual word. Each word is associated to a probability of being generated. The second assumption is that automata are not observable, or *hidden*, meaning that it is not possible to deterministically define the sequence of state transitions corresponding to the generation of a given word. A direct consequence is that even if states are partitioned in prefix and suffix sets, the position of the split point is not observable. Nevertheless, it is possible to compute the probability that, given a word, a split point occurs at a given position. As for the approach presented in Sect. 2, also this approach to stemming is then carried out as a maximization problem. Hidden Markov Models are the tool for representing the needed stochastic automata.

3.2 An Introduction to Hidden Markov Models

HMMs are stochastic finite-state automata, where transitions between states are ruled by probability functions. At each transition, the new state emits a symbol with a given probability density function. HMMs are called *hidden* because states cannot be directly observed, what is observed are only the symbols they emit. HMMs are Markovian because transitions and observations are assumed to depend only on the actual state. Moreover, it is assumed that the probability distributions do not change over time. HMMs are particularly useful in modeling processes that are, in general, unknown but that can be observed through a sequence of symbols. A HMM λ is completely defined by:

- a set of N states $Q = \{q_1, \ldots, q_N\}$, in which the initial and final states are identified;
- a probability distribution of initial states π_i, that is, the probability $Pr(q(1) = i)$ that a path starts from state i;

- a probability distribution for state transitions a_{ij}, that is, the probability $Pr(q_j|q_i)$ of going from state q_i to state q_j in a single step;
- a probability distribution for observations $b_j(r)$, that is, the probability $Pr(s|q_j)$ of observing the symbol r when in state q_j.

For the application to word generation, symbols are the letters of the alphabet, $s \in \Omega$ where Ω is the event space, and the sequences of observed symbols, $w = \{s_1 s_2 \dots s_L\}$, are possible words in a given language. States of the HMM can be partitioned in the two subsets described in the previous section, thus dividing them between the ones that contribute to the generation of prefixes and the ones that contribute to the generation of suffixes. It should be noted that it is possible to assign a transition probability of zero in order to not allow some transitions and forbid some paths across the states.

Even if states are not directly observable, it is possible to compute the probability of each state sequence given an observed word and choose the one that has the highest probability to correspond to the generation of a given word. This can be viewed as a way to reveal the hidden part of HMMs. The problem is known as *decoding* and can be stated as follows: given a model λ and a word w generated by the model, find the complete state sequence $q^\star = \{q(1), \dots, q(L)\}$ that most likely generated w, that is

$$q^\star = \arg\max_q P(q|w, \lambda) \tag{3}$$

Decoding can be solved efficiently using a dynamic programming approach proposed by Viterbi [17] in $O(LN^2)$ time, where L is the length of the word and N is the number of states, implying that to be efficient, HMMs should have a small number of states. It can be noted that there are other alternative approaches to decoding, based on a different criterion of optimality. For instance, instead of searching for the global optimal path, as for Viterbi decoding, it could be useful to find the state sequence that is locally optimal for each state $q(t)$. Yet, for the particular application to stemming, a globally optimal criterion seems more suitable because it takes into account the complete state evolution, including states of both the prefix and the suffix sets.

Another important problem related to HMMs is how to set the parameters of model λ, that is, the transition and emission probabilities, in order to maximize the probability that λ generates a set of observations $w \in W$. Also for this problem, which is usually called *training*, an efficient solution has been proposed, based on the Expectation-Maximization (EM) algorithm, which computes:

$$\lambda_L^* = \arg\max_\lambda \prod_{w \in W_L} Pr(w \mid \lambda) \tag{4}$$

Training a HMM using all the words of a given language may be computationally expensive, because the algorithm has to be iterated over all the examples until it converges to a suitable solution. Even HMMs need to be trained only once, and before indexing the collection, the computational complexity

of the EM algorithm is not an issue. In order to reduce its computational
cost, training could be carried out using only a subset $\hat{W} \subset W$ of the words
of a given language. It should be noted that the EM algorithm maximizes the
probability of the HMM to generate words w, but no assumption is made on
the internal evolution of the states. Therefore, training does not impose any
constraint on the optimal path as computed with Viterbi decoding. To this
end, some more assumptions have to be made on the language morphology in
order to apply HMM to stemming.

3.3 Applications of HMMs to Stemming

The behavior of a stemmer based on HMMs can be described through a simple
example. Figure 3 depicts the topology of a HMM made of 11 states, where all
the allowable transitions are represented by an arrow. It can be noted that this
simple topology follows the constraints described in Sect. 3.1, because states
are partitioned in two sets, initial states belong to the prefix set only, while no
transition is possibile from the suffix to the prefix set. Each state emits all the
letters of a given alphabet, with different probability distributions. For this
discussion, it can be assumed that these probability distributions are known,
and depend on a training based on a corpus of words in a given language.

Let us consider the stemming of the word `teaching`. Since the generation
of a symbol is forced by the transition from one state to another, `teaching`
is the result of a path of length 8. There is a number of possible paths that
generate the word, each one with a different probability. Table 1 reports some
of them and their probabilities, in decreasing order. These probabilities are
the results of transitions and emissions performed both in the prefix and in the
suffix sets. The first row reports the path with the highest probability, which
is the one highlighted by Viterbi decoding. The probability is computed as
the product of all the transition probabilities of the path and all the emission
probabilities of each state in the path, according to equation

$$Pr(w|q^{\star}\lambda) = \pi_{q(1)}b_{q(1)}(s_2)a_{q(1)q(2)}b_{q(1)}(s_2)\ldots a_{q(T-1)q(T)}b_{q(T)}(s_T) \qquad (5)$$

where $q^{\star} = \{q(1),\ldots,q(T)\}$ is the optimal path for word $w = s_1\ldots s_T$.

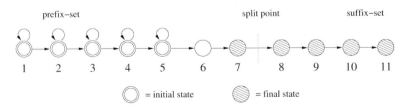

Fig. 3: The topology used as a reference for the stemming examples reported in
Table 1

Table 1: Different paths corresponding to the word `teaching` and their respective probability

Prefix-Suffix	t e a c h i n g	Probability
teach-ing	4 5 5 6 7 8 9 10	$6.30 \cdot 10^{-12}$
teach-ing	4 4 5 6 7 8 9 10	$2.69 \cdot 10^{-12}$
teach-ing	3 4 5 6 7 8 9 10	$2.44 \cdot 10^{-12}$
teachi-ng	2 3 4 5 6 7 8 9	$2.12 \cdot 10^{-12}$
teac-hing	4 5 6 7 8 9 10 11	$3.28 \cdot 10^{-13}$
teach-ing	5 5 5 6 7 8 9 10	$2.70 \cdot 10^{-13}$
teachi-ng	3 4 4 5 6 7 8 9	$2.18 \cdot 10^{-13}$
teaching-	1 2 2 3 4 5 6 7	$1.75 \cdot 10^{-13}$
teachin-g	1 2 3 4 5 6 7 8	$1.56 \cdot 10^{-13}$
teachin-g	2 3 4 5 5 6 7 8	$1.84 \cdot 10^{-14}$
teac-hing	5 5 6 7 8 9 10 11	$1.41 \cdot 10^{-14}$

As it can be seen, the first three paths have the same split-point, but there is a non negligible difference between the first one and the other two suggesting that the subpaths in the prefix-set also make an important contribution for the determination of the split-point. For example, the sixth path has the same subpath inside the suffix-set of the first one, but has a lower probability of the fourth and fifth paths because the subpath inside the prefix-set has a lower probability. From the example it can also be noted that the model takes into account that a word may have no derivation, like the decoding reported in the eighth row of Table 1. Moreover, another approach alternative to Viterbi decoding could be to consider all the possible paths and group the ones that share the same split point and select the group that has the highest overall probability. Yet this approach will not take advantage of the dynamic programming approach of Viterbi decoding, because all paths have to be computed, resulting in a higher computational cost.

3.4 Design of a HMM for Stemming

The discussion of HMM-based stemming has been carried out considering that it is possible to train the HMM parameters, namely the transition and emission probabilities. Since the goal is to fully develop automatic stemmers that do not require previous manual work, it is assumed that neither a formalization of morphological rules, expressed in the forms of probabilities distributions, nor a training set of manually stemmed words, which can be used to train the system to have the split point at the correct position, are available. In order to minimize manual work, and in parallel with the mutual reinforcement approach, the only assumption is that a corpus of words is available for a given language. The corpus can be based on the set of documents that are to be indexed, or even on a subset.

However, it has already been mentioned that the existing technique for training, the Expectation-Maximization algorithm, does not guarantee that the split point of the most probable path has any relationship with the prefix and the suffix of a given word. With the aim of creating such a relationship, we propose to inject some more knowledge about the general rules for the creations of word inflections. Thus, we make the reasonable assumption that for each language the number of different suffixes is smaller than the number of different prefixes. Suffixes are a set of letter sequences that can be modeled by chains of states of the HMM. This assumption suggests a particular topology for the states in the suffix-set, which can be made by a number of state chains with different lengths, where:

- transitions from the prefix-set are allowed only to the first state of each chain;
- the transition from one state to the next has probability one;
- each chain terminates with a final state.

The maximum length of state chains gives the maximum length of a possible suffix. Analogously, also the prefix-set topology can be modeled by a number of state chains, with the difference that a state can have non-zero self-transition probability. The minimum length of a chain gives the minimum length of a prefix. An example of this topology for the suffix-set is depicted in Fig. 4-a, where the maximum length of a suffix is set to four letters, and the minimum length of a prefix is set to three letters.

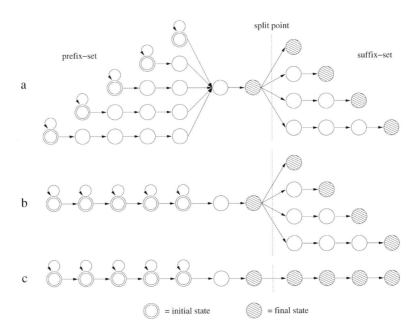

Fig. 4: Three topologies of the HMMs based on chains of states

After the definition of the suffix-set topology, the HMM can be trained using the EM algorithm on a set of words. Given the previous assumption, it is likely that a sequence of letters that corresponds to a suffix will be frequently present in the training set. For this reason, the EM algorithm will give to the states in the suffix-set a higher probability of emitting the letters of frequent suffixes. For example, considering the suffix-set chains, the state in the one-state chain will emit with the highest probability the last letter of each word, the states in the two-states chain will respectively emit the most frequent couple of ending letters of each word, and so on. Once the model has been trained, the most probable path that generates a word is the concatenation of two highly probable subpaths, respectively inside the prefix-set and the suffix-set. Hence, it is likely that the criterion based on the most probable path produces good retrieval results.

We tested our method using three different HMM topologies, which are depicted in Fig. 4. In particular, topology b simplifies the modeling of the chains of the prefix-set by collapsing them in a single chain; topology c, already introduced in Sect. 3.3, extends this same approach to the suffix-set. It should be noted that preliminary tests on alternative topologies, which for instance require chains of states only for the suffix set, showed that they are less effective.

4 Experimental Evaluation of Probabilistic Stemmers

The two probabilistic approaches to stemming were tested with the test collections available for CLEF 2003. In particular, five collections of documents written in Dutch, French, German, Italian, and Spanish were used for the experiments. The aim of the experiments for the monolingual track was to compare the retrieval effectiveness of the probabilistic stemmers with that of an algorithm based on a-priori linguistic knowledge – we chose the widely used Porter's stemmers [14]. The hypothesis was that the proposed probabilistic approaches generate stemmers that perform as effectively as Porter's stemmers. To evaluate stemming algorithms, the performances of different IR systems were compared by changing only the stemming algorithms for different runs, all other things being equal.

Our aim was to test the following hypotheses:

H': stemming does not hurt and can enhance the effectiveness of retrieval,
H'':the proposed probabilistic stemmers perform as effectively as Porter's ones.

For each track four different stemming algorithms were tested:

- **No Stem**: no stemming algorithm was applied;
- **Porter**: stemming carried out through algorithms freely available at the Snowball Web site edited by Martin Porter for different languages;
- **MF**: stemming based on the notion of mutual reinforcement;
- **HMM**: stemming based on Hidden Markov models.

Table 2: Relevant retrieved document number for CLEF 2003 Topics

Algorithm	Relevant Retrieved				
	Dutch	French	German	Italian	Spanish
No Stem	1,419	869	1,330	488	2,084
MF	1,420	886	1,376	497	2,122
HMM	1,386	891	1,384	503	2,148
Porter	1,416	911	1,434	492	2,202
Total Relevant Docs	1,577	946	1,825	809	2,368

For all the experiments the same stoplist was used. Retrieval was carried out using the Vector Space Model while the index terms occurring in the documents were weighted by the scheme proposed in [16].

For each language, the results over all the queries of the test collection have been summarized. Table 2 compares the number of relevant retrieved documents and the recall for the different algorithms under examination. Table 3 reports, for each language, the average precision attained by the system with the considered stemming algorithms. Table 4 reports the exact R-precision attained by the system for each language. The exact R-precision is the precision after R documents have been retrieved, where R is the number of relevant documents for the topic.

In general stemming improves the recall. The Dutch language is an exception to this note, since both the HMM and the Porter stemmer retrieve less relevant documents than without any stemmer.

Note that for French, German, Italian and Spanish stemming positively affects the precision, thus improving the overall performance of the system, since the recall has also improved. Dutch stemming does not degrade the overall performances of the system. Furthermore, when the stemming algorithms positively affect the performances, MF and HMM perform as effectively as Porter's stemmer.

Thus these figures give a positive answer to both hypotheses H′ and H″ since stemming does not hurt and sometimes improves the performance of an information retrieval system (IRS). The experimental evidence confirms the

Table 3: Average precision for CLEF 2003 Topics

Algorithm	Average Precision (%)				
	Dutch	French	German	Italian	Spanish
No Stem	42.11	42.86	34.92	34.76	39.27
MF	42.84	45.60	37.11	38.17	38.25
HMM	42.57	45.67	36.68	34.66	40.56
Porter	43.49	45.87	37.88	35.53	43.42

Table 4: Exact R-precision for CLEF 2003 Topics

Algorithm	Exact R-Precision (%)				
	Dutch	French	German	Italian	Spanish
No Stem	40.51	39.45	36.59	36.32	40.26
MF	41.54	43.22	37.80	38.39	39.85
HMM	39.66	42.20	37.53	33.26	39.90
Porter	40.55	41.68	38.73	34.79	42.70

hypothesis that it is possible to generate stemmers using probabilistic models without or with very little knowledge about the language.

5 Conclusions

The main conclusion of our research on probabilistic stemming is that a stemmer can be built for many European languages without much linguistic knowledge and with simple probabilistic models. This result has been confirmed by various experiments carried out using diverse standard test collections.

Acknowledgments

The authors are grateful to Dr. Michela Bacchin for the intense discussion and research collaboration done over the recent years on the subject of this chapter.

References

1. Bacchin, M., Ferro, N., Melucci, M.: A probabilistic model for stemmer generation. Information Processing and Management **41**(1), 121–137 (2005). Elsevier
2. Durbin, R., Eddy, S., Krogh, A., Mitchison, G.: Biological Sequence Analysis. Cambridge University Press, Cambridge, UK (2000)
3. Frakes, W.: Stemming algorithms. In: W. Frakes, R. Baeza-Yates (eds.) Information Retrieval: data structures and algorithms., chap. 8. Prentice Hall, Englewood Cliffs, NJ (1992)
4. Frakes, W., Baeza-Yates, R. (eds.): Information Retrieval: data structures and algorithms. Prentice Hall, Englewood Cliffs, NJ (1992)
5. Goldsmith, J.: Unsupervised learning of the morphology of a natural language. Computational Linguistics **27**(2), 154–198 (2001)
6. Hafer, M., Weiss, S.: Word segmentation by letter successor varieties. Information Storage and Retrieval **10**, 371–385 (1974)
7. Harman, D.: How effective is suffixing. Journal of the American Society for Information Science **42**(1), 7–15 (1991)

8. Kleinberg, J.: Authorative sources in a hyperlinked environment. Journal of the ACM **46**(5), 604–632 (1999)
9. Krovetz, R.: Viewing Morphology as an Inference Process,. In: Proceedings of the ACM International Conference on Research and Development in Information Retrieval (SIGIR), pp. 1–203 (1993)
10. Lovins, J.: Development of a stemming algorithm. Mechanical Translation and Computational Linguistics **11**, 22–31 (1968)
11. Melucci, M., Orio, N.: Design, implementation, and evaluation of a methodology for automatic stemmer generation. Journal of the American Society for Information Science and Technology **58**(5), 673–686 (2007)
12. Paice, C.: Constructing literature abstract by computer: techniques and prospects. Information Processing & Management **26**(1), 171–186 (1990)
13. Popovic, M., Willett, P.: The effectiveness of stemming for natural language access to Slovene textual data. Journal of the American Society for Information Science **43**(5), 384–390 (1992)
14. Porter, M.: An algorithm for suffix stripping. Program **14**(3), 130–137 (1980)
15. Rabiner, L., Juang, B.: Fundamentals of speech recognition. Prentice Hall, Englewood Cliffs, NJ (1993)
16. Singhal, A., Buckley, C., Mitra, M.: Pivoted document length normalization. In: Proceedings of the ACM International Conference on Research and Development in Information Retrieval (SIGIR), pp. 21–29. ACM Press, Zurich, Switzerland (1996)
17. Viterbi, A.: Error bounds for convolutional codes and an asymptotically decoding algorithm. IEEE Transactions on Knowledge and Data Engineering **IT**(13), 260–269 (1967)

Automated Text Categorization: The Two-Dimensional Probabilistic Model

Giorgio Maria Di Nunzio

Department of Information Engineering – University of Padua
Via Gradenigo, 6/b – 35131 Padua – Italy
dinunzio@dei.unipd.it

Abstract. In *Automated Text Categorization (ATC)*, a general inductive process automatically builds a classifier for the categories involved in the process by observing the properties of a set of pre-classified documents; from these properties, the inductive process learns the characteristics that a new unseen document should have in order to be categorized under a specific category. Probabilistic models, such as the *Naïve Bayes Models (NBs)*, achieve a performance comparable to more sophisticated models, and they prove to be very efficient.
We present the probabilistic model named *Two-Dimensional Probabilistic Model* (2DPM) which starts from different hypotheses from those of the NB models: instead of independent events, terms are seen as disjoint events, and documents are represented as the union of these events. The set of probability measures defined in this model work in such a way that a reduction of the vocabulary of terms in order to reduce the complexity of the problem is ultimately not necessary. Moreover, the model defines a direct relationship between the probability of a document given a category of interest and a point on a two-dimensional space. In this light, it is possible to graph entire collections of documents on a Cartesian plane, and to design algorithms that categorize documents directly on this two-dimensional representation. This graphical representation has been useful to give insights into the development of the theoretical aspects of the 2DPM. Experiments on traditional test collections for ATC show that the 2DPM performs with a greater degree of statistical significance than the multinomial NB model.

Key words: automated text categorization, probabilistic models, visualization of large data sets

1 Introduction

Today, solutions for the organization, access and interaction of digital contents are required in order to enable users to express their information needs, especially when the specific request is not clear in their mind [12]. In such situations, classification schemes, taxonomies, or subject hierarchies may be used to browse, explore, and retrieve resources from collections of objects.

When the digital content is of textual nature, this kind of organization of the information is typically done by means of automatic text categorizers [17]. Categorization systems which allow users to interact with them would be of help for: firstly, system designers during the process of raw data exploration; secondly, users to interpret results more clearly and possibly interact with them [10].

Probabilistic models for categorization, such as *Naïve Bayes Model (NB)*, are often used since they are simple to implement and give remarkable performances in terms of categorization accuracy [13]. Even though their accuracy does not reach the-state-of-the-art, they can be useful for obtaining a quick view of how difficult categorization is, especially in those cases where there are collections with millions of documents, and they can give directions for more complex methods, such as *Support Vector Machine (SVM)*; for example, when parameter tuning is needed.

Visualization frameworks that give a straightforward graphical explanation of the organization and classification of data of NB classifiers have been successfully designed and implemented [15]. However, these visualization approaches are mostly used in the area of bio-informatics and rarely in the area of textual document categorization where the number of features which describe the objects, that is the vocabulary of words in the documents, has an order of magnitude of hundreds of thousands. Moreover, even this kind of visualization technique only provides limited forms of guidance for the user when training and testing an *Automated Text Categorization (ATC)* system.

In this work, we present the 2DPM which represents documents on a two-dimensional space [3]. This model has proved to be a valid visualization tool for understanding the relationships between categories of textual documents, and for helping users to visually audit the classifier and identify suspicious training data [5, 6]. In addition, this model has the advantage of needing neither a reduction of the vocabulary of terms to reduce the complexity of the problem nor smoothing of probabilities to avoid zero probabilities during calculations. On the other hand, there is a lack of formalization which makes the comparison with other models difficult.

A formal explanation of this model is given to make the differences between the 2DPM and the NB models clear and demonstrate its advantages. In Sect. 1.1, we introduce the general definitions and notations of the problem of ATC [17]; in Sect. 2, we present the Two-Dimensional Probabilistic Model in detail; in Sect. 3 the experimental evaluation of the 2DPM is discussed and analyzed, and in Sect. 4 conclusions and final remarks are given.

1.1 Background on ATC

Given a finite set of pre-defined categories $C = \{c_1, ..., c_i, ..., c_{|C|}\}$, a finite set D of documents, and two boolean values that we indicate with T, true, and F, false, ATC may be formalized as the task of approximating the unknown target function

$$\Phi : D \times C \rightarrow \{T, F\} \,,$$

that describes how documents ought to be categorized, according to a reputed authoritative expert, by means of a function

$$\hat{\Phi} : D \times C \rightarrow \{T, F\} \,,$$

called the categorizer.

The function Φ is general and does not pose any limit to the number of categories one may assign to a document d; d may also not belong to any of the pre-defined categories of the chosen set C. This situation is known in the literature as *multi–label* categorization to indicate that the same document d may belong to more than one category (or that we may "stamp" d with different labels, where each label corresponds to a category). On the other hand, *single-label* categorization happens when the constraint of assigning at most one category is put on the number of categories that Φ may assign to a document.

In practice, the learning of a categorizer consists in the definition of a function for each category c_i of this kind:

$$CSV_i : D \rightarrow [0, 1] \,.$$

In this case, a categorizer returns a "degree of membership" of a document d for a category c_i, that is to say, given a document $d \in D$, CSV_i returns a *categorization status value* (CSV) for the document with respect to the category c_i. However, when the decision to assign or not d to c_i has to be taken, a threshold t may be needed such that if $CSV_i > t$, d is assigned to category c_i, otherwise it is not assigned to c_i. In the first case, the document d is said to be a *positive* example for the category c_i, i.e. d has been *accepted* for c_i; in the second case, the document d is said to be a *negative* example for the category c_i, i.e. d has been *rejected* for c_i.

As already mentioned, a constraint may be put on the number of categories that a document may belong to. The case where exactly one category must be assigned to each document is usually named *single-label* categorization, which means that d is assigned to the category with the highest CSV; the result of this choice is that categories do not overlap, that is to say a document d cannot be considered as a *positive* example for two or more categories.

There is an important case of the single-label categorization that is called *binary* categorization, also known as *one-vs-all* categorization [16]. In this case, there are $|C|$ independent binary categorization problems where each document of D must be assigned either to category c_i or its complement $\bar{c}_i = C - c_i$. For a document d, the i-th independent problem is assigning d either to category c_i or to the complementary $\bar{c}_i$. When we approach the problem in terms of binary categorization, we actually build $|C|$ binary classifiers, one for each category in C.

In order to train and estimate the parameters of each category, and test the effectiveness of this estimate, in a supervised learning approach the initial set D, which is the set of pre-classified documents, is split into two main subsets: the *training* set D_{tr}, where the subscript tr stands for training; the *test* set D_{te}, where the subscript te stands for test and $D_{te} = D - D_{tr}$. D_{tr} is used to train the system while D_{te} is used to measure performance. The documents in D_{te} cannot participate in any way in the inductive construction of the classifiers; if this condition were not satisfied, the experimental results obtained would be biased and would likely be unrealistically good.

The CSV function takes on different meanings according to the learning method used: in the NB approach, the CSV_i is defined in terms of the probability that a document d belongs to the category c_i. For example, Bayesian classifiers view $CSV_i(d)$ in terms of the conditional probability $P(c_i|d)$, that is, the probability that a document d belongs to c_i.

2 The Two-Dimensional Model

The Two-Dimensional representation of documents [3], which allows documents to be represented on a two-dimensional Cartesian plane, is based on the definition of two parameters for each term that appears in a document. These parameters are called *presence* and *expressiveness* and their purpose is to capture the fact that the importance of a term in a generic category is not only given by the relative frequency of the term in the documents of the category, but also by the relative frequency of the term in the documents of all the other categories [7]. These measures are used to define the coordinates of a point in the two-dimensional space which is directly related to the probability that a document belongs to a category. This direct relation between the probability of a document and a point on a two-dimensional space makes possible the visualization of entire collections of documents on a Cartesian plane, and the design of ad-hoc algorithms that categorize documents directly on this two-dimensional representation.

The main advantages of this representation are: no explicit need for feature selection to reduce dimensionality [20]; limited space required to store objects, comparable to the NB models, as well as the computational cost for training the classifier; 2-D visualization of collections to analyze performance and find possible relations among categories.

The 2DPM that we present here is a probabilistic model, and it differs from the NB models in the main assumptions which are formally addressed in Sect. 2.1. The NB classifier assumes that all attributes of the examples, that is to say the terms t of a document d, are independent of each other given the context of the category c. This is usually expressed in formula as

$$P(d|c) = \prod P(t|c) .$$

This is the so-called NB assumption; because of it, the parameters for each attribute can be learned separately [11].

The hypotheses of the 2DPM are different from those of the NB models: instead of independent events, terms are seen as disjoint events, and documents are represented as the union of these events. The set of probability measures defined in this model work in such a way that a reduction of the vocabulary of terms in order to reduce the complexity of the problem is ultimately not necessary. In order to progressively familiarize the reader with the 2DPM, and in particular with the non-common use of the hypothesis of disjoint events, we present the definition of the probabilities step-by-step.

2.1 Basic Probabilities for the 2DPM

Let us assume we have a set of known categories that we indicate with

$$C = \{c_1, c_2, \ldots, c_i, \ldots, c_{|C|}\} ,$$

and let us assume we have a vocabulary of terms

$$V = \{t_1, t_2, \ldots, t_k, \ldots, t_{|V|}\} .$$

The sample space Ω we want to study is the following:

$$\Omega = \{(t_k, c_i) \mid t_k \in V, \ c_i \in C\} ,$$

where the elementary events represent the fact that a term is present in the documents of a category. For example, (t_k, c_i) represents the fact that the term t_k appears in the documents of category c_i. In the following, sentences like "find the term t_k in c_i", or "draw the term t_k in c_i", or "choose the term t_k in c_i", are used to summarize the meaning of the event (t_k, c_i).

Without losing generality, we consider an example with three categories and six terms in order to show the basic events which are used to build the model. The sample space becomes

$$\begin{aligned}
\Omega = \{ &(t_1, c_1), (t_2, c_1), (t_3, c_1), (t_4, c_1), (t_5, c_1), (t_6, c_1) , \\
&(t_1, c_2), (t_2, c_2), (t_3, c_2), (t_4, c_2), (t_5, c_2), (t_6, c_2) , \\
&(t_1, c_3), (t_2, c_3), (t_3, c_3), (t_4, c_3), (t_5, c_3), (t_6, c_3)\} ,
\end{aligned}$$

each elementary event can be seen as the intersection of two events of this kind:

choose category c_i, with $i \in \{1, 2, 3\}$, and *choose term* t_k, with $k \in \{1, 2, 3, 4, 5, 6\}$.

Therefore, with the event *choose a category* c_1, that in the space Ω is equal to:

$$c_1 = \{(t_1, c_1), (t_2, c_1), (t_3, c_1), (t_4, c_1), (t_5, c_1), (t_6, c_1)\} ,$$

we indicate the fact that the category c_1 was chosen during the experiment. With the event *choose the term* t_1, that in the space Ω is equal to

$$t_1 = \{(t_1, c_1), (t_1, c_2), (t_1, c_3)\} \,,$$

we indicate the fact that the term t_1 was chosen during the experiment. The intersection of these two events returns an elementary event of Ω:

$$t_1 \cap c_1 = \{(t_1, c_1)\} \,.$$

We want to underline this passage because there is the possibility of confusing the probability of the elementary event $P(\{(t_1, c_1)\})$ with the probability of the conditional event $P(t_1|c_1)$.

Finally, we indicate a document with the symbol d and we define it in the following way:

a document d is the event constituted by the union of all and only the events which are equivalent to the terms in the document.

For example, if the document d contains the terms t_1 and t_3, it can be represented as the event

$$d = \{(t_1, c_1), (t_1, c_2), (t_1, c_3), (t_3, c_1), (t_3, c_2), (t_3, c_3)\} \,.$$

If we try to decompound the sample space Ω into the product space of Ω_C (the sample space of the categories), and Ω_V (the sample space of the terms of the vocabulary), it is immediately clear that the two spaces are not independent, because the probability of a term is strongly connected to the category in which it appears. Therefore, no multiplication rule can be applied and, for this reason, we have to start from the calculation of the conditional probabilities which are explained in the following paragraphs.

Probability of a Term, Given a Category or a Set of Categories

The simplest situation is when we want to calculate the probability of finding the term t_k after having chosen the category c_i. This probability is equal to the conditional probability $P(t_k|c_i)$, which we can write as

$$P(t_k|c_i) = \frac{\text{frequency of } t_k \text{ in the document of } c_i}{\text{total frequency of all the terms in the documents of } c_i} \,.$$

Now, assuming that a set of categories has been chosen, what is the probability of choosing the term t_k? Given a set of categories $\bigcup_{i\in\gamma} c_i$, where γ is a set of integers in the interval $[1, |C|]$, the conditional probability becomes:

$$P\left(t_k \Big| \bigcup_{i\in\gamma} c_i\right) = \frac{P\left(t_k \cap \left(\bigcup_{i\in\gamma} c_i\right)\right)}{P\left(\bigcup_{i\in\gamma} c_i\right)} = \frac{P\left(\bigcup_{i\in\gamma}(t_k \cap c_i)\right)}{P\left(\bigcup_{i\in\gamma} c_i\right)}$$

$$= \frac{\sum_{i\in\gamma} P(t_k|c_i) P(c_i)}{P\left(\bigcup_{i\in\gamma} c_i\right)} = \frac{1}{|\gamma|} \sum_{i\in\gamma} P(t_k|c_i) \,,$$

where the ratio between the probability of a category, $P(c_i)$, and the probability of a set of categories, $P\left(\bigcup_{i\in\gamma} c_i\right)$, is constant and equal to $\frac{1}{|\gamma|}$.

Probability of a Set of Terms, Given a Category or a Set of Categories

More generally, we want to calculate the probability of a set of terms, that is to say a document, having chosen one or more categories. Given a set of terms $\bigcup_{k \in v} t_k$, where v is a set of integers in the interval $[1, |V|]$, the conditional probability for one category becomes:

$$\mathrm{P}\left(\bigcup_{k \in v} t_k \Big| c_i\right) = \frac{\mathrm{P}\left((\bigcup_{k \in v} t_k) \cap c_i\right)}{\mathrm{P}(c_i)} = \frac{\mathrm{P}\left(\bigcup_{k \in v}(t_k \cap c_i)\right)}{\mathrm{P}(c_i)}$$

$$= \sum_{k \in v} \frac{\mathrm{P}(t_k \cap c_i)}{\mathrm{P}(c_i)} = \sum_{k \in v} \mathrm{P}(t_k | c_i) \ .$$

If we consider a set of terms $\bigcup_{k \in v} t_k$, and a set of categories $\bigcup_{i \in \gamma} c_i$, the conditional probability can be re-written as

$$\mathrm{P}\left(\bigcup_{k \in v} t_k \Big| \bigcup_{i \in \gamma} c_i\right) = \frac{\mathrm{P}\left((\bigcup_{k \in v} t_k) \cap \left(\bigcup_{i \in \gamma} c_i\right)\right)}{\mathrm{P}\left(\bigcup_{i \in \gamma} c_i\right)}$$

$$= \frac{\mathrm{P}\left(\bigcup_{k \in v}\left(t_k \cap \left(\bigcup_{i \in \gamma} c_i\right)\right)\right)}{\mathrm{P}\left(\bigcup_{i \in \gamma} c_i\right)}$$

$$= \sum_{k \in v} \frac{\mathrm{P}\left(t_k \cap \left(\bigcup_{i \in \gamma} c_i\right)\right)}{\mathrm{P}\left(\bigcup_{i \in \gamma} c_i\right)} = \frac{1}{|\gamma|} \sum_{k \in v} \sum_{i \in \gamma} \mathrm{P}(t_k | c_i) \ .$$

2.2 "Peculiarity" of a Term, Having Chosen a Set of Categories

Now that the basic tools to calculate the probabilities of interest have been presented, we need to introduce another key concept of this model, the "peculiarity" of a term having chosen a set of categories. In order to have a compact notation, we indicate with Γ the set of categories of interest, where $\Gamma = \bigcup_{i \in \gamma} c_i$ and $|\Gamma| = |\gamma|$, while $\bar{\Gamma}$ indicates the set of all the remaining categories, $\bar{\Gamma} = C - \bigcup_{i \in \gamma} c_i$ and $|\bar{\Gamma}| = |C| - |\gamma|$.

The peculiarity of a term t_k for a set of categories is proportional to the probability of finding t_k from the set of categories Γ and the probability of not finding t_k from the set of categories $\bar{\Gamma}$. We give the name *presence* of a term t_k having chosen a set of categories Γ to the first probability, while we give the name *expressiveness* of a term t_k chosen the set of categories Γ to the second probability. Therefore, the peculiarity of a term can be related in terms of its presence in the set of categories, i.e. how frequently we see the term in the categories, and its expressiveness, i.e. how distinctive the term is for that set of categories.

The situation presented here indeed implies two distinct experiments: drawing a term from Γ and drawing a term from $\bar{\Gamma}$. The building of the new sample space and the definition of the peculiarity of a term in terms of probability is presented in the following sections.

Probability of a Term, Given Complementary Sets of Categories

The experiments that we want to observe are the following: choosing a term t_k from a set of categories Γ, and choosing the term t_k from the remaining categories $\bar{\Gamma}$. Doing so, we can consider two separate and independent sample spaces Ω_Γ and $\Omega_{\bar{\Gamma}}$, that are subsets of the initial space Ω.

To better understand the two new spaces, we give the example of the three categories, considering $\Gamma = c_1$ and $\bar{\Gamma} = C - \Gamma = c_2 \cup c_3$. In this way the two spaces are:

$$\Omega_\Gamma = \{(t_1, c_1), (t_2, c_1), (t_3, c_1), (t_4, c_1), (t_5, c_1), (t_6, c_1)\} , \quad .$$
$$\Omega_{\bar{\Gamma}} = \{(t_1, c_2), (t_2, c_2), (t_3, c_2), (t_4, c_2), (t_5, c_2), (t_6, c_2) ,$$
$$(t_1, c_3), (t_2, c_3), (t_3, c_3), (t_4, c_3), (t_5, c_3), (t_6, c_3)\} .$$

The sample space of the experiment "find a term t_k in a set of categories Γ and find the term t_k in the set of remaining categories $\bar{\Gamma}$", which we indicate with e, is given by the product of the two spaces Ω_Γ and $\Omega_{\bar{\Gamma}}$. In the example of the three categories, it becomes:

$$\Omega_\Gamma \times \Omega_{\bar{\Gamma}} = \left\{ \left((t_k, c_i), (t_j, c_h) \right) \mid (t_k, c_i) \in \Omega_\Gamma, \ (t_j, c_h) \in \Omega_{\bar{\Gamma}} \right\} .$$

A generic event $\left((t_k, c_i), (t_j, c_h) \right)$ of the product space has to be interpreted as "finding the term t_k from category $c_i \in \Gamma$", which we indicate with e_1, and "finding the term t_j from category $c_h \in \bar{\Gamma}$", which we indicate with e_2. The probabilities of such events are:

$$P_{\Omega_\Gamma \times \Omega_{\bar{\Gamma}}}(e_1 \times \Omega_{\bar{\Gamma}}) = P_{\Omega_\Gamma}(e_1) = P\left(t_k | \Gamma\right)$$
$$P_{\Omega_\Gamma \times \Omega_{\bar{\Gamma}}}(\Omega_\Gamma \times e_2) = P_{\Omega_{\bar{\Gamma}}}(e_2) = P\left(t_k | \bar{\Gamma}\right) .$$

The probability of the joint event $e = e_1 \cap e_2$ is equal to:

$$P_{\Omega_\Gamma \times \Omega_{\bar{\Gamma}}}(e) = P_{\Omega_\Gamma \times \Omega_{\bar{\Gamma}}}(e_1 \cap e_2) = P_{\Omega_\Gamma \times \Omega_{\bar{\Gamma}}}((e_1 \times \Omega_{\bar{\Gamma}}) \cap (\Omega_\Gamma \times e_2))$$
$$= P_{\Omega_\Gamma \times \Omega_{\bar{\Gamma}}}(e_1 \times \Omega_{\bar{\Gamma}}) \cdot P_{\Omega_\Gamma \times \Omega_{\bar{\Gamma}}}(\Omega_\Gamma \times e_2) = P_{\Omega_\Gamma}(e_1) \cdot P_{\Omega_{\bar{\Gamma}}}(e_2)$$
$$= P\left(t_k | \Gamma\right) \cdot P\left(t_k | \bar{\Gamma}\right) .$$

The last passage shows that the probability of the joint event $e_1 \cap e_2$ is equal to the product of two conditional probabilities, which can be calculated in the way presented in the previous subsection.

In this example, we have considered the events of drawing a term t_k from Γ and a term t_j from $\bar{\Gamma}$. However, the definition of peculiarity of a term for a set of categories considers a different event, that is "drawing the term t_k from Γ and *not* drawing t_k from $\bar{\Gamma}$". The explanation of this probability is presented in the following paragraph.

Peculiarity of a Term, Having Chosen a Set of Categories

Consider the new event "finding the term t_k from Γ and *not* finding t_k from $\bar{\Gamma}$", which we indicate with e', equal to $e' = e_1 \cap e_3$, where e_3 is the event "*not* finding the term t_k from the set of categories $\bar{\Gamma}$".

The probability of e' is equal to:

$$
\begin{aligned}
P_{\Omega_\Gamma \times \Omega_{\bar{\Gamma}}}(e') &= P_{\Omega_\Gamma \times \Omega_{\bar{\Gamma}}}(e_1 \cap e_3) = P_{\Omega_\Gamma \times \Omega_{\bar{\Gamma}}}((e_1 \times \Omega_{\bar{\Gamma}}) \cap (\Omega_\Gamma \times e_3)) \\
&= P_{\Omega_\Gamma \times \Omega_{\bar{\Gamma}}}(e_1 \times \Omega_{\bar{\Gamma}}) \cdot P_{\Omega_\Gamma \times \Omega_{\bar{\Gamma}}}(\Omega_\Gamma \times e_3) = P_{\Omega_\Gamma}(e_1) \cdot P_{\Omega_{\bar{\Gamma}}}(e_3) \\
&= P(t_k|\Gamma) \cdot P(\bar{t}_k|\bar{\Gamma}) \ .
\end{aligned}
$$

Moreover, since the probability of the union of all the terms of the vocabulary given a set of categories is equal to one:

$$
P \left(\bigcup_{j=1}^{|V|} t_j | \bar{\Gamma} \right) = \sum_{j=1, j \neq k}^{|V|} P(t_j|\bar{\Gamma}) + P(t_k|\bar{\Gamma}) = 1 \ ,
$$

we can rewrite the probability of $P(\bar{t}_k|\bar{\Gamma})$ in the following way:

$$
P(\bar{t}_k|\bar{\Gamma}) = \sum_{j=1, j \neq k}^{|V|} P(t_j|\bar{\Gamma}) = 1 - P(t_k|\bar{\Gamma}) \ .
$$

We can finally define the peculiarity, indicated here with $\mathcal{P}(t_k, \Gamma)$, of a term t_k for a set of categories Γ as

$$
\mathcal{P}(t_k, \Gamma) = P(t_k|\Gamma) \cdot P(\bar{t}_k|\bar{\Gamma}) = P(t_k|\Gamma) \cdot \left(1 - P(t_k|\bar{\Gamma}) \right) \ .
$$

This last formula gives a measure of the importance of a term with respect to the set of categories of interest and the remaining categories. In particular, we can associate the two probabilities $P(t_k|\Gamma)$ and $(1 - P(t_k|\bar{\Gamma}))$ with the definitions we gave earlier in this section of presence and expressiveness, respectively.

Peculiarity of a Set of Terms, Given a Set of Categories

Since the final goal is to find the probability of a document given a category, or a set of categories, we want to consider the probability of the union of the events of the kind of e', which we indicate with $\bigcup_{k \in \upsilon} e'_k$ where e'_k is the event "finding the term t_k from Γ and *not* finding t_k from $\bar{\Gamma}$". The events e'_k and e'_j are disjoint for each $k \neq j$, and the peculiarity of a set of terms given a set of categories is defined as

$$
\mathcal{P} \left(\bigcup_{k \in \upsilon} t_k, \Gamma \right) = \sum_{k \in \upsilon} P(t_k|\Gamma) \cdot \left(1 - P(t_k|\bar{\Gamma}) \right) \ .
$$

At this point, we would like to use the peculiarity as the new estimate of the probability for the term t_k given a set of categories Γ, instead of the conditional probability $P(t_k|\Gamma)$. Nevertheless, $\mathcal{P}(\cdot, \Gamma)$ is not a probability measure on Ω_Γ because $\mathcal{P}(\Omega_\Gamma, \Gamma) \neq 1$, and the reason for this is given by the fact that elementary events of the product space $\Omega_\Gamma \times \Omega_{\bar{\Gamma}}$ like $((t_k, c_i), (t_k, c_j))$ are never taken into account by the function $\mathcal{P}(\cdot, \Gamma)$. In order to overcome this problem, we define a normalized version of the peculiarity as

$$\mathscr{P}\left(\bigcup_{k \in v} t_k, \Gamma\right) = \frac{\mathcal{P}\left(\bigcup_{k \in v} t_k, \Gamma\right)}{\mathcal{P}(\Omega_\Gamma, \Gamma)} ,$$

which is indeed a probability measure on the space Ω_Γ. Note that $\mathscr{P}(\cdot, \Gamma)$ is indeed a set of probability measures, one for each Γ.

Strictly speaking, $\mathscr{P}(\cdot, \Gamma)$ can be defined in terms of a conditional probability:

$$\mathscr{P}\left(\bigcup_{k \in v} t_k, \Gamma\right) = P_{\Omega_\Gamma \times \Omega_{\bar{\Gamma}}}\left(\bigcup_{k \in v} e'_k \mid \bigcup_{k=1}^{|V|} e'_k\right)$$

where the given event $\bigcup_{k=1}^{|V|} e'_k$ ensures that only events of the kind of e'_k can occur, i.e. elementary events of the product space $\Omega_\Gamma \times \Omega_{\bar{\Gamma}}$ like $((t_k, c_i), (t_k, c_j))$ are not taken into account.

2.3 Document Coordinates

In Sect. 2.1, we defined a document d as the event constituted by the union of all and only the events which are equivalent to the terms in the document, such as $d = \bigcup_{k \in \delta} t_k$, where δ is the set of indices of the terms that appear in the document.

Using $\mathscr{P}(\cdot, \Gamma)$, the probability of such an event, given a set of categories Γ, is equal to

$$\mathscr{P}(d, \Gamma) = \mathscr{P}\left(\bigcup_{k \in \delta} t_k, \Gamma\right) = \sum_{k \in \delta} \mathscr{P}(t_k, \Gamma) .$$

The definition of the probability of a document given a set of categories Γ of the last equation is general, and we need to instantiate it in the case of c_i and $\bar{c}_i$ for the binary categorization approach.

Using this set of new probability measures we can define the $X_i(d)$ and $Y_i(d)$ coordinates of a document d as:

$$X_i(d) = \mathscr{P}\left(\bigcup_{k \in \delta} t_k, c_i\right) , \quad Y_i(d) = \mathscr{P}\left(\bigcup_{k \in \delta} t_k, \bar{c}_i\right) .$$

According to the set of measures $\mathscr{P}(\cdot, \Gamma)$, we expect a document belonging with high probability to category c_i with respect to $\bar{c}_i$ to have a high value of $X_i(d)$ and a low value of $Y_i(d)$, and the opposite for a document belonging with low probability to category c_i with respect to $\bar{c}_i$.

2.4 2-D Representation and Categorization

So far we have defined a set of probability measures in order to estimate the probability that a document d belongs to a category c_i or to $\bar{c}_i$. In particular, we named these two probabilities $X_i(d)$ and $Y_i(d)$, respectively. These two measures will be used as the two-dimensional coordinates for the document d in a two-dimensional Cartesian plane.

Suppose for a moment that $X_i(d)$ and $Y_i(d)$ are indeed the probabilities of a category given a document; this means that $X_i(d) = P(c_i|d)$ and $Y_i(d) = P(\bar{c}_i|d)$. With this hypothesis, the more natural way to assign d to c_i would be when:

$$Y_i(d) < X_i(d) .$$

In the two-dimensional plane, this inequality means to assign all the documents below the bisecting line of the first quadrant to c_i. This situation is shown in Fig. 1 where crosses represent the documents belonging to c_i, dots those belonging to $\bar{c}_i$, and the continuous line is the bisecting line. This choice is clearly not the optimal one; with a simple count, it can immediately be seen that almost all the documents of c_i fall below this bisecting line, but so too do a relevant number of documents of $\bar{c}_i$.

One then might imagine introducing a threshold to improve the separation between the points of the two sets of documents:

$$Y_i(d) < X_i(d) + q .$$

In the two-dimensional space, this means shifting the bisecting line and finding that intercept q such that when the last inequality holds, we assign d to c_i. Different lines according to different intercepts are represented in Fig. 1 with dashed lines. Nevertheless, the separation would clearly be improved if the line could rotate in order to adjust the separation.

Hence, a better separation of the documents in c_i and $\bar{c}_i$ is reached when the best intercept together with the best angular coefficient m of the separating line is found. In this way, the plane is split into two regions according to the following inequality:

$$Y_i(d) < X_i(d) \cdot m + q .$$

In Fig. 1 a dash-dotted line shows the best separation according to the best q and m.

Two-Dimensional Categorization

Now that the idea of how documents should be categorized in the two-dimensional plane has been presented, we want to formalize it properly. The condition for which a document d is assigned to category c_i is that the inequality $P(\bar{c}_i|d) < P(c_i|d)$ is satisfied. However, we want to introduce a threshold q such that

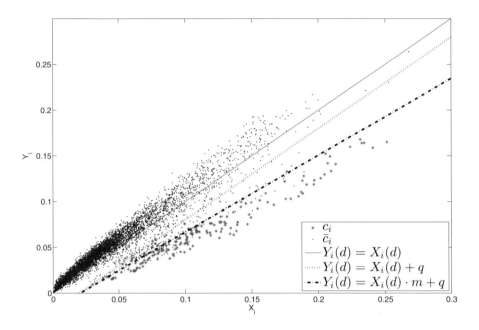

Fig. 1: Example of separation of documents using different lines

$$P(\bar{c}_i|d) < P(c_i|d) + q \ .$$

If we expand the probabilities, and suppose that in each document d there is at least one term of the vocabulary, $P\left(d\right) \neq 0$, and in each category at least one document, $P\left(c\right) \neq 0$, we have:

$$P(d|\bar{c}_i) < P(d|c_i)\frac{P(c_i)}{P(\bar{c}_i)} + q \cdot \frac{P(d)}{P(\bar{c}_i)} \ .$$

Using $\mathscr{P}(\cdot, \Gamma)$ to estimate the probability $P(\cdot|\Gamma)$ we get

$$Y_i(d) < X_i(d) \cdot \mathcal{M} + \mathcal{Q} \ ,$$

where $\mathcal{M} = \frac{P(c_i)}{P(\bar{c}_i)}$ and $\mathcal{Q} = q \cdot \frac{P(d)}{P(\bar{c}_i)}$. $\mathcal{Q}$ is the intercept and $\mathcal{M}$ is the angular coefficient of the separating straight line given by the inequality. Both are calculated experimentally, and the question is how to estimate these two parameters in order to optimize the categorization, an optimization that will be achieved according to some cost function.

Finding the optimal $\mathcal{M}$ and $\mathcal{Q}$ without any guidance and restriction would be impractical. For this reason, advantage can be taken of the analysis of the particular distribution of the documents on the two-dimensional plane. From now on, we will use the symbols $m = \mathcal{M}$, $q = \mathcal{Q}$, for simplicity, to indicate the angular coefficient and the intercept. The particular distribution of the documents, as shown in Fig. 1, suggests searching for the optimal separating line within the region of the two dimensional space covered by the documents. This distribution recalls the shape of a triangle, with one of the vertices very close to the origin of the space. We expect that the separating line crosses this area of the space.

The *Focused Angular Region* algorithm [8] iteratively searches for the optimal straight line that best separates the two sets c_i and $\bar{c}_i$, and the general idea may be stated as follows: let $(0, q)$ be a point close to the origin, $|q| < \varepsilon$. Let $Y_{c_i} = Y_{c_i}(X_{c_i})$ be the interpolating line of category c_i constrained to pass through the point $(0, q)$, and let $Y_{\bar{c}_i} = Y_{\bar{c}_i}(X_{\bar{c}_i})$ be the interpolating line of the complementary set $\bar{c}_i$ constrained to pass through the point $(0, q)$:

$$Y_{c_i} = Y_{c_i}(X_{c_i}) = m_{c_i} \cdot X_{c_i} + q \, , \quad Y_{\bar{c}_i} = Y_{\bar{c}_i}(X_{\bar{c}_i}) = m_{\bar{c}_i} \cdot X_{\bar{c}_i} + q \, .$$

In both cases, the interpolating lines of positive and negative documents, that is to say the documents belonging to c_i and $\bar{c}_i$ respectively, are found by means of standard vertical least square fitting procedures. Consider the angular region whose vertex is the point $(0, q)$, bounded by the semi-lines Y_{c_i} and $Y_{\bar{c}_i}$. Within this region the optimal separating straight line should be found according to some cost function. The equation of the line is:

$$Y_i = m_i \cdot X_i + q \quad ,$$

Figure 2 shows an example of the line found by the algorithm on the same documents as Fig. 1.

This approach leads to a computational cost which is linear with respect to the number of training documents, and it is independent from the size of the vocabulary of terms. The comparison in terms of complexity with other approaches in text classification [19, 21] shows that this algorithm is close to the best cost performers like NB and Rocchio, while at the same time being much more efficient compared to other complex methodologies like SVM (see [4] for an analysis of the order of magnitude of the difference between the two-dimensional approach and SVM).

2.5 Feature Selection and Term Weights

At the end of this analysis, we would like emphasize the effects a feature selection could have on 2DPM, and why using one is to be avoided.

The effect of a feature selection function on a single document would be to shift the position of a document on the two dimensional plane. Therefore, thinking of the whole collection of documents, the selection of terms would produce a translation and rotation of the points. The roto-translation would be favorable for the classification if the new position taken by positive and negative documents is better with respect to the bisecting line of the first quadrant.

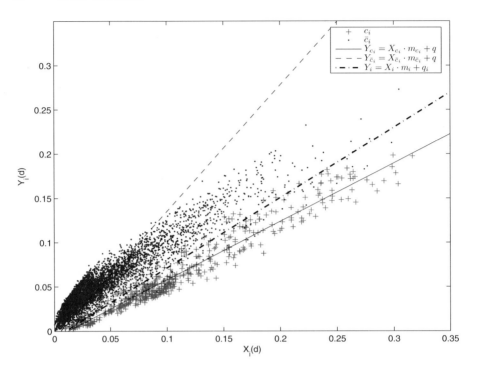

Fig. 2: Example of possible plots using the 2DPM

On the other hand, our approach is to maintain the information of all the vocabulary and to move the separating line, instead of moving the cloud of points. We consider this aspect very important because, in this way, the vocabulary of terms is not impoverished in an arbitrary way, i.e. selecting only the *n-thousands* terms and discarding the rest of the vocabulary. Moreover, from a computational cost point of view, our approach is comparable to the separate training required by the feature selection phase, which is often ignored in the literature.

In addition, from the point of view of probabilities as term weights, at first sight, presence and expressiveness may call to mind the tf × idf weighting scheme. Although the fundamental idea is similar to the one of tf × idf, there are significant differences: term frequency (tf) gives the relative frequency of the term in the document while presence gives the relative frequency of the documents of the category under observation that contain the term; inverse document frequency (idf) calculates the relative frequency of the documents of the collection that contain the term while expressiveness keeps count of the relative frequency of the documents of a subset of the collection that contain the term.

In the literature, an experimental study was carried out to mix in the definition of term weights, the frequency of terms, such as tf, with a feature selection function, such as Information Gain [9]. The main advantage of the way 2DPM defines probabilities is to embody in a formal, not empirical, and correct way a kind of selection of terms, that is to say the relative importance of t_k in c_i (its presence) is discredited or given credence by an amount proportional to its relative importance in $\bar{c}_i$ (its expressiveness).

3 Experiments

In this section the experimental results which compare the 2DPM to the multinomial NB model are presented.

3.1 Datasets

There are standard benchmark collections that can be used for experimental purposes for ATC. The most widely used are the Reuters datasets that collect Reuters newswire agencies that are classified under different categories. They are the Reuters-21578[1] and the Reuters RCV1[2]. The description of the collections follows, and particular stress is given to the Reuters-21578 which has been widely used in the past by different researchers.

Reuters-21578: Of the 135 potential categories, we used the following subsets in the experiments: the 10 most frequent categories; the 90 most frequent categories, that is the categories with at least one training document and one test document; the 115 most frequent categories, that is the categories with at least one training document and possibly no test documents.

Reuters Collection Volume 1 (RCV1): the new Reuters corpus consists of almost 810 thousand newswires covering a whole year of Reuters news agencies, from August 20, 1996 to August 19, 1997. For the RCV1, a sample of 16 categories, which approximately follow the distribution of the documents in the whole collection [14], were chosen out of the 103 potential categories. The training set consisted of the first month of the Reuters year (20th August 1996, 19th September 1996) with 30,529 documents, while the test set consisted of the last Reuters month (20th July 20 1997, 19th August 1997) with 36,243 documents. A similar choice on the months was made in one of the experiments of [1].

3.2 Pre-Processing and Performance Measures

Before indexing terms, some text preprocessing was carried out on the documents of both collections: a first cleaning was made removing all the punctuation marks and converting all the letters to lower case. A standard stoplist

---

[1] http://www.daviddlewis.com/resources/testcollections/reuters21578/
[2] http://about.reuters.com/researchandstandards/corpus/

of 571 terms[3] was used to remove the most frequent terms of the English language; finally, the English Porter stemmer[4] was used as the only method to reduce the number of terms of the vocabulary. No feature selection function was used to reduce the vocabulary of terms.

For the 2DPM, a k-fold cross validation with $k = 5$ was used to find the best separating line with the FAR algorithm [8]. The multinomial NB model was used as baseline since it performs in general better than the Bernoulli model. The Laplacian prior was used to smooth probabilities, and the whole vocabulary was used in both cases.

Standard IR evaluation measures like recall ρ_i, precision π_i were computed for each category c_i together with a combination of them into a single measure given by the F_1 measure [18]. Macro-averages and micro-averages of these measures were computed. Table 1 summarizes the definitions for all the measures and averages presented in the results, using the superscript M to indicate a macro-averaged measure, and μ to indicate a micro-averaged measure, where TP_i indicates the number of *true positives* for category c_i, FN_i the number of *false negatives* for category c_i, and FP_i the number of *false positives* for category c_i.

3.3 Analyses of Results

Table 2 reports the outcomes of the experiments in tables that are divided into two parts: the results of the 2DPM, and the results of the NB multinomial model. In each part, the performance of each model in terms of averaged recall, precision, and F_1 measure for each category is shown.

Table 2a compares the performance of the two models on the 10 most frequent categories of Reuters-21578. Both the classifiers show a F_1 measure constantly over 0.70, except in the case of category *corn* (not shown in the

Table 1: Evaluation measures

	macro-averaging	micro-averaging
recall	$\rho^M = \dfrac{\sum_{i=1}^{|C|} \rho_i}{|C|}$	$\rho^\mu = \dfrac{\sum_{i=1}^{|C|} TP_i}{\sum_{i=1}^{|C|} (TP_i + FN_i)}$
precision	$\pi^M = \dfrac{\sum_{i=1}^{|C|} \pi_i}{|C|}$	$\pi^\mu = \dfrac{\sum_{i=1}^{|C|} TP_i}{\sum_{i=1}^{|C|} (TP_i + FP_i)}$
F_1 measure	$F_1^M = \dfrac{2\pi^M \rho^M}{\pi^M + \rho^M}$	$F_1^\mu = \dfrac{2\pi^\mu \rho^\mu}{\pi^\mu + \rho^\mu}$

[3] http://www.cs.utk.edu/~cs460.is&r/labs/perl/english.stop
[4] http://www.tartarus.org/~martin/PorterStemmer/

Table 2: Results of experiments

measure	2DPM F_1	ρ	π	Multinominal F_1	ρ	π
micro-aver.	.8828	.9031	.8635	.9055	.9383	.8749
macro-aver.	.8082	.8313	.7864	.8144	.8615	.7722

(a) Reuters-21578, 10 categories.

measure	2DPM F_1	ρ	π	Multinominal F_1	ρ	π
micro-aver.	.7564	.7252	.7904	.7640	.7121	.8241
macro-aver.	.3543	.2714	.5100	.1868	.1430	.2693

(b) Reuters-21578, 90 categories.

measure	2DPM F_1	ρ	π	Multinominal F_1	ρ	π
micro-aver.	.7214	.7868	.7527	.7645	.7113	.8262
macro-aver.	.4273	.5923	.4965	.3736	.3282	.4337

(c) Reuters-21578, 115 categories.

measure	2DPM F_1	ρ	π	Multinominal F_1	ρ	π
micro-aver.	.8140	.8100	.8181	.8811	.8880	.8742
macro-aver.	.6319	.5838	.6885	.5517	.5143	.5949

(d) RCV1, 16 categories.

table). This category is the smallest one in terms of the number of training and test documents together with another category, category *wheat*. The multinomial NB model performs slightly better than the 2DPM

Table 2b compares the performance of the 2DPM against the multinomial NB model on the 90 most frequent categories of Reuters-21578. These categories have at least one training document and one test document. Micro-averaged measures are over 0.70, while macro-averaged measures are halved with respect to the experiments with 10 categories. This is an indication of the behavior of the classifier that tends to perform better on categories with a significant number of training samples, at least twenty documents, and worse in extreme cases with categories with few documents. In particular, situations with only a couple of test documents are misleading in terms of performance analyses since the classifier behaves either with scores of 1.00 or 0.00, which means it either did everything well or everything wrong. The macro-averaged performances of the 2DPM are almost double with respect to the NB model, while micro-averaged performances are almost equal.

Table 2c compares the performance of the 2DPM against the multinomial NB model on the 115 most frequent categories of Reuters-21578. These categories have at least one training document, but possibly no test documents. Building a classifier for the 115 categories of Reuters-21578 is a challenging task, even from the evaluation point of view [2]. There are a number of categories without any positive test documents, in these cases we assigned by default a recall equal to one. Then, we verified if the number of false positive documents was equal to zero or not. In the first case we assigned a precision of one; otherwise, zero. Results are similar to the case of 90 categories. However, the macro-averages increased significantly. This is due to those categories without positive test documents where the classifier behaves like a perfect rejector achieving a perfect score of one. This result has also been underlined by [2].

Table 2d presents the performance of the 2DPM on the 16 categories of RCV1 proposed by [14], compared with that of the multinomial NB model. Once again, the multinomial NB tends to perform better than the 2DPM on the micro-average measures, while worse on the macro-average measures. In particular, the multinomial model suffers from those categories that have an unbalanced number of documents compared to the rest of the collection. For example categories like *C313*, *E132*, *E142*, *GOBIT*, which have less than 100 training documents, have a recall and precision of zero.

In order to understand the difference of performances of the two models, we performed a Wilcoxon signed rank test for zero median. In particular, given the two vectors, the 2DPM and the multinomial NB, of performances for each category, we performed a two-sided paired test of the hypothesis that the difference between the matched samples in the two vectors comes from a distribution whose median is zero, at the 5% significance level. The result of this analysis is that the only case where the difference is not statistically significant is the Reuters-21578 10 categories. In all the other cases, the 2DPM performs significantly better than the multinomial model.

4 Conclusions

A new probabilistic model for ATC, the 2DPM, has been presented and particular attention given to the comparison with the NB models. The 2DPM starts from the hypothesis of disjointness of events: terms are disjoint events and documents are the union of these events. In order to estimate the probability of these events, a probability measure, $\mathscr{P}(t, c_i)$ is defined in a way that terms which appear frequently in the documents of c_i are much more discriminative for c_i if they appear *less* frequently in the documents in the complementary set $\bar{c}_i$. It is with the combination of this twin information that a term t_k gains or loses strength (in terms of discriminative power) in a particular category.

The experimental analyses on standard benchmark collections showed that the performance of the 2DPM is at least equal to that for NB models. In general, there is strong evidence of the fact that the 2DPM performs better on macro-averaged F_1 measures which is a consequence of this model's characteristic of considering categories equally important. The Wilcoxon test carried out on different experiments showed that the performance of the 2DPM has a greater degree of statistical significance than the multinomial NB model.

It is important to underline the graphical aspects of this model and their possible use. When plotted on the Cartesian plane according to this formulation, the documents that are constantly shifted along the x-axis and the y-axis can be seen. This graphical representation makes the understanding of the classifier decision very easy and helps find a better decision when possible. A translation and a rotation of the decision line would result in a better separation of the two classes of points. This is the idea of the *Focused Angular Region* algorithm used to improve the performances of the two-dimensional representation.

Moreover, it is possible to find *overlapping* categories, that is categories that are distributed similarly on the plane; Fig. 3 shows a category of interest c_i, and another category c_j which clearly overlaps with c_i. These are the cases where the 2DPM could give advice to other more complex methods to use more computational resources.

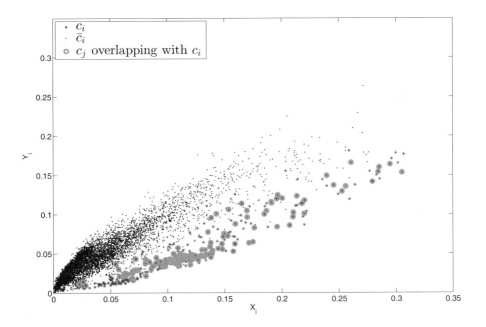

Fig. 3: Example of graphical analysis of two categories which overlap

Finally, current works on the application of the idea of the 2DPM show that this model might be more general than expected and could be used to explain the behavior of different probabilistic models.

References

1. Damerau, F., Zhang, T., Weiss, S., Indurkhya, N.: Text Categorization for a Comprehensive Time-Dependent Benchmark. Information Processing and Management **40**(2), 209–221 (2004)
2. Debole, F., Sebastiani, F.: An Analysis of the Relative Hardness of Reuters–21578 Subsets. Journal of the American Society for Information Science and Technology **56**(6), 584–596 (2005)
3. Di Nunzio, G.M.: A Bidimensional View of Documents for Text Categorization. In: S. McDonald, J. Tait (eds.) Proceedings of the 26th European Conference on Information Retrieval (ECIR 2004), *Lecture Notes in Computer Science (LNCS)*, Vol. 2997, pp. 112–126. Springer, Heidelberg, Germany (2004)
4. Di Nunzio, G.M.: Cross–comparison for Two-dimensional Text Categorization. In: A. Apostolico, M. Melucci (eds.) Proceedings of the 11th Symposium on String Processing and Information Retrieval (SPIRE 2004), *Lecture Notes in Computer Science (LNCS)*, Vol. 3246, pp. 125–126. Springer, Heidelberg, Germany (2004)
5. Di Nunzio, G.M.: 3–D Environment to Represent Textual Documents for Duplicate Detection and Collection Examination. In: T. Catarci, S. Christodoulakis, A. Del Bimbo (eds.) Seventh International Workshop of the EU Network of Excellence DELOS on Audio-Visual Content and Information Visualization in Digital Libraries (AVIVDiLib-05), pp. 12–21. Centromedia, Capannori (Lucca), Italy, Cortona (AR), Italy (2005)
6. Di Nunzio, G.M.: Visualization and Classification of Documents: A New Probabilistic Model to Automated Text Classification. Bulletin of the IEEE Technical Committee on Digital Libraries (IEEE-TCDL) **2**(2) (2006)
7. Di Nunzio, G.M., Micarelli, A.: Does a New Simple Gaussian Weighting Approach Perform Well in Text Categorization? In: G. Gottlob, T. Walsh (eds.) Proceedings of the 18th International Joint Conference of Artificial Intelligence (IJCAI 2003), pp. 581–586. Morgan Kaufmann, San Francisco, CA, USA (2003)
8. Di Nunzio, G.M., Micarelli, A.: Pushing "Underfitting" to the Limit: Learning in Bidimensional Text Categorization. In: R.L. de Mántaras, L. Saitta (eds.) Proceedings of the 16th Eureopean Conference on Artificial Intelligence (ECAI 2004), including Prestigious Applicants of Intelligent Systems (PAIS 2004), pp. 465–469. IOS Press (2004)
9. Dumais, S.: LSI meets TREC: A Status Report. In: G.B. Lamont, H. Haddad, G.A. Papadopoulos, B. Panda (eds.) Proceedings of 2003 ACM Symposium on Applied Computing (SAC 2003), pp. 137–152. ACM Press, New York, USA (2003)
10. Ferreira de Oliveria, M., Levkowitz, H.: From Visual Data Exploration to Visual Data Mining: A Survey. IEEE Transactions on Visualization and Computer Graphics **9**(3), 378–394 (2003)

11. Fuhr, N.: Models in Information Retrieval. In: M. Agosti, F. Crestani, G. Pasi (eds.) Lectures on Information Retrieval, *Lecture Notes in Computer Science (LNCS)*, Vol. 1980, pp. 21–50. Springer, Heidelberg, Germany (2000)
12. Krowne, A., Halbert, M.: An Initial Evaluation of Automated Organization for Digital Library Browsing. In: M. Marlino, T. Sumner, F. Shipman III (eds.) ACM/IEEE Joint Conference on Digital Libraries (JCDL 2005), pp. 246–255. ACM Press, New York, NY, USA, Denver, CO, USA (2005)
13. Lewis, D.: Naive (Bayes) at Forty: The Independence Assumption in Information Retrieval. In: C. Nedellec, C. Rouveirol (eds.) Machine Learning: ECML-98, 10th European Conference on Machine Learning, *Lecture Notes in Computer Science (LNCS)*, Vol. 1398, pp. 4–15. Springer, Heidelberg, Germany (1998)
14. Mladenič, D., Brank, J., Grobelnik, M., Milic-Frayling, N.: Feature Selection using Linear Classifier Weights: Interaction with Classification Models. In: J. Callan, N. Fuhr, W. Nejdl (eds.) Peer-to-Peer Information Retrieval, pp. 234–241. ACM Press, New York, NY, USA (2004)
15. Poulin, B., Eisner, R., Szafron, D., Lu, P., Greiner, R., Wishart, D.S., Fyshe, A., Pearcy, B., Macdonell, C., Anvik, J.: Visual Explanation of Evidence with Additive Classifiers. In: Proceedings of the 21st National Conference on Artificial Intelligence (AAAI) and the 18th Innovative Applications of Artificial Intelligence (IAAI) Conference, July 16-20, 2006, Boston, Massachusetts, USA. AAAI Press (2006)
16. Rifkin, R., Klautau, A.: In Defense of One-Vs-All Classification. Journal of Machine Learning Research **5**, 101–141 (2004)
17. Sebastiani, F.: Machine Learning in Automated Text Categorization. ACM Computing Surveys **34**(1), 1–47 (2002)
18. Van Rijsbergen, C.: Information Retrieval. Butterworth-Heinemann, Newton, MA, USA (1979)
19. Webb, G., Boughton, J., Wang, Z.: Not So Naive Bayes: Aggregating One-Dependence Estimators. Machine Learning **58**(1), 5–24 (2005)
20. Yang, Y., Pedersen, J.: A Comparative Study on Feature Selection in Text Categorization. In: D. Fisher (ed.) Proceedings of the Fourteenth International Conference on Machine Learning (ICML 1997), pp. 412–420. Morgan Kaufmann Publishers, San Francisco, CA, USA, Nashville, Tennessee, USA (1997)
21. Yang, Y., Zhang, J., Kisiel, B.: A Scalability Analysis of Classifiers in Text Categorization. In: C. Clarke, G. Cormack, J. Callan, D. Hawking, A. Smeaton (eds.) Proceedings of the 26th Annual International ACM SIGIR Conference on Research and Development in Information Retrieval (SIGIR 2003), pp. 96–103. ACM Press, New York, USA (2003). DOI http://doi.acm.org/10.1145/860435.860455

Analysis of Web Link Analysis Algorithms: The Mathematics of Ranking

Luca Pretto

Department of Information Engineering – University of Padua
Via Gradenigo, 6/b – 35131 Padua – Italy
luca.pretto@dei.unipd.it

Abstract. Link analysis ranking algorithms were originally designed to enhance the performance of Web search engines by exploiting the topological structure of the digraph associated to the Web; now they are also used in many other fields, sometimes far removed from that of Web searching. In many of their applications, their *ranking* capabilities are of prime importance; from here the need arises to perform a mathematical analysis of these algorithms from the perspective of the *rank* they induce on the nodes of the digraphs on which they work. In this chapter the main theoretical results for the questions that arise when ranking is under investigation are presented. Furthermore, future directions for research in this field are conceived and discussed.

Key words: analysis of algorithms, link analysis ranking, mathematics of ranking

1 Introduction

Link analysis ranking algorithms use the information provided by the topological structure of the digraph representing the Web, or a subset of it, to try to infer the "importance" of web pages. These algorithms assign a score to every web page they consider as a measure of its importance; these scores are used by Web search engines to rank the web pages given in response to a user's query.

These algorithms are generally categorized as query-independent and query-dependent algorithms. Query-independent link analysis algorithms work on a digraph representing the whole Web as it is known to the search engine, and rank the web pages off-line before a query is sent. Later, when a query is sent to the search engine, the web pages are filtered on the basis of their relevance to the query, and the scores provided by the algorithm are subsequently used to rank the filtered pages. The celebrated PageRank algorithm is the most famous query-independent algorithm [9]. Query-dependent link analysis algorithms, on the other hand, work on a much smaller digraph, which is a subgraph of the Web built on the basis of the query sent to the search engine; the ranking induced by the scores accorded to each web page by the algorithm is the ranking in which pages are presented. The HITS [17] and SALSA [19] algorithms are the most famous query-dependent algorithms. After PageRank, HITS and SALSA were put forward, a plethora of Web link analysis algorithms were proposed and tested ([4, 6, 8, 14, 23, 24, 27, 30, 31] to name just a few).

Since every link analysis algorithm assigns a score to each web page it considers, with the goal of ranking the web pages given in response to a user's query, a mathematical study of these algorithms naturally leads to an analysis of their behaviour with respect to the *rank* they induce on web pages. It should be noted that this is certainly true for query-dependent algorithms, for which the scores provided by the algorithms are directly used to rank the web pages given in response to a user's query. This is also true for query-independent algorithms when the scores they provide are the only scores used to rank web pages given in response to a user's query: for instance, when pages are previously filtered on the basis of their relevance through a boolean model, i.e. a model that does not assign a relevance score to the pages. Moreover, many of the known alternative usages of query-independent link analysis algorithms use these algorithms as pure ranking algorithms: for instance, in the field of crawling, PageRank is used to decide in 'what order a crawler should visit the URLs it has seen, in order to obtain more "important" pages first' [11]. Indeed, a further reason to study these algorithms is that, rather surprisingly, link analysis algorithms – in some cases with slight variations – have lately been used with success in many other fields, such as that of personalized Web search [14], crawling [11], automatic construction of Web directories [10], word stemming [2,3] and automatic synonym extraction in a dictionary [5]. In many of these applications their ranking capabilities are of prime importance.

Despite its intrinsic theoretical interest and practical importance, the study of the behaviour of these algorithms with respect to the ranking they induce has been rather neglected. The very small number of formal studies on this subject is probably due to its intrinsic mathematical difficulty. Indeed, when the *scores* provided by these algorithms are studied, their behaviour can be analysed either with traditional linear algebra or mathematical analysis tools – for the wider class of algebraic link analysis algorithms – or with traditional tools from calculus of probability – for the class of probabilistic link analysis algorithms [18]. In particular, the most important and most frequently used link analysis algorithms can be mathematically formalized as linear dynamical systems, so their behaviour with respect to the scores can be analysed with traditional linear algebra and computational linear algebra tools. For instance, the scores provided by the PageRank algorithm change according to a linear law when the damping factor changes. This is no longer true when *ranking* is under observation: a change in the damping factor may or may not affect the ranking induced by PageRank on the web pages, and, for some graphs, the induced ranking does not change, whatever the damping factor values in its allowed range. Moreover, the effects on ranking of two damping factor changes are not given by the sum of the effects of each individual change – a fact that is actually insignificant when ranking is under investigation. The above mentioned loss of linearity and the loss of continuity in the mathematical model describing the behaviour of the algorithms when ranking is under investigation force us to use the more complicated tools provided by discrete mathematics in this kind of analysis.

The aim of this chapter is twofold: First, it provides an outline of all the mathematical studies on the ranking induced by link analysis algorithms undertaken up to now, and to the most promising directions for research in this field. Second, it gives a more detailed description of the author's contribution to this subject, namely on the study of PageRank-induced ranking changes when the damping factor varies; in this regard, some novel extensions are presented. The only prerequisite required of the reader is a basic knowledge of PageRank, HITS, SALSA and INDEGREE algorithms. The algorithms will be studied in the abstract, independently of their applications: for this reason, a graph theory terminology will be preferred over a Web terminology. In the rest of this chapter, any link analysis algorithm will be considered according to the following formal definition. Let $\mathbb{R}_+$ be the set of nonnegative real numbers. If $\mathcal{G}_n$ is the set of the directed graphs with n nodes, a *link analysis ranking algorithm* A is a function

$$A : \mathcal{G}_n \to \mathbb{R}_+^n$$

which maps a generic digraph G of $\mathcal{G}_n$ in a vector of n nonnegative real numbers. If G is a digraph in $\mathcal{G}_n$, $A(G)$ is the vector that gives the ranking scores of each node of G, i.e. $A(G)(i)$ is the ranking score of node i.

The chapter is organized as follows. Sect. 2 contains citations of the related works. Existing results for the questions of rank similarity and rank stability are presented in Sect. 3. The main theoretical results on the sensitivity of PageRank-induced ranking to the damping factor changes are provided in Sect. 4. In Sect. 5 the question of ranking convergence as a future direction for research is outlined. In Sect. 6 conclusions are drawn.

2 Related Works

The idea of exploiting the hyperlinked structure of the Web to try to enhance the performance of Web search engines was first suggested in [21]. The PageRank algorithm is presented in [9] and discussed in [25]. HITS and SALSA are illustrated in [17] and [19], respectively. Many other link analysis algorithms have been put forward since 1998 [4,6,8,14,23,24,27,30,31]: some of them are completely new, others are modifications of existing algorithms, sometimes with the purpose of solving specific problems, such as that of personalization. Recently, link analysis algorithms have been applied in different fields, sometimes far removed from that of Web searching [2,3,5,10,11,14].

Although some works exist on the analysis of these algorithms (e.g. [1,7, 8]), only a few focus their attention on the *ranking* induced by link analysis algorithms. Existing works include studies on rank similarity of link analysis algorithms [8, 20] and on their rank stability [8, 20, 29]. The only other works which are specifically about link analysis algorithms and the ranking they induce regard the dependence of the PageRank-induced ranking on damping factor variations. The problem was first addressed in [26], and was then treated in [7] and especially in [22], which provides the most complete theoretical and experimental study on this subject.

3 Previous Work: Rank Similarity and Rank Stability

Previous work on the ranking induced by link analysis algorithms focusses on two aspects, that is *rank similarity* – how similar the rankings produced by two different link analysis algorithms are when working on the same digraph – and *rank stability* – how minor changes to the topology of the digraph on which they work can affect the ranking induced by these algorithms. The main results on these subjects will be briefly presented in this section; our presentation follows [8].

When ranking problems are studied, rank correlation measures must be used to measure the correlations between rankings provided by vectors of scores. In the context of rank similarity and rank stability slight modifications of Kendall's τ measure [16] are generally used. Let us define these measures. Let

$$\mathbf{v} = \begin{bmatrix} v_1 \\ v_2 \\ \vdots \\ v_n \end{bmatrix} \qquad \mathbf{w} = \begin{bmatrix} w_1 \\ w_2 \\ \vdots \\ w_n \end{bmatrix}$$

be two vectors of scores, $\mathbf{v}, \mathbf{w} \in \mathbb{R}^n$. Let us define the indicator function $I_{\mathbf{vw}}^{(0)}$ as

$$I_{\mathbf{vw}}^{(0)}(i,j) = \begin{cases} 1 & \text{if } (v_i > v_j \text{ and } w_i < w_j) \text{ or } (v_i < v_j \text{ and } w_i > w_j) \\ 0 & \text{otherwise} \end{cases}$$

while

$$I_{\mathbf{vw}}^{(1)}(i,j) = \begin{cases} 1 & \text{if } (v_i > v_j \text{ and } w_i < w_j) \text{ or } (v_i < v_j \text{ and } w_i > w_j) \\ & \text{or } (v_i = v_j \text{ and } w_i \neq w_j) \text{ or } (v_i \neq v_j \text{ and } w_i = w_j) \\ 0 & \text{otherwise.} \end{cases}$$

The weak rank distance, $d_r^{(0)}$, is defined as follows:

$$d_r^{(0)}(\mathbf{v}, \mathbf{w}) = \frac{1}{n(n-1)/2} \sum_{i=j}^{n} \sum_{j=1}^{n} I_{\mathbf{vw}}^{(0)}(i,j)$$

while the strict rank distance, $d_r^{(1)}$, is defined as follows:

$$d_r^{(1)}(\mathbf{v}, \mathbf{w}) = \frac{1}{n(n-1)/2} \sum_{i=j}^{n} \sum_{j=1}^{n} I_{\mathbf{vw}}^{(1)}(i,j) \ .$$

Now the following definitions can be stated:

Definition 1. *Two algorithms, A_1 and A_2, are weakly rank similar on the class of digraphs $\bar{\mathcal{G}}_n \subseteq \mathcal{G}_n$, if as $n \to +\infty$*

$$\max_{G \in \bar{\mathcal{G}}_n} d_r^{(0)}(A_1(G), A_2(G)) = o(1) \ .$$

Definition 2. *Two algorithms, A_1 and A_2, are strictly rank similar on the class of digraphs $\bar{\mathcal{G}}_n \subseteq \mathcal{G}_n$, if as $n \to +\infty$*

$$\max_{G \in \bar{\mathcal{G}}_n} d_r^{(1)}(A_1(G), A_2(G)) = o(1) \ .$$

As an obvious consequence of these definitions, if two algorithms are strictly rank similar on $\bar{\mathcal{G}}_n$, then they are also weakly rank similar on $\bar{\mathcal{G}}_n$. Equivalently, if two algorithms are not weakly rank similar on $\bar{\mathcal{G}}_n$, then they are not strictly rank similar on $\bar{\mathcal{G}}_n$, either. The main results on the rank similarity of link analysis algorithms are provided in [8,20]. In particular, in [8] it is proved that the HITS, INDEGREE and SALSA algorithms are not weakly rank similar on the class $\mathcal{G}_n$. In other words, these algorithms can provide considerably different rankings when working on the same digraph. In [20] the analysis is performed on a specific, but particularly important, set of digraphs: the so-called authority connected digraphs.

On the other hand, when rank stability is examined, only *one* fixed algorithm per time is studied. In this case, the effects on the algorithm-induced ranking of a small change in the digraph on which the algorithm works are studied. These small changes consist of *arc* addition or removal, while *node* addition or removal have never been taken into account. Let us remember the main results in this field. Let $G = (N, E)$ and $G' = (N, E')$ be two digraphs in $\mathcal{G}_n$. The link distance d_l between digraphs G and G' is defined as follows:

$$d_l(G, G') = |(E \cup E') - (E \cap E')| \ .$$

That is, $d_l(G, G')$ is the minimum number of arcs that must be added or removed so as to change one digraph into the other.

Definition 3. *An algorithm A is weakly rank stable on the class of digraphs $\bar{\mathcal{G}}_n \subseteq \mathcal{G}_n$, if for every fixed positive integer k, when $n \to +\infty$*

$$\max_{G, G' \in \bar{\mathcal{G}}_n, \ d_l(G, G') \leq k} d_r^{(0)}(A(G), A(G')) = o(1) \ .$$

Definition 4. *An algorithm A is strictly rank stable on the class of digraphs $\bar{\mathcal{G}}_n \subseteq \mathcal{G}_n$, if for every fixed positive integer k, when $n \to +\infty$*

$$\max_{G,G' \in \bar{\mathcal{G}}_n,\ d_l(G,G') \leq k} d_r^{(1)}(A(G), A(G')) = o(1) \ .$$

Clearly, if an algorithm A is strictly rank stable on a certain class of digraphs $\bar{\mathcal{G}}_n$, then A is weakly rank stable on the same class of digraphs. Equivalently, if A is not weakly rank stable on $\bar{\mathcal{G}}_n$, then A is not strictly rank stable on $\bar{\mathcal{G}}_n$. The main results on rank stability prove that the HITS and SALSA algorithms are not weakly rank stable on $\mathcal{G}_n$, while the INDEGREE algorithm is strictly rank stable on $\mathcal{G}_n$. In [20] more results are provided, while focussing on the class of authority connected digraphs. A question in some way related to the one of rank similarity is addressed in [29]; in this article it is experimentally shown that the addition of just *one outgoing arc* to a node can significantly change its PageRank-induced rank.

4 On PageRank-Induced Ranking Changes

Although PageRank can be applied in many different fields, it is convenient to use some terms from a Web context when describing the algorithm. Let us consider the *Web Markov chain*, i.e. the Markov chain represented by the Web digraph; let us assume the dangling nodes problem has been solved. In order to obtain irreducibility and aperiodicity, the Web Markov chain is modified: when in a state i, an existing arc is followed with probability α, while a jump towards a randomly chosen state is performed with probability $1 - \alpha$, where $\alpha \in [0, 1)$ is the damping factor. This modification of the Web Markov chain will be called *PageRank Markov chain*, and its associated digraph will be called *PageRank digraph*. Let

$$\mathbf{p}(\alpha) = \frac{(1-\alpha)}{N}\mathbf{1} + \alpha\mathbf{W}^T\mathbf{p}(\alpha) \tag{1}$$

be the formula which gives the PageRank vector. In this formula, α is the damping factor, N is the total number of considered nodes, and $\mathbf{W}$ is the $N \times N$ transition probability matrix of the Web Markov chain. Moreover, let us denote by $p_i(\alpha)$ the i-th entry of the PageRank vector, that is the PageRank value of node i. When PageRank is used for ranking purposes, it is of prime interest to know how the ranking induced by PageRank is affected by a change in the damping factor. More precisely, it is of interest to answer questions like: If $p_i(\alpha) < p_j(\alpha)$, does α' such that $p_i(\alpha') > p_j(\alpha')$ exist? What are the mechanisms that hinder ranking variations and what are the mechanisms that favour them? Do Web digraphs exist in which a ranking change is impossible?

To answer these questions, it is of use to perform some algebraic manipulations on Formula (1). Formula (1) gives

$$(\mathbf{I} - \alpha \mathbf{W}^T)\mathbf{p}(\alpha) = \frac{(1-\alpha)}{N}\mathbf{1}$$

where $\mathbf{I}$ is the $N \times N$ identity matrix. When $\alpha < 1$, the matrix $(\mathbf{I} - \alpha \mathbf{W}^T)$ is non-singular [28, Lemma B.1], so that

$$\mathbf{p}(\alpha) = \frac{(1-\alpha)}{N}(\mathbf{I} - \alpha \mathbf{W}^T)^{-1}\mathbf{1} = \frac{(1-\alpha)}{N}(\sum_{k=0}^{+\infty}(\alpha \mathbf{W}^T)^k)\mathbf{1} . \qquad (2)$$

When only the ranking is studied, the factor $1 - \alpha$ is irrelevant, as is the first member of the power series, and ranking changes are governed by:

$$\alpha \mathbf{W}^T \frac{1}{N}\mathbf{1} + \alpha^2(\mathbf{W}^T)^2 \frac{1}{N}\mathbf{1} + \alpha^3(\mathbf{W}^T)^3 \frac{1}{N}\mathbf{1} + \cdots . \qquad (3)$$

It can easily be seen that the generic member $(\mathbf{W}^T)^k \frac{1}{N}\mathbf{1}$ gives the probability vector of the Web Markov chain $x(\cdot)$ after k steps when the initial distribution is the uniform one, that is the PageRank-induced ranking changes are strictly related to the transitory behaviour of the Web Markov chain with an initial uniform distribution. This result, however, is hardly useful unless it is translated into observable properties of the Web digraph; this translation is our main task in the rest of this section.

4.1 Limit Behaviour

Since our analysis regards PageRank-induced ranking changes which occur when α moves from 0 to 1, the question of first studying the PageRank behaviour when $\alpha \to 0^+$ and $\alpha \to 1^-$ naturally arises. Before beginning this study let us call *weighted in-degree of node i* the sum $\sum_{h \to i} \frac{1}{d_h}$ where "$h \to i$" means that the sum is extended to all the nodes h with an outgoing arc towards the node i, and d_h is the out-degree of node h. Now, when $\alpha \to 0^+$ Formula (1) gives:

$$\lim_{\alpha \to 0^+} \mathbf{p}(\alpha) = \frac{1}{N}\mathbf{1}$$

i.e. all the PageRank entries have the same value $\frac{1}{N}$. When $\alpha > 0$, but $\alpha \approx 0$, the PageRank-induced ranking is governed by the term $\mathbf{W}^T\mathbf{1}$ in (3). This means that when $\alpha \approx 0$, $p_i(\alpha) > p_j(\alpha)$ if and only if the weighted in-degree of the node i is greater than the weighted in-degree of the node j. When $\alpha \to 1^-$ the mathematical study is more difficult. Only partial results are known for this limit. To get these results, let us call

$$\mathbf{Q}(\alpha) = \alpha \mathbf{W}^T + \frac{(1-\alpha)}{N}\mathbf{1}\mathbf{1}^T$$

the transition probability matrix of the PageRank Markov chain, where $\alpha \in [0, 1)$. Formula (1) can be written as

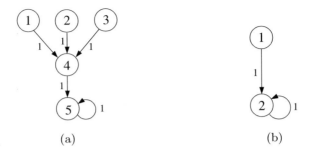

(a)   (b)

Fig. 1: **(a)** A Web digraph in which a ranking change occurs when α moves from 0 to 1. **(b)** A Web digraph in which a ranking change does not occur when α moves from 0 to 1

$$\mathbf{p}(\alpha) = \mathbf{Q}(\alpha)\mathbf{p}(\alpha) \tag{4}$$

since $\mathbf{1}^T\mathbf{p}(\alpha) = 1$. Now, when $\alpha \to 1^-$, an interesting situation comes to light, since the limit

$$\lim_{\alpha \to 1^-} \frac{(1-\alpha)}{N}(\mathbf{I} - \alpha\mathbf{W}^T)^{-1}\mathbf{1} \tag{5}$$

certainly exists, as each entry of the vector is a rational function bounded by 0 and 1 when $\alpha \in [0,1)$, while (4) when $\alpha = 1$ has, in general, an infinite number of solutions, one of which certainly agrees with (5), since $\mathbf{p}(\alpha)$ is a continuous function in $[0,1]$. And since each solution of (4) when $\alpha = 1$ has a zero value for each entry corresponding to a transient state, each entry of the limit vector (5) corresponding to a state which is not in a rank sink is zero.

To sum up, when $\alpha \to 0^+$ all the PageRank vector entries have the same value $\frac{1}{N}$, while when $\alpha \to 1^-$ all the PageRank values are swallowed up by the rank sinks. This PageRank shift towards the rank sinks may produce a ranking change, as can be seen in Fig. 1(a), where the smallest Web digraph in which this kind of ranking change occurs is shown. It can easily be seen, in fact, that in this case $p_1(\alpha) = p_2(\alpha) = p_3(\alpha) = \frac{1-\alpha}{5}$, $p_4(\alpha) = \frac{1+2\alpha-3\alpha^2}{5}$ and $p_5(\alpha) = \frac{1+\alpha+3\alpha^2}{5}$, so that, while p_1, p_2, p_3 are always less than p_4 and p_5, $p_4 > p_5$ when $\alpha < \frac{1}{6}$, and $p_4 < p_5$ when $\alpha > \frac{1}{6}$. It should be noted, however, that in other cases the PageRank shift towards the rank sinks could not produce a ranking change: this is what happens, for instance, in the digraph in Fig. 1(b), which is the smallest Web digraph in which this occurs.

4.2 Local Behaviour

In the previous section it was proved that when α moves from 0 to 1 a ranking change may occur, due to a PageRank shift towards the rank sinks. Now some questions naturally arise: What happens between these two values? Are

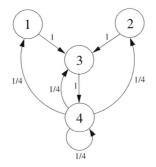

Fig. 2: A strongly connected digraph in which a ranking change occurs when α moves from 0 to 1

ranking changes only due to a shift towards the rank sinks, or can they also be due to other mechanisms? Fig. 2 provides an example of a digraph in which a ranking change occurs, even when the digraph is strongly connected, and no rank sink exists: when $\alpha < \frac{1}{2}$, $p_3 > p_4$, while when $\alpha > \frac{1}{2}$, $p_3 < p_4$. This counterexample proves that there are mechanisms other than a shift towards rank sinks which cause a ranking change. To study these mechanisms, let us return to Formula (3). Since the factor $\frac{1}{N}$ is irrelevant when the ranking is studied, it is of use to concentrate our attention on the formula:

$$\alpha \mathbf{W}^T \mathbf{1} + \alpha^2 (\mathbf{W}^T)^2 \mathbf{1} + \alpha^3 (\mathbf{W}^T)^3 \mathbf{1} + \cdots .$$

Let us now consider the entries i and j of this limit vector. The contribution to the entry i of the k-th addend is given by:

$$\alpha^k \sum_{i_k \to i_{k-1}} \sum_{i_{k-1} \to i_{k-2}} \cdots \sum_{i_1 \to i} \frac{1}{d_{i_k}} \frac{1}{d_{i_{k-1}}} \cdots \frac{1}{d_{i_1}} = \alpha^k B(k,i) .$$

Leaving the factor α^k aside, this addend gives the sum of the probabilities of all and only the oriented paths of k steps which lead to the node i. The subgraph of the digraph made of the nodes from which a path leading to node i in k steps exists will henceforth be called *back digraph* of the node i in k steps. Let us now state the following definition.

Definition 5. *The back digraph of a node i is said to* expand *at step k with regard to node j if $B(k,i) > B(k,j)$. $B(k,i) - B(k,j)$ is the* size *of the* expansion.

Now, it can easily be seen that a necessary condition for a rank change to occur between nodes i and j is that, if the back digraph of node i expands at step k with regard to node j, then the back digraph of node j should expand at another step k' with regard to node i. For instance, in the digraph depicted in Fig. 2, the back digraph of node 3 expands with regard to node 4 at step 1, while the back digraph of node 4 expands with regard to node 3 at step 2.

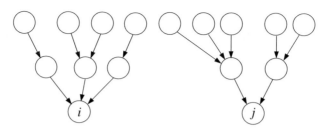

Fig. 3: The two nodes i and j are liable to change their relative ranks

The concept of expansion defined above helps to understand which mechanisms allow a ranking change, by defining them on the basis of the digraph topology. For instance, in Fig. 3, it is evident that nodes i and j are liable to change their relative ranks, since two opposite expansions take place on the back digraphs of node i and j at steps 1 and 2. Nevertheless, the above defined condition is far from being a *sufficient* condition for a ranking change to take place. This happens substantially for two reasons:

1. The size of the expansions should be taken into account. In fact, an expansion of a given size can only be compensated for by a subsequent expansion of a larger size; moreover, the size of the subsequent expansion must be larger the further the second expansion is from the first.
2. The more subsequent expansions of the back digraph of node i with regard to node j occur, the more difficult it becomes to compensate for them.

4.3 Effects of Truncation

The mathematical analysis performed until now is also of use in answering questions regarding the effects of a truncation in the computation of PageRank performed through the power series (2). Indeed, for obvious reasons, when PageRank is computed through the power series (2), a truncation occurs in the actual computation. How does this truncation affect the final result? Can a ranking change between the real limit vector and the vector obtained with the truncated computation occur? And, if the answer to the previous question is yes, which nodes are favoured as a consequence of this truncation to the detriment of others?

The mathematical theory developed up to now allows us to answer, at least qualitatively, all these questions. Indeed, when α is small, i.e. $\alpha \ll 1$, only the first few members of (2) give their contribution to the computation of $\mathbf{p}(\alpha)$ – a truncation, in a sense. This allows us to say that when a truncation occurs, the effects of the PageRank shift towards the rank sinks are removed, and only the first expansions are involved: more precisely, if the truncation occurs at step k, only the expansions which take place at a step no further than k are sensitive. As a consequence of this, even if in general it is impossible to foresee the effects of the removal of some expansions, some conclusions can be drawn; the most important is that the final ranking of the nodes in a rank sink is liable to be damaged by truncation.

4.4 Modified PageRank

After PageRank was originally presented in 1998 [9], many different proposals to modify PageRank were put forward [4,6,12,14,15,27]. These proposals have the purpose of improving the quality of the algorithm, or of biasing PageRank to boost the PageRank values of some nodes to the detriment of others, on the basis of the expected tastes of each user or group of users. In the second case, modifications of the classic formulation of PageRank were suggested, with the purpose of obtaining different PageRank values which best reflect the characteristics of the group of users of the algorithm – in general, a different value for the same node for each group of users: a kind of "personalization". In the rest of this section the behaviour of the ranking induced by these modified algorithms when the damping factor varies is studied. As usual, our work will focus on the mathematical analysis of the algorithms, trying to extract their common properties.

From a mathematical perspective, all the modified PageRank algorithms act on two aspects of the original PageRank formulation:

1. The matrix $\mathbf{W}$, which is changed into another stochastic matrix $\mathbf{V} = [v_{ij}]$, by increasing some transition probabilities to the detriment of others.
2. The personalization vector $\mathbf{v}$, which is initially set to $\mathbf{1}$, is changed to bias the transition probability towards some of the nodes of the Web digraph, to the detriment of others. In all cases, a Web Markov chain with only one closed communicating class must be obtained. Generally, $\mathbf{v} > \mathbf{0}$, so that the only closed communicating class is made of all the nodes of the digraph.

After these variations have been carried out, the new transition probability matrix of the PageRank Markov chain is given by:

$$\mathbf{Q}'(\alpha) = (1 - \alpha)\mathbf{v}\mathbf{1}^T + \alpha\mathbf{V}^T$$

and the modified PageRank vector $\mathbf{p}'(\alpha)$ satisfies:

$$\mathbf{p}'(\alpha) = (1 - \alpha)\mathbf{v} + \alpha\mathbf{V}^T\mathbf{p}'(\alpha)$$

that is, when $\alpha < 1$ [28, Lemma B.1]:

$$\mathbf{p}'(\alpha) = (1 - \alpha)(\mathbf{I} - \alpha\mathbf{V}^T)^{-1}\mathbf{v} = (1 - \alpha)(\sum_{k=0}^{+\infty} \alpha^k(\mathbf{V}^T)^k)\mathbf{v} \ . \tag{6}$$

Formula (6) shows that – in analogy with the classic case – in all the modified versions of PageRank, PageRank-induced ranking variations are related to the transitory effect of the Web Markov chain when $\mathbf{v}$ gives its initial probability distribution. Moreover, all the results previously obtained for the classic version (limit behaviour, local behaviour) are substantially maintained for the modified versions, with the only difference that, in the modified version, the expansion of the back digraph of a node i with regard to node j is defined on the basis of the quantity:

$$B'(k,i) = \sum_{i_k \to i_{k-1}} \sum_{i_{k-1} \to i_{k-2}} \cdots \sum_{i_1 \to i} v_{i_k} v_{i_k i_{k-1}} v_{i_{k-1} i_{k-2}} \cdots v_{i_1 i} .$$

where common notations are used.

5 Ranking Convergence: A Mathematical Challenge

The mathematical issues tackled until now, i.e. the similarity of the ranking induced by different link analysis algorithms working on the same digraph, the sensitivity of link analysis algorithm-induced ranking to the structure of the digraph, and the PageRank-induced ranking changes when the damping factor varies, have been studied in depth recently and are now quite well understood. There is another issue related to ranking problems, however, which has important practical consequences and which is interesting theoretically: the issue of ranking convergence. This issue has not been studied until now, although it should be, at least in so far as a correct and conscious usage of link analysis algorithms is desired. In this section this issue and its related problems are briefly presented. Our aim here is to highlight the problem and some related questions; their study is likely to become a non-trivial and exciting question in the field of applied mathematics.

Many link analysis algorithms, and certainly the most important of them, on the basis of their actual applications or their degree of innovation – PageRank, HITS, SALSA – calculate the scores output vector, which is used to rank the nodes of the digraph on which they work, by using an iterative procedure – typically the power method applied to a matrix obtained from the digraph. Now, while the 'usual' convergence rate of the iterative procedures in a normed vector space is well known [13], no known results are provided for their ranking convergence – intuitively, the number of steps beyond which the ranking provided by the scores does not change any more. Moreover, no formal definition of ranking convergence and no discussion about the connection between ranking convergence and usual convergence have been undertaken until now. This question raises many important related questions: Is it possible for an algorithm to converge quickly in the usual way, yet slowly in ranking, or vice versa? What are the intrinsic properties of a digraph which make an algorithm converge on it quickly or slowly in ranking? Given a random digraph, what is the probability that a given algorithm converges quickly on it? And the probability that a given algorithm converges on it quickly in ranking?

Do accelerations of the iterative procedures exist that ensure that the algorithms will always converge quickly in ranking, or is it always possible to find a digraph which makes the iterative procedure converge slowly in ranking, whatever acceleration is applied?

These are deep questions, intrinsically related to the actual applicability of these algorithms, which should be addressed but have not been addressed until now: they are likely to be the next, and perhaps final, step in the mathematical study of ranking problems in link analysis.

6 Conclusions

The introduction of link analysis algorithms in Information Retrieval and in other fields has raised some new mathematical questions. Some of the most interesting and important for their practical consequences regard the study of the *ranking* induced by these algorithms on the nodes of the digraph on which they work. In this chapter all these questions have been addressed in the abstract, from a mathematical perspective. First, the main results regarding the similarity of the ranking induced by different link analysis algorithms working on the same digraph have been presented. Second, the main results regarding the sensitivity of the ranking induced by link analysis algorithms on digraph topology variations have been shown. Then, the problem of PageRank-induced ranking variations as a function of a change in the damping factor value has been illustrated, and the main results with respect to this problem have been illustrated; in this regard, some novel extensions have been presented. Finally, the open question of the convergence in ranking of the iterative link analysis algorithms — regarding the number of steps beyond which the ranking induced by the scores provided by the algorithms does not change any more — has been posed; at the moment this seems to be the last open question on this subject, and it appears to be both non-trivial and theoretically interesting.

References

1. Agosti, M., Pretto, L.: A theoretical study of a generalized version of Kleinberg's HITS algorithm. Information Retrieval **8**, 219–243 (2005). Special topic issue: Advances in Mathematical/Formal Methods in Information Retrieval.
2. Bacchin, M., Ferro, N., Melucci, M.: The effectiveness of a graph-based algorithm for stemming. In: E.P. Lim, C.S.G. Khoo, H. Chen, E.A. Fox, S.R. Urs, C. Thanos (eds.) Proceedings of the 5th International Conference on Asian Digital Libraries: People, Knowledge, and Technology, ICADL 2002, No. 2555 in Lecture Notes in Computer Science, pp. 117–128. Springer, Berlin Heidelberg New York (2002)
3. Bacchin, M., Ferro, N., Melucci, M.: A probabilistic model for stemmer generation. Information Processing and Management **41**(1), 121–137 (2005)

4. Baeza-Yates, R., Davis, E.: Web page ranking using link attributes. In: Proceedings of the World Wide Web Conference, pp. 328–329 (2004)
5. Berry, M.W. (ed.): Survey of Text Mining: Clustering, Classification, and Retrieval. Springer, New York (2004)
6. Bharat, K., Henzinger, M.R.: Improved algorithms for topic distillation in a hyperlinked environment. In: Proceedings of the 24th Annual International ACM SIGIR Conference on Research and Development in Information Retrieval, pp. 104–111. ACM (1998)
7. Bianchini, M., Gori, M., Scarselli, F.: Inside PageRank. ACM Transactions on Internet Technology **5**(1), 92–128 (2005)
8. Borodin, A., Roberts, G.O., Rosenthal, J.S., Tsaparas, P.: Link analysis ranking: Algorithms, theory, and experiments. ACM Transactions on Internet Technology **5**(1), 231–297 (2005)
9. Brin, S., Page, L.: The anatomy of a large scale hypertextual Web search engine. In: Proceedings of the World Wide Web Conference (1998). `http://www7.scu.edu.au/programme/fullpapers/1921/com1921.htm`
10. Chakrabarti, S., Dom, B.E., Gibson, D., Kumar, R., Raghavan, P., Rajagopalan, S., Tomkins, A.: Experiments in topic distillation. In: Proceedings of the ACM SIGIR Workshop on Hypertext Information Retrieval on the Web, pp. 117–128. ACM, New York (1998)
11. Cho, J., Garcia-Molina, H., Page, L.: Efficient crawling through URL ordering. Computer Networks **30**(1–7), 161–172 (1998)
12. Diligenti, M., Gori, M., Maggini, M.: Web page scoring systems for horizontal and vertical search. In: Proceedings of the World Wide Web Conference, pp. 508–516 (2002)
13. Golub, G.H., Van Loan, C.F.: Matrix Computations, third edn. Johns Hopkins Studies in the Mathematical Sciences. The Johns Hopkins University Press, Baltimore (1996)
14. Haveliwala, T.H.: Topic-Sensitive PageRank. In: Proceedings of the World Wide Web Conference (2002). `http://www2002.org/CDROM/refereed/127`
15. Jeh, G., Widom, J.: Scaling personalized Web search. In: Proceedings of the World Wide Web Conference, pp. 271–279 (2003)
16. Kendall, M.G.: Rank Correlation Methods, fourth edn. Charles Griffin & Co. Ltd., London (1970)
17. Kleinberg, J.M.: Authoritative sources in a hyperlinked environment. Journal of the ACM **46**(5), 604–632 (1999)
18. Lee, H.C., Borodin, A.: Perturbation of the hyper-linked environment. In: T. Warnow, B. Zhu (eds.) Computing and Combinatorics, no. 2697 in Lecture Notes in Computer Science, pp. 272–283. Springer, Berlin Heidelberg New York (2003)
19. Lempel, R., Moran, S.: SALSA: The stochastic approach for link-structure analysis. ACM Transactions on Information Systems **19**(2), 131–160 (2001)
20. Lempel, R., Moran, S.: Rank-stability and rank-similarity of link-based Web ranking algorithms in authority-connected graphs. Information Retrieval **8**, 219–243 (2005). Special topic issue: Advances in Mathematical/Formal Methods in Information Retrieval.
21. Marchiori, M.: The quest for correct information on the Web: Hyper search engines. Computer Networks and ISDN Systems **29**(8–13), 1225–1235 (1997)

22. Melucci, M., Pretto, L.: PageRank: When order changes. In: G. Amati, C. Carpineto, G. Romano (eds.) ECIR2007, no. 4425 in Lecture Notes in Computer Science, pp. 581–588. Springer, Berlin Heidelberg New York (2007)

23. Miller, J.C., Rae, G., Schaefer, F., Ward, L.H., LoFaro, T., Farahat, A.: Modifications of Kleinberg's HITS algorithm using matrix exponentiation and Web log records. In: W.B. Croft, D.J. Harper, D.H. Kraft, J. Zobel (eds.) Proceedings of the 24th Annual International ACM SIGIR Conference on Research and Development in Information Retrieval, pp. 444–445. ACM (2001)

24. Ng, A.Y., Zeng, A.X., Jordan, M.I.: Stable algorithms for link analysis. In: W.B. Croft, D.J. Harper, D.H. Kraft, J. Zobel (eds.) Proceedings of the 24th Annual International ACM SIGIR Conference on Research and Development in Information Retrieval, pp. 258–266. ACM (2001)

25. Page, L., Brin, S., Motwani, R., Winograd, T.: The PageRank citation ranking: bringing order to the Web (1998). Unpublished manuscript. http://google.stanford.edu/~backrub/pageranksub.ps (downloaded: January 2002)

26. Pretto, L.: A theoretical analysis of Google's PageRank. In: A.H.F. Laender, A.L. Oliveira (eds.) String Processing and Information Retrieval, No. 2476 in Lecture Notes in Computer Science, pp. 131–144. Springer, Berlin Heidelberg New York (2002)

27. Richardson, M., Domingos, P.: The intelligent surfer: Probabilistic combination of link and content information in PageRank. In: Advances in Neural Information Processing Systems, pp. 1441–1448. MIT Press, Cambridge, MA (2002)

28. Seneta, E.: Non-negative Matrices and Markov Chains, second edn. Springer, New York (1981)

29. Sydow, M.: Can one out-link change your PageRank? In: P.S. Szczepaniak, J. Kacprzyk, A. Niewiadomski (eds.) Advances in Web Intelligence, no. 3528 in Lecture Notes in Computer Science. Lecture Notes in Artificial Intelligence, pp. 408–414. Springer, Berlin Heidelberg New York (2005)

30. Tomlin, J.A.: A new paradigm for ranking pages on the World Wide Web. In: Proceedings of the World Wide Web Conference, pp. 350–355 (2003)

31. Tsaparas, P.: Using non-linear dynamical systems for web searching and ranking. In: A. Deutsch (ed.) Proceedings of the Twenty-third ACM SIGACT-SIGMOD-SIGART Symposium on Principles of Database Systems, pp. 59–70. ACM (2004)

Digital Annotations: a Formal Model and its Applications

Nicola Ferro

Department of Information Engineering – University of Padua
Via Gradenigo, 6/b – 35131 Padua – Italy
`ferro@dei.unipd.it`

Abstract. We discuss various issues and viewpoints concerning the annotation of digital contents, such as textual documents, images, and multimedia documents in general. The discussion shows how fragmentary the picture is about the annotation and how its definition changes according to the different applicative contexts in which it is used. Therefore, we propose a formal model of the annotation which provides us with a unified and integrated picture on the annotation which takes into account the different viewpoints and uses of it. Finally, we present various possible application areas of the proposed formal model and we introduce the next steps we can undertake by using it as a starting point.

Key words: annotation, digital content, foundations, hypertext, information management system

1 Introduction

The possibility of enriching and personalizing digital contents by adding and sharing annotations has attracted many researchers, who have looked at this opportunity from many different perspectives and with a number of purposes in mind.

Almost everybody is familiar with annotations and has his own intuitive idea about what they are, drawn from personal experience and the habit of dealing with some kind of annotation in every day life, which ranges from jottings for the shopping to taking notes during a lecture or even adding a commentary to a text. This intuitiveness makes annotations especially appealing for both researchers and users: the former propose annotations as an easy understandable way of performing user tasks, while the latter feel annotations to be a familiar tool for carrying out their own tasks. Therefore, annotations have been adopted in a variety of different contexts, such as content enrichment, data curation, collaborative and learning applications, and social networks, as well as in various information management systems, such as the Web (semantic and not), digital libraries, and databases. Surprisingly, all these approaches have not led us to deep knowledge and comprehension of the annotation but, on the contrary, the picture about the annotation of digital contents is still quite fragmentary.

Even though this concept is so familiar, it turns out to be especially elusive when it comes to explicitly and formally defining it, mainly because it is a far more complex and multifaceted concept than one might imagine at a first glance. Indeed, we usually derive what an annotation is from the particular task to which it is applied, rather than investigating the annotation by itself in order to understand its features and how to use it. To cite a few examples, if we deal with the Semantic Web, annotations are considered as metadata [43, 70]; in collaborative applications annotations are a seen as a discourse [34] and might be considered even like e-mails [35]; in the field of digital libraries annotations are treated as an additional content [2, 8]; when we talk about scientific databases, annotations represent both provenance information about the managed data and a way of curating the database itself [26, 28]; in the case of data minining and data visualization, annotations are seen as a means for recording the history of user explorations in visualization environments [40]; finally, in social networks and collaborative tagging, annotations are tags or keywords on different kinds of digital content, e.g. photos or bookmarks [37]. It can be noted as these different notions of annotation partially overlap or share commonalities.

This flourishing of different viewpoints about the annotation, which are often considered as separated, reveals a lack of a clear comprehension of what an annotation is, prevents us from exploiting synergies and complementarities among the different approaches, and makes it more difficult to determine what the differences between annotations and other concepts are, and what the advantages or disadvantages of using annotations are, even when they seem so similar to other concepts.

Moreover, we should consider that the tools we adopt influence the way we work, may change the way we approach a problem, and may impact on our findings. Thus, if we are not able to define annotations and determine their features by themselves, we will not be able to understand whether and when annotations are the tool of choice for a given task, whether and when we can perform a task by using annotations better than by using other approaches, or what we lose or gain when we introduce the use of annotations with respect to other approaches to the same problem.

Therefore, we discuss the different perspectives regarding annotations in order to gather some key features about them. These key features can help us to better distinguish between the different uses of annotations and to understand the case at hand when dealing with annotations. Furthermore, they can be used as a support if we need to make design choices for developing an annotation management system. Finally, we use conducted analyses for proposing a comprehensive and unifying formal model of annotations on digital contents, which only recently has been introduced in the literature [13, 33].

The proposed formal model intends to formalize the main concepts concerning annotations and define the relationships among annotations and annotated information resources. In addition, the formal model constitutes the necessary groundwork to be able to design and formalize search algorithms and to express query languages which take annotations into account, such as those proposed in [11, 12, 35, 38]. Finally, the formal model provides us with the basis for designing and developing an annotation service which can be easily integrated into a wider *Information Management System (IMS)*. Indeed, a clear definition of the concepts related to the annotation allows us to separate the functionalities needed to manage, access, and search annotations, which constitute the core of an annotation service, from the functionalities needed to integrate such an annotation service into IMSs.

The paper is organized as follows: Sect. 2 provides an overview of the different viewpoints about annotations; Sect. 3 provides an introduction to the proposed formal model and discusses different applications of it; Sect. 4 explains and formalizes the various concepts of the formal model; finally, Sect. 5 draws some conclusions and wraps up the discussion.

2 Viewpoints on Annotations

This section aims at giving readers a sample of the different viewpoints about annotations so that they can figure out the range of issues involved with annotations. Indeed, when we talk about annotations, we deal with a concept that has been stratified over a long period of time in our culture and comprises pre-existing knowledge from our cultural heritage. On the other hand, analysing the present use of annotations helps us to understand the current trends in developing annotation management systems as well as comprehend user requirements and expectations.

Therefore, we will discuss the annotation from three perspectives: the user perspective, as it is gained from user studies; the historical perspective on annotations, which provides us with additional information that users may not be able to point out because they often overlook what they have naturally absorbed from their cultural heritage or studies; finally, the perspective of the current annotation systems, which differently model annotations according to the tasks they aim at supporting. For each viewpoint, we will provide some relevant examples and related discussion.

Please note that this section does not intend to be a fully exhaustive survey on annotations, for which the interested reader can refer to [5, 13, 31, 43, 55, 58, 60].

2.1 User Viewpoint

[51] studied personal annotative practices of American college students to point out the form the annotations have in the textbooks and the function of

the annotations, which is derived from their form. [51, pp. 237–238] discovered that:

> First, annotations are *procedural signals*, cluing in the student to where an assignment starts, what material is important (and as we will see, unimportant), and what material might require a second (or successive readings). Second, annotations are *placemarks*; they hold the quotes that are being reserved for the paper that the student will write at the end of the term, the chemical reactions and term definitions the student must memorize for the final, the theorem that is key to the proof in the homework assignment. Third, they are an *in situ way of working problems*. Fourth, annotations record *interpretive activity*, either from another reader (e.g. a professors explanation), or as the result of careful reading (the student has interpreted it him or herself). Fifth, and most elusively, these markings act as a *visible trace of a reader's attention*, a focus on the passing words, and a marker of all that has already been read (as if these words are now possessed). Finally, the markings may just be incidental, *reflecting the material circumstance of reading.*

[52] carries on her research work and categorizes annotations along several dimensions which reflect the form annotations may take on: formal versus informal annotations, explicit versus tacit annotations, annotations as writing versus annotations as reading, hyperextensive versus extensive versus intensive annotations, permanent versus transient annotations, published versus private annotations. Finally, [53], [54], and [65] investigate the relationship between private, shared and public annotations and how they can be exploited to find useful passages in the text.

Recently, [46] conducted a study on the impact of annotations in improving the learning achievements of students. A four-month experimentation was performed, where the learning achievements of student who did not use annotations and students who used a Web-based annotation system for learning material were compared. By using a questionnaire, they found that most of the students agree that the annotation system improved their online reading performances and was easy to use; furthermore, using the annotation system improved the interaction between learners and the provided materials, by increasing students' interest in learning; finally, students reported that the possibility of sharing annotations both between groups and publicly improved their motivation to learn. In addition, [46] conducted a series of statistical analyses to determine the impact of the use of annotations in different learning scenarios, namely individual reading, group annotation sharing, public annotation sharing, and final examination. They report that, in general, the use of annotations can raise a student's learning achievements in most scenarios, even though in the final examination scenario the high motivation of students to pass the exam produced similar results with and without using annotations. Finally, [46] note a positive correlation between the quantity of annotations made and the learning achievements: the greater the number of annotations, the higher the learning achievements. Interestingly enough, they discovered that this effect is more prominent in the group annotation sharing scenario with respect to the public annotation sharing scenario and they argue that this is due to the fact that public annotations may reduce learner's desire to make their own annotations.

2.2 Historical Viewpoint

In order to give an idea of the purport of the annotation in our cultural heritage, we discuss how the gloss, a particular kind of annotation, has been used with the passing of time and what the impacts of its use have been. A full discussion on the historical viewpoint on annotations can be found in [5].

The word gloss derives from the ancient Greek word γλῶσσα (glôssa), that means *tongue, language, idiom, spoken word, foreign or obsolete word* [44, p. 620] and [62, p. 393].

As reported in [48, pp. 652–653], at the time of the ancient Greeks, the term gloss meant an obscure, archaic, dialect, or rare locution that required an additional explanation. These locutions were the object of study by grammarians or the object of research by scholarly poets, especially the Alexandrian poets, who enriched their compositions with these terms. Therefore, gloss meant the explanations themselves of such locutions, either collected in wide-ranging lexicons or as interlinear notes placed above the words to be explained. This methodology of study and a lexicographical practice dates back to ancient times (there were glosses to Homer as early as the V century B.C.) and was fully developed by the grammarians of the Alexandrian age. During the Bizantine age and the Middle Ages, the term gloss meant an interlinear or marginal note to a biblical or juridical codex. For the biblical codices, the gloss was a very short paraphrase to explain a passage of the Bible, sometimes together with a mention to its allegorical interpretation. On the other hand, for the juridical codices, the glosses were explanatory annotations which constituted a thorough commentary to the text.

The gloss was a practice that flourished especially in the juridical context, as reported by [47, pp. 427–429]. During the Roman Empire, one of the usual literary forms of Roman jurisprudence was the comment to the works of former jurists, so that it is often possible to distinguish the annotated text from the annotation to the text; furthermore, the glosses were sometimes physically separated from the annotated text. However, the most famous use of this kind of method of study is credited to the Bolognese school: indeed, the word gloss denoted the way of studying the Justinian Code practised in Bologna, which began in the 12th century A.D.. The Bolognese gloss passed from a simpler form to a more complex one by passing from simple interlinear notes to a real theoretical treatment of the subject. The glossarist reveals the contradictions (*contrarietates*) of the Justinian books, raises doubts (*dubiationes* or *dubietates*), which often give rise to controversies (*dissensiones*).

The contradictions often find an explanation (*solutio*) and the doubts disappear by means of an appropriate distinction (*distinctio* or *differentia*). The glossarist teaches the Justinian books and creates cases in point and examples that originate glosses pointing out the different cases (*casus*); furthermore, the glossarist establishes and defines rules derived from the texts he studies, and, accordingly, creates glosses that report such rules (*regulae*) and definitions (*definitiones*). In conclusion, the Bolognese gloss was a way of doing research aimed at defining and elucidating the law.

The glosses were usually arranged on a page around the text, as shown in Fig. 1, which reproduces a page from the work *Ars notariae* (Handbook for notaries) written by Salatiele, one of the professors at the University of Bologna in the Middle Ages [36, 63].

The intellectual work entailed by the gloss is of very high quality, because it is a method of both study and research. This kind of intellectual work gives

Fig. 1: The photo shows the typical structure of the gloss: the author's commentary, written in smaller characters, is placed around the text, written in greater characters (Italia, Bologna, Biblioteca Comunale dell'Archiginnasio, Salatiele, *Ars notariae*, ms B 1484, c. 12r – published with the permission of Biblioteca Comunale dell'Archiginnasio di Bologna – taken from [5])

us an idea of how strong the active involvement required by the gloss is: it does not concern only the authors themselves, but it is also capable of involving and stimulating a wide community of people who work, study and do research on a subject. Therefore, it turns out that an annotation may comprise a public dimension, because it becomes the vehicle for carrying and transmitting ideas and knowledge to other people, or it may comprise a shared dimension only, if the recipients of the annotation are less numerous.

The research or study aspects and the public or shared dimension entailed by the gloss help us to understand how long-lasting and recordable the annotations are. Indeed, not only are they comments and remarks to a text, but also an autonomous intellectual work which is worth recording.

This important lesson learned from the past should also be taken into account when we design an annotation management system, because the possibility of digitally annotating and quoting can be a valid support to the research work in a networked and distributed environment.

2.3 System Viewpoint

This section discusses the two main approaches that have been adopted to deal with annotations when designing an annotation management system: we can consider them as either *metadata* or *content*.

Table 1 summarizes and presents systems along two dimensions. One is the degree of structure of the content and the other is the degree of structure of the annotation. The structure of the content can range from loosely structured documents, as in the case of the Web, to highly structured data, as in the case of a database[1]. Similarly, the structure of the annotation can vary from unstructured or loosely structured annotations, as in the case of content annotations, to very structured annotations, as in the case of metadata annotations.

When annotations are considered as metadata, they are additional data which relate to an existing content and clarify the properties and semantics of the annotated content. With this aim in mind, annotations have to conform to some specifications which define the structure, the semantics, the syntax, and even the values that annotations can assume. The recipients of this kind of annotation are both people and computing devices. On the one hand, metadata can benefit people because, if they are expressed in a human-readable form and their format and fields are known, they can be read by people and used to obtain useful and well-structured information about an existing content. On the other hand, metadata offer computing devices the means for automatically processing the annotated contents.

In the Web, the most relevant example of this kind of annotations is the Semantic Web [43, 70], which aims at enhancing human-understandable data,

---

[1] Note that we have put the NoteCards system under the Web box, even though it was developed before the Web, because a hypermedia system is much more closer to the Web than to DBMSs or DLMSs.

Table 1: Summary of the different viewpoints about annotations with respect to their use in the Web, DLMSs, and DBMSs

increasing structure of the content ↓ / increasing structure of the annotation →	Content	Metadata
Web	CoNote [32] MADCOW [24,25] NoteCards [41,42]	Annotea [50,69] Semantic Web [43,70]
DLMS	COLLATE [34,67] DiLAS [2,14,19] FAST [8,10–12]	IPSA [3,16,17] SCHOLNET [31]
DBMS		BIODAS [66] Data Provenance [23,27,28,40]

namely Web pages, with computer-understandable data, namely metadata, and this process is called *semantic annotation*. The Annotea project [50,69] represents a first step in the direction of creating a shared metadata infrastructure.

In the context of *Digital Library Management Systems (DLMSs)*, SCHOLNET [31] uses annotations as metadata to support communication and interaction within scholarly communities by introducing a semantic annotation model, where annotations are treated as documents themselves, the semantics of which is captured by a controlled vocabulary of annotation types. In a similar context, IPSA [3,16,17] supports the annotation and personalization of a digital archive of images taken from *illuminated manuscripts* [29]. The goal is supporting the research on illuminated manuscripts which unveils hidden connections between illustrations belonging to different manuscripts. In IPSA annotations are links that connect one image to another and they are drawn from a link taxonomy which specifies the relationship between the two images.

Annotations are also used in the context of *DataBase Management Systems (DBMSs)* and, in particular, in the case of *curated databases* and *scientific databases*. For example, BIODAS [66] provides a distributed annotation system, which is a system based on Web servers for sharing lists of annotations across a certain segment of the genome. In this context, annotations are often employed for addressing the wider problem of *data provenance* which is the description of the origins of a piece of data and the process by which it arrived in a database [27,28]. Data provenance is undoubtedly an open and challenging research issue in the field of DBMSs, as [1] points out, and annotations have different applications in this regards: tracing the provenance and flow of data, reporting errors or remarks about a piece of data, and describing the quality or the security level of a piece of data [23]. Recently, [40] uses annotations in interactive visualization systems as a means for both capturing the history of user interaction with the visualization system and keeping track of the observations that a user may make while exploring the visualization.

When annotations are regarded as additional content which relates to an existing content, they increase the existing content by providing an additional layer of elucidation and explanation. However, this elucidation does not happen, as in the case of annotations as metadata, by means of some kind of constrained or formal description of the semantics of the annotated object. On the contrary, the explanation itself takes the shape of an additional content which can help people understand the annotated content. However, the semantics of the additional content may be no more explicit for a computing device than the semantics of the annotated content. This view of annotations is comparable to the activity of reading a document and adding notes to it: explanation and clarification of words or passages of the document by expounding on it, providing a commentary on it, and finally completing it with personal observations and ideas.

Therefore, the final recipients of this kind of annotation are people, because a content annotation does not make the annotated object more readily processable by a computer than the same object without annotations. In fact, from the point of view of a computer, the semantics of content annotations needs to be in some way processed, e.g. indexed, before it can be used to deal with the semantics of the annotated object; this is quite different from the case of metadata annotations, which are pieces of information ready to be used for interpreting the semantics of the annotated object. In contrast, the additional semantics provided by content annotations can offer people useful interpretations and comments for the annotated object, making it easier to understand its hidden facets.

In the field of hypermedia/hypertext systems, NoteCards [41,42] is a system designed for helping people to work with ideas: authors, researchers, and intellectual work practitioners can analyze information, construct models, formulate topics, and elaborate ideas by using a network of electronic notecards interconnected by typed links. One of the famous "seven issues" mentioned by [41] concerns support for collaborative work: he highlighted how annotations are part of the "activities that form the basis of any collaboration effort" [41, p. 848]. Moving forward in the context of the Web, the CoNote [32] is a cooperative system for supporting communications within groups of users by using shared annotations on a set of documents. CoNote offers plain text or *HyperText Markup Language (HTML)* [68] annotations on Web pages and pays particular attention in structuring annotations on the same part of a document as a tree, in order to ease the discussion among the users by supporting replies to previously inserted annotations. Finally, a recent example of this kind of annotation system in the Web is *Multimedia Annotation of Digital Content Over the Web (MADCOW)* [24, 25], which enables multimedia annotation on Web pages and is based on a client-server architecture.

As an example of this use of annotations in DLMSs, *Collaboratory for Annotation Indexing and Retrieval of Digitized Historical Archive Material (COLLATE)* [34, 67] supports the collaboration among film scientists and archivists who are annotating historical film documentation, dealing with digitized versions of documents about European films from the 1920s and 1930s. In COLLATE annotations are *dialog acts*, part of a discourse about film documentation, and these constitute the document context, intended as the context of the collaborative discourse in which the document is placed. *Flexible Annotation Service Tool (FAST)* [8–12] is a flexible system designed to support its integration into a wide range of different DLMSs. Annotations in FAST allow users to merge their personal content with the information resources managed by diverse DLMSs: annotations can span and cross the boundaries of a single DLMS, annotating digital objects that are part of different digital libraries. In this way, by using annotations, users may link digital objects that otherwise would have remained separated because they are managed by different DLMSs. [49] recently noted this as an advantage for users and a challenge for the next generation DLMSs. Finally, FAST also constitutes the underlying infrastructure of the *Digital Library Annotation Service (DiLAS)* project [2, 14, 19], which is an ongoing project in the framework of DELOS, the European Network of Excellence on Digital Libraries. The goal of DiLAS is to design and develop a generic annotation service which can be easily used in different DLMSs; the annotation service is being evaluated as a new way of interacting with a *Digital Library (DL)* and cooperating among DL users and stakeholders.

Summing up, the final recipients of annotations can be computing devices and people. The former is mainly the case of metadata annotations which allow annotated objects to be automatically processed, integrated and reused in different applications, even though these metadata annotations can be understandable and useful for people too. The latter is mainly the case of content annotations which elucidate and expound on an annotated object. Note that, also in this latter case, a computing device can become the recipient of such annotations, provided that some further step of processing is performed, e.g. indexing. However, in both cases, the semantics of the annotation itself needs to be taken into consideration and modeled. This can happen formally and precisely by agreeing on metadata standards which describe how annotations should be interpreted and used; alternatively, support can be provided for identifying different pre-defined annotation types, perhaps with varying levels of detail.

The medium of the annotation can vary a lot: it can range from textual annotations, to image, audio, and video annotations; in a general setting, we may need to deal with multimedia rich annotations, composed of different parts, each with its own medium. All of these different kinds of media have to be considered and properly modeled, in a uniform way where possible.

Both annotations and annotated objects need to be uniquely identified. Moreover, annotations comprise a temporal dimension that is often not explicit, but which limits the creation of the annotation to the existence of another object. This temporal relationship between the annotation and the annotated object does not mean that the annotation cannot be considered a stand–alone intellectual work, but it does impose a temporal ordering between the existence of an annotated object and the annotation annotating it which cannot be overlooked. In addition, once we have identified both the annotation and the annotated object, we need to link and anchor the annotation to the part of the annotated object in question. This can happen in a way that mainly depends on the medium of the annotated object. On the whole, we need to model how annotations and annotated objects are uniquely identified and linked together, maybe with a varying degree of granularity in the anchoring, paying particular attention to the temporal dimension that regulates the relationships between annotations and annotated objects.

As far as co-operation is concerned, almost all of the analyzed systems show that annotations have great potential for supporting and improving interaction among users, and even among computing devices. Therefore, there is a need for modeling and offering different scopes of annotations, e.g. private, shared, or public, and managing the access rights of various groups of users.

Finally, a relevant aspect of annotations is that they can take a part of a hypertext [15, 41, 52] since they enable the creation of new relationships among existing objects, by means of links that connect annotations together with existing objects, as we will see later in more detail. The hypertext viewpoint about annotations is common to different systems, such as Annotea, MADCOW, and NoteCards in the hypermedia/Web context, or DiLAS, FAST, and IPSA in the DLMS context. [41] points out that annotations are one of the activities that form the basis of any collaborative effort and for which hypermedia systems are ideally suited, while [52] considers annotations a natural way of creating and growing hypertexts that connect information resources by actively engaging users.

3 Overview of the Formal Model

In this section we provide a description and overview of the formal model, explaining the main concepts around which it is build, and give an idea of its possible application areas and the next steps we can undertake by using it as a starting point.

3.1 Modeling Approach

Figure 2 provides both an overview of the areas covered and the detail of the definitions introduced within each area. The figure clearly shows how these areas correspond to the very basic issues that emerge when we think about annotations: we need to identify annotations and annotated objects in order to link them together, perhaps providing facilities for supporting cooperation, and we have to deal with both the actual contents of an annotation and the semantics expressed by those contents.

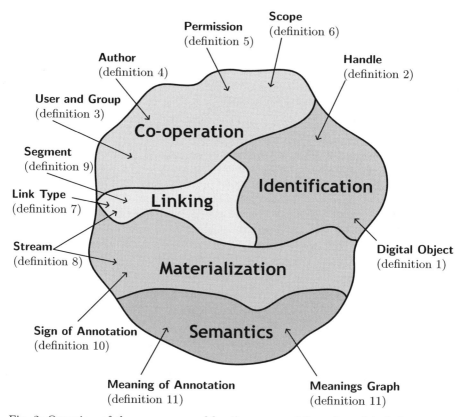

Fig. 2: Overview of the areas covered by the proposed formal model of the annotation – from [13]

In the remainder of this section, we will briefly introduce the areas shown in Fig. 2, which can be used as a map of the concepts dealt with in the formal model.

Identification This is the problem of uniquely identifying both the annotation and the annotated objects, highlighting the temporal constraints between them. This area is built around the concept of *handle*, which is defined as a unique identifier of both digital objects and annotations, and the proposed notation for dealing with the time dimension involved by annotations.

Co-operation This is about annotations as a co-operation tool among users. It introduces the definitions of *user* and *group* of users, together with the associated concept of *scope* of annotation and access *permission*, which regulate the access policies for a given annotation.

Linking This deals with the allowed linking patterns between digital objects and annotations, and the problem of correctly anchoring annotations to digital objects. It defines the concepts of *link type*, which is defined as the allowed methods of linking annotations to annotated objects, *stream*, which abstracts the notion of content of a digital object, and *segment*, which represents a given portion of a stream, useful for anchoring an annotation to a digital object.

Semantics This concerns the meaning of the annotation and what it stands for, trying to make explicit the semantics of the different parts of the content of an annotation. It introduces the notions of *meaning of annotation*, which is part of the semantics of the whole annotation, and *meanings graph*, which is a graph which allows for interoperability between the different meanings.

Materialization This deals with the way in which the semantics carried by an annotation can take shape, that is, the actual content of the annotation perceived by the user. It describes the *sign of annotation*, which is a particular type of stream representing part of the content of an annotation.

Finally, we will discuss the hypertext between annotated objects and annotations, which is build on top of the previously introduced concepts and can also be thought of as a kind of concise view of the main relationships between annotations and annotated objects.

3.2 Applications and Uses of the Formal Model

A first application of the formal model is to use it as an analysis tool for studying and having a better comprehension of an existing annotation management system. Indeed, the main areas identified above act as main questions which can be asked about the annotation management system: which mechanism is used for identifying annotations and annotated objects? Which kind of support is offered for the co-operation of the users and which degree of visibility for annotations are available? How are annotations linked to annotated objects? Are they embedded in the annotated objects or kept separated? What is the granularity available for anchoring an annotation to an annotated object? How is the semantics of an annotation expressed, by using fixed annotation types or a more flexible mechanism? What about the content of the annotation: can different media be mixed together? All these question and even more detailed ones can be derived from the formal model and can be useful for analysing and comparing annotation management systems in a qualitative way.

A step further is to apply the definitions of the model to describe an annotation management system. In this way, we can formally compare different annotation management systems and spot differences and commonalities, by using the model as a kind of landmark which allows us to determine the features of each system.

Another interesting possibility is to use the formal model as the starting point for defining and creating more refined and specialized models, which may be more tailored to specific applicative contexts. In this context, the formal model provides a kind of template which outlines the main areas and concepts which can be further specialized. In addition, the formal model ensures the comparability and compatibility of the derived models. In this way, we avoid the flourishing of unrelated annotation models, as has happened to date, while maintaining both the coherence among different specialistic annotation models and the possibility of passing from one to another in a clearly defined way.

We successfully applied the above mentioned strategy in the context of illuminated manuscripts [17, 18]. Image digital archives of illuminated manuscripts can become a useful tool for researchers in different disciplines and we proposed to provide them with tools for annotating images to disclose hidden relationships between illustrations belonging to different works. Relationships can be modeled as typed annotative links, which induce a hypertext over the archive. In this context, we defined a model for annotations which is derived from the one presented here and represents the basis for building methods for automatically processing existing relationships among link types and exploiting the properties of the graph which models the hypertext between annotations and annotated images.

The hypertext between annotations and annotated objects can be exploited for providing alternative navigation and browsing capabilities. In particular, DLMSs usually offer some basic hypertext and browsing capabilities based on the available structured data, such as authors or references. On the other hand, DLMSs do not normally provide users with advanced hypertext functionalities, where the information resources are linked on the basis of the semantics of their content. Therefore, annotations can turn out to be an effective way of associating this kind of hypertext to a DLMS to enable the active and dynamic use of information resources. In addition, this hypertext can span and cross the boundaries of the single DLMS, if users need to interact with the information resources managed by diverse DLMSs [9,10]. This latter possibility is quite innovative, because it offers the means for interconnecting various DLMSs in a personalized and meaningful way for the end-user, and, as [49] point out, this is a major challenge for the next generation DLMSs.

Moreover, the proposed formal model constitutes the necessary ground-work for designing and formalizing search algorithms and expressing query languages which take annotations into account in order to retrieve more and better ranked objects in response to a user query. Indeed, annotations provide us with an additional source of evidence, which is complementary to that already contained in the set of documents. Therefore, we can exploit annotations with the two final goals of retrieving more relevant documents and ranking them better. Furthermore, the paths that connect annotations to documents become the vehicle for moving this further source of evidence towards the documents. In this context, the hypertext between annotations and annotated objects is the basic infrastructure for combining the sources of evidence which come from annotated objects and annotations. We have already started to work on this problem in the context of *data fusion* [11,12]. This is because we need to combine the source of evidence which comes from annotations with the source which comes from documents. For the future, we plan to employ both hypertext information retrieval [6, 20] and *link fusion* techniques [71] for designing advanced search algorithms which involve annotations based on our formal model.

Once we have developed search strategies that exploit annotations, we will therefore need to evaluate their retrieval performances by using standard information retrieval methodologies. We plan to adopt the Cranfield method-ology [30], which makes use of experimental collections to measure the performances of an information retrieval system. The performances are measured by using the standard precision and recall figures [61,64], but according to [10] we also need a statistical methodology for judging whether the measured performances can be considered statistically significant. The next step will be to investigate the possibility of using measures that differ from precision and recall and are better tailored to the features of annotations. Finally, there is a lack of experimental test collections with annotated digital contents. We have already started to work on this problem [7] and the future research work will also concern the design and development of this kind of test collection.

Finally, the formal model provides us with sound bases for designing and developing an annotation service which can be easily integrated into a wider IMS. Indeed, a clear definition of the concepts related to the annotation allows us to modularly design the functionalities of such service. In particular, we can separate the functionalities needed to manage, access, and search annotations, which constitute the core of an annotation service, from the functionalities needed to integrate such annotation service into an IMS. In addition, the formal model can be used as a starting point for deriving conceptual and logical models of the annotation suitable for managing the persistence of the annotations, for example, by using a DBMS.

We successfully adopted this approach for designing and developing the FAST annotation service, whose conceptual and logical model of annotation [15, 16] has been derived from our formal model, which is independent from any particular IMS [10], offers advanced search functionalities based on annotations [11,12], and has been successfully integrated into different systems [2,4].

4 The Formal Model

4.1 Identification

In order to uniquely identify both the annotation and the annotated objects, we need to proceed as follows: firstly, we need to define the objects we deal with; then, we also have to be able to deal with objects whose relationships are constrained by a temporal dimension; finally, a suitable identification mechanism has to be provided.

Document, Annotation, and Digital Object Sets

According to widely accepted terminology, we adopt the term digital object to refer to information resources managed by an IMS. In the following, we need terminology to distinguish between two kinds of digital objects: the generic ones managed by the IMS, which we call *documents*, and the ones that are *annotations*. Therefore, when we use the generic term digital object, we mean a digital object that can be either a document or an annotation. The following definition introduces the different sets of digital objects we will need to deal with.

Definition 1. *Let us define the following sets:*

- D *is a **set of documents** and* $d \in D$ *is a generic **document**.* U_D *is a **universe set of documents**, which is the set of all the possible documents, so that* $D \subseteq U_D$.
- A *is a **set of annotations** and* $a \in A$ *is a generic **annotation**.* U_A *is a **universe set of annotations**, which is the set of all the possible annotations, so that* $A \subseteq U_A$.
- $DO = D \cup A$ *is a **set of digital objects** and* $do \in DO$ *is either a document or an annotation.* $U_{DO} = U_A \cup U_D$ *is a **universe set of digital objects**, so that* $DO \subseteq U_{DO}$.

Expressing the Temporal Dimension Involved by Annotations

The universe sets U_D, U_A, and U_{DO} are abstract sets, since they contain all the possible needed objects, whether they actually exists or not in any given moment; on the other hand, the sets D, A, and DO are tangible sets that contain the objects that already exist in a given moment: if we pick out an element from D, A, or DO we are dealing with a digital object that has been created even before we start working on it; in other words, the element already exists. The D, A, and DO sets can be considered *time–variant sets*, since we can add, delete or modify elements of these sets over time. On the other hand, the U_D, U_A, and U_{DO} sets can be considered *time–invariant sets*, since they already contain every possibile object we may need to deal with.

The annotation is the result of an intellectual task performed on an existing digital object and it follows an already existing digital object. Therefore, the annotation comprises a temporal dimension which is often not explicit, but which limits the creation of the annotation to the existence of another digital object. This temporal relationship between the annotation and the annotated digital object does not mean that the annotation cannot be considered a stand–alone intellectual task, but it does impose a temporal ordering between the existence of an annotated digital object and its annotation which cannot be overlooked.

In conclusion, we need some mechanism for rendering the time dimension explicit, if necessary. We will illustrate this mechanism by means of an example concerning the creation of a new digital object. Although, this example makes use of the set DO, it does have a more general validity.

The creation of a new digital object consists of the following events:

1. we start with the set of digital objects at time k: $DO(k)$;
2. we create a new digital object, that is, we pick out an element from the universe set of digital objects that does not belong to $DO(k)$: $do \in \overline{DO}(k) \subseteq U_{DO}$;
3. we end up with a new set of digital objects at time $k+1$, which contains the newly created digital object: $DO(k+1) = \big(DO(k) \cup \{do\}\big) \in 2^{U_{DO}}$.

Therefore, we have the following temporal ordering:

$$\underbrace{DO(k)}_{\text{event 1}} \dashrightarrow \underbrace{do \in \overline{DO}(k)}_{\text{event 2}} \dashrightarrow \underbrace{DO(k+1) = DO(k) \cup \{do\}}_{\text{event 3}}$$

with overbraces labeled $\text{time } k$ (over events 1 and 2) and $\text{time } k+1$ (over event 3).

both events 1 and 2 happen at time k, but at that time the newly created digital object does not yet belong to the set $DO(k)$ of digital objects at time k; event 3 happens at time $k+1$ and represents the new set of digital objects that now also contains the newly created and existing digital object.

$DO(k)$ and $DO(k+1)$ unambiguously identify the digital objects we are dealing with: the newly created digital objects are given by $DO(k+1) \setminus DO(k)$. Therefore, we can talk about the digital objects identified by the transition from $DO(k)$ to $DO(k+1)$. We assume that the operations previously shown are atomic, i.e. no operation can occur during the execution of another operation, so as to avoid concurrency issues.

In conclusion, this mechanism provides us with a means to clearly identify which objects are involved in a given operation, when they can be utilized, and the ordering among the different events involved by an operation. For a more detailed discussion on this approach, please refer to [13].

In the following sections, we will use the notation $DO(k)$, which explicitly points out the time dimension, only when needed; otherwise we will use the simpler notation DO, without explicitly pointing out the time dimension. We will also use a similar notation for the other sets we will define below.

Handle

According to the previous discussion, we can assume that each digital object is identified by a *unique handle*, which is a name assigned to a digital object to identify and to facilitate the referencing process to the digital object. Over the past years, various syntaxes, mechanisms, and systems have been developed to provide handles or identifiers for digital objects: *Uniform Resource Identifier (URI)* [21,22], *Digital Object Identifier (DOI)* [59]; OpenURL [57]; *Persistent URL (PURL)*[2]; and *PURL-based Object Identifier (POI)*[3].

The following definition introduces the notion of handle, compatible with the mechanisms described above, and its relationship with digital objects.

Definition 2. *H is a **set of handles** such that $|H| = |DO|$ and $h \in H$ is a generic **handle**. U_H is a **universe set of handles**, which is the set of all the possible handles, such that $|U_H| = |U_{DO}|$; it follows that $H \subseteq U_H$.*

We define a bijective function $\mathrm{h} : U_H \to U_{DO}$ *which maps a handle to the digital object identified by it:*

$$\forall do \in U_{DO}, \exists! h \in U_H \mid \mathrm{h}(h) = do \Rightarrow \mathrm{h}^{-1}(do) = h$$

The relationship between the sets H and U_H is the same as the one between the sets DO and U_{DO}, described in Sect. 4.1.

4.2 Co-operation

In order to provide users with annotations as an effective co-operation tool, we need to proceed as follows: firstly, we need to define the notion of user, group of users, and author; then, we have to deal both with different scopes of annotation, and various access permissions.

User, Group of Users and Author

Definition 3. *Let USR be a **set of users** and usr $\in USR$ is a generic user; U_{USR} is a **universe set of users**, which is the set of all the possible users, so that $USR \subseteq U_{USR}$.*

---

[2] http://purl.oclc.org/

[3] http://www.ukoln.ac.uk/distributed-systems/poi/

$GR \subseteq 2^{USR}$ is a **set of groups of users** and $G \in GR$ is a generic group of users; $U_{GR} = 2^{U_{USR}}$ is a **universe set of groups of users**, which is the set of all the possible groups of users, so that $GR \subseteq U_{GR}$.

We define a function $\text{gr} : USR \rightarrow 2^{GR}$ which maps a user to the groups of users he belongs to. The following constraint must be adhered to:

$$\forall\, usr \in USR,\ \text{gr}(usr) \neq \varnothing$$

i.e. each user in USR must belong to at least one group of users.

The relationship between the sets USR and GR and the sets U_{USR} and U_{GR} is the same as the one between the sets DO and U_{DO}, described in Sect. 4.1.

Digital objects – both documents and annotations – always have at least one author who authored them. Therefore, the author is a specialization of the more general concept of user, introduced in the definition above, i.e. an author is a user who authored one or more digital objects.

Definition 4. *Let us define a function* $\text{au} : USR \rightarrow 2^{H}$ *which maps a user to the handles of the digital objects authored by him. Let the* **set of authors** *AU be the following set:*

$$AU = \{usr \in USR \mid \text{au}(usr) \neq \varnothing\}$$

we denote with $au \in AU \subseteq USR$ *a generic author. The following constraint must be adhered to:*

$$\forall\, h \in H\ \exists\, au \in AU \mid h \in \text{au}(au)$$

i.e. each digital object must be authored by at least one author.

The function au characterizes the authors, distinguishing them from generic users; indeed, if a generic user $usr \in USR$ has not authored any digital object, it follows that $\text{au}(usr) = \varnothing$ and thus $usr \notin AU$.

Permission

An annotation can have different access permissions, as introduced in the following definition.

Definition 5. *Let* $P = \{Denied, ReadOnly, ReadWrite\}$ *be a* **set of access permissions** *and* $p \in P$ *is an access permission. Let us define the following relations:*

- **equality relation** $=$

$$\{(p, p) \in P \times P \mid p \in P\} = \{(Denied, Denied), (ReadOnly, ReadOnly),$$
$$(ReadWrite, ReadWrite)\}$$

- **strict ordering relation** $\prec$

$$\{(Denied, ReadOnly), (Denied, ReadWrite), (ReadOnly, ReadWrite)\}$$

- **ordering relation** $\preceq$

$$\{(p_1, p_2) \in P \times P \mid p_1 = p_2 \lor p_1 \prec p_2\}$$

In contrast to the set of the previous definitions, the set of access permissions P is a time–invariant set which does not need the notation for taking into account the temporal dimension. Indeed, we assume that an annotation can only have the access permissions listed above. Note that $(P, \preceq)$ is a totally ordered set.

Scope

An annotation can have one of the following scopes, as introduced in the following definition.

Definition 6. *Let* $SP = \{Private, Shared, Public\}$ *be a **set of scopes** and* $sp \in SP$ *is a scope. Let us define the following relations:*

- **equality relation** $=$

$$\{(sp, sp) \in SP \times SP \mid sp \in SP\} = \{(Private, Private), (Shared, Shared),$$
$$(Public, Public)\}$$

- **strict ordering relation** $\prec$

$$\{(Private, Shared), (Private, Public), (Shared, Public)\}$$

- **ordering relation** $\preceq$

$$\{(sp_1, sp_2) \in SP \times SP \mid sp_1 = sp_2 \lor sp_1 \prec sp_2\}$$

As in the case of the set of access permissions, the set of scopes SP is also a time–invariant set, because we assume that an annotation can have only one of the three scopes listed above. Note that $(SP, \preceq)$ is a totally ordered set.

4.3 Linking

In order to link annotations to digital objects and to correctly anchor annotations to digital objects, we need to proceed as follows: firstly, we need to choose a linking mechanism and define the link types that can exist between annotations and digital objects; then, since annotations are usually linked to specific parts of a digital object, we need to model the content of digital objects; finally, a suitable anchoring mechanism for annotations has to be provided.

Linking Annotations to Digital Objects

Handles can be used not only for the purpose of uniquely identifying a digital object, but they can also provide us with a means for linking an annotation to a digital object. This use of handles is particularly clear if we think about *Uniform Resource Locators (URLs)*, but it is also still valid in the case of the other types of handles presented in Sect. 4.1.

Once we have decided to use handles as basic mechanism for linking annotations to digital objects, we still have to consider the kind of links an annotation can have with a digital object. Annotations can be linked to digital objects with two main types of links:

- *annotate link*: an annotation annotates a digital object, which can be a document or another annotation.
  The "annotate link" is intended to allow an annotation only to annotate one or more parts of a given digital object. Therefore, this kind of link lets the annotation express *intra–digital object relationships*, meaning that the annotation creates a relationship between the different parts of the annotated digital object;
- *relate-to link*: an annotation relates to a digital object, which can be a document or another annotation.
  The "relate-to link" is intended to allow an annotation only to relate to one or more parts of other digital objects, but not the annotated one. Therefore, this kind of link lets the annotation express *inter–digital object relationships*, meaning that the annotation creates a relationship between the annotated digital object and the other digital objects related to it.

With respect to these two main types of link, we introduce the following constraint:

> an annotation must annotate one and only one digital object, which can be either a document or another annotation, i.e. an annotation must have one and only one "annotate link".

This constraint means that an annotation can be created only for the purpose of annotating a digital object and not exclusively for relating to a digital object. An annotation, then, can annotate one and only one digital object, because the "annotate link" expresses intra–digital object relationships and thus it cannot be mutual to multiple digital objects different from the annotated one. Finally, this constraint does not prevent the annotation from relating to more than one digital object, i.e. from having more than one "relate-to link".

Definition 7. *Let LT be a **set of link types**; an element lt ∈ LT corresponds to one of the allowed link types. The set LT contains the following link types: LT = {Annotate, RelateTo}.*

As in the case of the set of access permissions and the set of scopes, the set of link types LT is a time–invariant set too, because we assume that an annotation can be linked to digital objects only with the link types listed above.

Stream

Digital objects can be very different – texts, images, audio, video, hypertexts, multimedia objects, and so on – and the way in which their structure and content is modeled and expressed can also vary widely across different conceptual and logical models of IMS and digital object. Nevertheless, many of these types of models share the idea that beyond representing the structure of the digital object the model also has to take into account a mechanism for representing the actual content of the digital object.

The following definition introduces the concept of stream in order to represent the actual content of a digital object or a part of it. The definition of stream is inspired by [39,56] but with some differences which will be discussed below.

Definition 8. *A **stream** sm is a finite sequence:*

$$\text{sm} : I = \{1, 2, \ldots, n\} \to \Sigma, \quad n \in \mathbb{N}$$

*where Σ is the alphabet of symbols. We allow the existence of an **empty stream** esm $= \varnothing$. SM is a **set of streams** and sm $\in SM$ is a stream. U_{SM} is a **universe set of streams**, that is, the set of all the possible streams. It follows that $SM \subseteq U_{SM}$.*

We define a function hsm $: H \to 2^{SM}$ *which maps a handle of a digital object to the streams contained in that digital object. The following constraint must be adhered to:*

$$\forall h \in H, \text{hsm}(h) \neq \varnothing$$

i.e. each digital object must contain at least one stream, which could also be the empty stream.

The relationship between the sets SM and U_{SM} is the same as the one between the sets DO and U_{DO}, described in Sect. 4.1.

Segment

The handles discussed in Sect. 4.1 may be capable not only of uniquely identifying a digital object, but also of indicating a part of the identified digital object. For example, a URL can point to any given anchor within a HTML document, or we can use an XPath expression to point to a specific element within an *eXtensible Markup Language (XML)* document. On the other hand, parts of a digital object cannot always be identified with an arbitrary degree of detail; for example, a URL cannot point to a given word of a HTML document, if this word is not marked with an anchor. Therefore, we need some further mechanism for identifying parts of a digital object with the necessary degree of detail.

The following definition introduces the notion of *segment*, which is a mechanism for selecting parts of a stream; this mechanism can be partnered with the handle of a digital object to provide access to a digital object with the necessary degree of detail.

Definition 9. *Given a stream* $\mathrm{sm} : I = \{1, 2, \ldots, n\} \rightarrow \Sigma$, $n \in \mathbb{N}$, $\mathrm{sm} \in SM$, *a **segment** is a pair:*

$$st_{\mathrm{sm}} = (a, b) \mid 1 \leq a \leq b \leq n, \quad a, b \in \mathbb{N}$$

*A **stream segment** is a restriction* $\mathrm{sm}_{|[a,b]}$ *of the stream* sm *to interval* $[a, b]$ *associated with the segment* st_{sm}. *ST is a **set of segments** and* $st_{\mathrm{sm}} \in ST$ *is a generic segment;* U_{ST} *is a **universe set of segments**, which is the set of all the possible segments, so that* $ST \subseteq U_{ST}$.

The relationship between the sets ST and U_{ST} is the same as the relationship between the sets DO and U_{DO}, described in Sect. 4.1. Definition 9 resembles the definition of segment provided in [39, 56].

All of the introduced concepts, namely handle, stream, and segment, provide us with the formal means needed to deal with the linking and anchoring problem related to annotations. By using a *handle h* we can link an annotation to a digital object; then, the function $\mathrm{hsm}(h)$ allows us to select the desired *stream* sm of the digital object identified by h, be it a physical or a logical view of the actual content of the digital object; finally, a *segment* st_{sm} enables the fine-tuned anchoring of the annotation to the digital object.

4.4 Materialization

We call *sign of annotation* the basic way in which an annotation can take shape, i.e. the way of representing and materializing the semantics of annotation.

Definition 10. *A **sign of annotation** is a stream. $SN \subseteq SM$ is a **set of signs of annotation** and* $\mathrm{sn} \in SN$ *is a sign.* $U_{SN} \subseteq U_{SM}$ *is a **universe set of signs of annotation**, which is the set of all the possible signs of annotation, so that $SN \subseteq U_{SN}$.*

The relationship between the sets SN and U_{SN} is the same as the relationship between the sets DO and U_{DO}, described in Sect. 4.1.

Henceforth we will use the term *sign of annotation*, or briefly stated as *sign*, to indicate a stream that belongs to an annotation. On the other hand, we will use the term *stream* to indicate a stream that belongs to a digital object without the need of specifying if the digital object is a document or an annotation.

4.5 Semantics

We call *meaning of annotation* a main feature of the concept of annotation which identifies conceptual differences within the semantics of the annotation or part of it.

Definition 11. *M is a **set of meanings of annotations**, and $m \in M$ is a generic **meaning of annotation**.*

*The **meanings graph** is a labeled directed graph (G_M, l_M), where $G_M = (M, E_M \subseteq M \times M)$ and $l_M : E_M \to L_M$ with L_M set of labels.*

*The **meanings function** $m : SN \to 2^M$ associates each sign of annotation with its corresponding meanings of annotation. The following constraint must be satisfied:*

$$\forall \, sn \in SN, m(sn) \neq \varnothing$$

i.e. each sign of annotation has at least one meaning of annotation.

As in the case of the set of access permissions, the set of scopes and the set of link types LT, the set of meanings M is a time–invariant set, because we assume that meanings represent a pre-existing knowledge which does not change over time. Therefore, all the needed meanings of annotation are already elements of the set M.

The goal of the meanings graph is to provide structure and hierarchy among the meanings of annotation in order to navigate and browse through them. The relation E_M can be constrained in many ways to obtain the necessary structure of meanings, which can represent some domain specific knowledge. The labelling function l_M can be further exploited to distinguish different kinds of arcs in the set E_M in order to better explain the kind of relationship between two different meanings.

The meanings function allows us to associate each sign of annotation with its corresponding meanings in order to clarify the semantics of the sign. Note that the meanings function is neither injective nor surjective. In conclusion, an annotation is expressed by one or more signs of annotation, which in turn are characterised by one or more meanings of annotation, thus defining the overall semantics of the annotation.

4.6 Annotation

We are now ready to introduce the definition of annotation. Summing up the concepts introduced in the previous sections, we can briefly say that an annotation is expressed by one or more signs of annotation, such as a piece of text or some graphic mark, which are the way an annotation takes shape. The semantics of each sign is, in turn, defined by one or more meanings of annotation. With respect to the linking issue, an annotation must annotate one and only one digital object, identified by its handle, while it may relate to one or more digital objects. Lastly, the mechanism introduced in Sect. 4.1

on how to address the time dimension is now fundamental to properly define the relationship between the annotation and the annotated digital object.

Definition 12. *An **annotation** $a \in A(k)$ is a tuple:*

$$a = \Big(h_a \in H(k), au_a \in USR(k-1), G_a \in 2^{GR(k-1)} \times P, sp_a \in SP,$$

$$\mathcal{A}_a \subseteq SN(k) \times LT \times ST(k) \times SM(k-1) \times H(k-1)\Big)$$

where:

- h_a *is the unique handle of the annotation* a, *i.e.* $\mathrm{h}(h_a) = a$;
- au_a *is the author of the annotation* a, *i.e.* $h_a \in \mathrm{au}(au_a)$;
- G_a *are the groups of users with their respective access permissions for the annotation* a, *specified by the pairs* (G, p) *with* $G \in G_a$ *and* $p \in P$;
- sp_a *is the scope of the annotation* a;
- *each n-ple of the* $\mathcal{A}_a$ *relation means that the annotation* a *by means of a sign in* $SN(k)$ *and a link type in* LT *is annotating or relating to a segment in* $ST(k)$ *of a stream in* $SM(k-1)$ *of a digital object identified by its handle in* $H(k-1)$.
  Note that since $\forall \mathrm{sm} \in SM(k-1) \mid \exists \alpha \in \mathcal{A}_a, \alpha = (\mathrm{sn}, t, st_{\mathrm{sm}}, \mathrm{sm}, h)$ *must be* $\mathrm{sm} \in \mathrm{hsm}(h)$; *in other words, the stream* sm *must be contained in the digital object identified by the handle* h.

We introduce the following auxiliary sets to simplify the following discussion:

- *the set of the signs of annotation that belong to the annotation* a:
  $SN_a = \{\mathrm{sn} \in SN(k) \mid \exists \alpha \in \mathcal{A}_a, \alpha = (\mathrm{sn}, lt, st_{\mathrm{sm}}, \mathrm{sm}, h)\} = \mathrm{hsm}(h_a)$
- *the set of the handles of digital objects that are subject to the tasks of the annotation* a:
  $H_a = \{h \in H(k-1) \mid \exists \alpha \in \mathcal{A}_a, \alpha = (\mathrm{sn}, lt, st_{\mathrm{sm}}, \mathrm{sm}, h)\}$

The following constraints must be adhered to:

1. *the annotation* a *must annotate one and only one digital object, and it cannot also relate to this digital object, hence:*

   $\exists ! \, h \in H_a \mid$

   $$\Big(\forall \mathrm{sn} \in SN_a, \exists ! \, \alpha \in \mathcal{A}_a, \alpha = (\mathrm{sn}, Annotate, st_{\mathrm{sm}}, \mathrm{sm}, h)\Big) \wedge$$

   $$\Big(\nexists \alpha_1 \in \mathcal{A}_a, \alpha_1 = (\mathrm{sn}_1, RelateTo, st_{\mathrm{sm}_1}, \mathrm{sm}_1, h)\Big)$$

2. *a sign in* SN_a *cannot relate to more than one digital object, hence:*

   $\forall \mathrm{sn} \in SN_A \mid \exists \alpha_1, \alpha_2 \in \mathcal{A}_a,$
   $\alpha_1 = (\mathrm{sn}, RelateTo, st_{\mathrm{sm}_1}, \mathrm{sm}_1, h_1), \alpha_2 = (\mathrm{sn}, RelateTo, st_{\mathrm{sm}_2}, \mathrm{sm}_2, h_2)$
   $\Rightarrow \alpha_1 = \alpha_2$

3. *there is no other annotation $a_1 \in A(k-1)$ that shares signs of annotation with a, hence:*

$$\nexists\, a_1 \in A(k-1) \mid SN_a \cap SN_{a_1} \neq \varnothing$$

4. *if the annotation $a \in A(k)$ annotates or relates to another annotation $a_1 \in A(k-1)$, then scope and access permission conflicts have to be avoided. Let us define the* conflict detector *function*, cd $: A(k) \times A(k-1) \rightarrow \{0,1\}$, *so that:*

$$\mathrm{cd}(a, a_1) = \begin{cases} 0 & \textit{if there are neither scope conflicts nor} \\ & \textit{access permission conflicts} \\ 1 & \textit{if there are either scope conflicts or} \\ & \textit{access permission conflicts} \end{cases}$$

Therefore, the following condition must be satisfied:

$$\forall\, h \in H_a \mid \mathrm{h}(h) = a_1 \in A(k-1) \;\Rightarrow\; \mathrm{cd}(a, a_1) = 0$$

In conclusion, the first part of the annotation tuple is devoted to providing information about the annotation itself, because it specifies the handle of the annotation, its author, its groups of users with their respective access permissions, its scope, the signs of the annotation, and the link types. On the other hand, the second part of the annotation tuple provides information about the annotated or related digital objects, specifying which segment of which stream of which digital object is being annotated or related to, as shown below (we do not use the time dimension notation for space reasons, as it is not needed for this observation):

$$a = \left(\underbrace{h_a, au_a, G_a \times P, sp_a, \mathcal{A}_a \subseteq SN \times LT}_{\text{information about the annotation}} \times \underbrace{ST \times SM \times H}_{\text{information about the digital object}} \right)$$

4.7 Document–Annotation Hypertext

As explained in Sect. 3, we consider that existing digital objects and annotations constitute a hypertext. The definition and the properties of this hypertext directly follow from the definition of annotation we provided in the previous sections. Therefore, we can consider the document–annotation hypertext as a kind of view on the set of documents and annotations. The aim is to mask all of the details involved by the definition of the annotation itself, and to provide us with a more abstract representation of the objects we dealt with and of their structural relationships.

Definition 13. *The* document–annotation hypertext *is a labeled directed graph:*

$$\left(H_{da} = (DO, E_{da} \subseteq A \times DO), \mathrm{l}_{da} \right)$$

where:

- $DO = A \cup D$ *is a set of vertices;*
- $E_{da} = \{(a, do) \in A \times DO \mid \exists \alpha \in \mathcal{A}_a, \alpha = (\mathrm{sn}, t, st_{\mathrm{sm}}, \mathrm{sm}, \mathrm{h}^{-1}(do)\}$ *is a set of edges;*
- $\mathrm{l}_{da} : E_{da} \to LT$ *is a labelling function, such that for each* $e = (a, do) \in E_{da}$ *there is a lt-labeled edge from the annotation a to the generic digital object do:*

$$\mathrm{l}_{da}(a, do) = \begin{cases} Annotate & if\ \exists \alpha \in \mathcal{A}_a \mid \alpha = \left(\mathrm{sn}, Annotate, st_{\mathrm{sm}}, \mathrm{sm}, \mathrm{h}^{-1}(do)\right) \\ RelateTo & if\ \exists \alpha \in \mathcal{A}_a \mid \alpha = \left(\mathrm{sn}, RelateTo, st_{\mathrm{sm}}, \mathrm{sm}, \mathrm{h}^{-1}(do)\right) \end{cases}$$

The document–annotation hypertext is constructed by putting an edge between an annotation vertex and a digital object vertex, if the annotation is annotating or relating to that digital object. Note that we used $\mathrm{h}^{-1}(do)$ in E_{da} to track the digital object back to its handle; the edge is then labeled with the corresponding link type. Each edge $e = (a, do) \in E_{da}$ always starts from an annotation $a \in A$, while $e \in E_{da}$ which starts from a document $d \in D$ does not exist.

Figure 3 shows an example of document–annotation hypertext H_{da}. In the figure, continuous lines, labeled with "A", indicate "annotate" links, while dotted lines, labeled with "R", indicate "relate to" links; annotations are labeled with the letter "a", while documents are labeled with the letter "d".

- $D = \{d_1, d_2, d_3, d_4, d_5\}$, we can assume that the subscript of each document indicates the time in which the document became an element of the set D;
- $A = \{a_1, a_2, a_3, a_4, a_5, a_6, a_7, a_8, a_9, a_{10}, a_{11}, a_{12}, a_{13}, a_{14}\}$, we can assume that the subscript of each annotation indicates the time in which the annotation became an element of the set A;
- we can express, for example:
  - *annotation sets concerning a document:* $\{a_1, a_2\}$ is an annotation set concerning the document d_1;
  - *annotation sets concerning an annotation:* $\{a_8, a_9\}$ is an annotation set concerning the annotation a_7;
  - *annotation threads concerning a document:* $\{a_1, a_3, a_4\}$ is an annotation thread concerning the document d_1;
  - *annotation threads concerning an annotation:* $\{a_8, a_{10}\}$ is an annotation thread concerning the annotation a_7;
  - *multiple annotation threads concerning a document:* $\{a_7, a_8, a_{10}\}$ and $\{a_{12}, a_{13}, a_{14}\}$ are two different annotations threads both concerning the document d_3;
  - *multiple annotation threads concerning an annotation:* $\{a_8, a_{10}\}$ and $\{a_9, a_{11}\}$ are two annotation threads both concerning the annotation a_7;
  - *nested annotation threads concerning a document:* $\{a_8, a_{10}\}$ and $\{a_9, a_{11}\}$ are two different and nested annotation threads both concerning the document d_3.

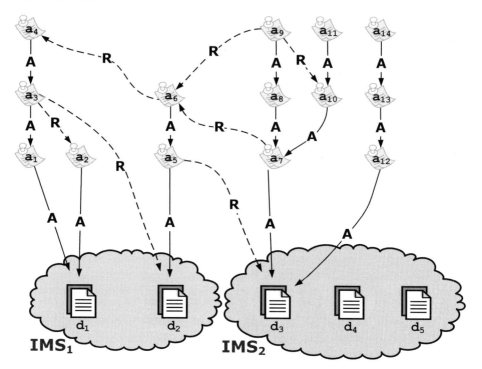

Fig. 3: Example of document–annotation hypertext H_{da}

Figure 3 also points out another important feature of the document–annotation hypertext. It can span and cross the boundaries of the single IMS, as discussed in Sect. 3. The IMS_1 manages d_1 and d_2, while the IMS_2 manages d_3, d_4, and d_5. There are annotations that act as a bridge between two IMSs: for example, a_5 annotates d_2, which is managed by IMS_1, and refers to d_3, which is managed by IMS_2.

5 Conclusions

We have presented different issues which concern the annotation of digital contents and we have shown how differently this seemingly simple and intuitive concept is perceived by users and designers, who often vary their definition of annotation according to the task at hand. In order to give an idea of how fragmentary the picture about annotations is, we have presented the different and coexisting perspectives on annotations with which we deal today.

Therefore, we have proposed a formal model of annotations on digital content, which not only captures all the aspects described above, but also effectively formalizes the time dimension entailed by annotations and explicitly introduces the notion of document–annotation hypertext.

Finally, we have thoroughly discussed different application areas of the proposed formal model, which range from qualitative and formal comparison of existing system, definition of more specialized models derived from it, and design of advanced search algorithms which exploit annotations, to the development of flexible annotation services which can be easily integrated into existing IMSs in order to add annotation functionalities to them.

References

1. Abiteboul, S., Agrawal, R., Bernstein, P., Carey, M., Ceri, S., Croft, B., De-Witt, D., Franklin, M., Garcia-Molina, H., Gawlick, D., Gray, J., Haas, L., Halevy, A., Hellerstein, J., Ioannidis, Y., Kersten, M., Pazzani, M., Lesk, M., Maier, D., Naughton, J., Schek, H.J., Sellis, T., Silberschatz, A., Stonebraker, M., Snodgrass, R., Ullman, J.D., Weikum, G., Widom, J., Zdonik, S.: The Lowell Database Research Self-Assessment. Communications of the ACM (CACM) **48**(5), 111–118 (2005)

2. Agosti, M., Albrechtsen, H., Ferro, N., Frommholz, I., Hansen, P., Orio, N., Panizzi, E., Pejtersen, A.M., Thiel, U.: DiLAS: a Digital Library Annotation Service. In: J.F. Boujut (ed.) Proc. International Workshop on Annotation for Collaboration – Methods, Tools, and Practices (IWAC 2005), pp. 91–101. CNRS - Programme société de l'information (2005)

3. Agosti, M., Benfante, L., Orio, N.: IPSA: A Digital Archive of Herbals to Support Scientific Research. In: T.M.T. Sembok, H.B. Zaman, H. Chen, S.R. Urs, S.H. Myaeng (eds.) Proc. 6th International Conference on Asian Digital Libraries – Digital Libraries: Technology and Management of Indigenous Knowledge (ICADL 2003), pp. 253–264. Lecture Notes in Computer Science (LNCS) 2911, Springer, Heidelberg, Germany (2003)

4. Agosti, M., Berretti, S., Brettlecker, G., del Bimbo, A., Ferro, N., Fuhr, N., Keim, D., Klas, C.P., Lidy, T., Norrie, M., Ranaldi, P., Rauber, A., Schek, H.J., Schreck, T., Schuldt, H., Signer, B., Springmann, M.: DelosDLMS – the Integrated DELOS Digital Library Management System. In: C. Thanos, F. Borri (eds.) DELOS Conference 2007 Working Notes, pp. 71–80. ISTI-CNR, Gruppo ALI, Pisa, Italy (2007)

5. Agosti, M., Bonfiglio-Dosio, G., Ferro, N.: A Historical and Contemporary Study on Annotations to Derive Key Features for Systems Design. International Journal on Digital Libraries http://dx.doi.org/10.1007/s00799-007-0010-0 (2007)

6. Agosti, M., Colotti, R., Gradenigo, G.: A Two-Level Hypertext Retrieval Model for Legal Data. In: E.A. Fox (ed.) Proc. 14th Annual International ACM SIGIR Conference on Research and Development in Information Retrieval (SIGIR 1991), pp. 316–325. ACM Press, New York, USA (1991)

7. Agosti, M., Coppotelli, T., Ferro, N., Pretto, L.: Exploiting Relevance Assessment for the Creation of an Experimental Test Collection to Evaluate Systems that Use Annotations. In: C. Thanos, F. Borri (eds.) DELOS Conference 2007 Working Notes, pp. 195–202. ISTI-CNR, Gruppo ALI, Pisa, Italy (2007)

8. Agosti, M., Ferro, N.: Annotations: Enriching a Digital Library. In: T. Koch, I.T. Sølvberg (eds.) Proc. 7th European Conference on Research and Advanced

Technology for Digital Libraries (ECDL 2003), pp. 88–100. Lecture Notes in Computer Science (LNCS) 2769, Springer, Heidelberg, Germany (2003)

9. Agosti, M., Ferro, N.: An Information Service Architecture for Annotations. In: M. Agosti, H.J. Schek, C. Türker (eds.) Digital Library Architectures: Peer-to-Peer, Grid, and Service-Orientation, Pre-proceedings of the 6th Thematic Workshop of the EU Network of Excellence DELOS, pp. 115–126. Edizioni Libreria Progetto, Padova, Italy (2004)

10. Agosti, M., Ferro, N.: A System Architecture as a Support to a Flexible Annotation Service. In: C. Türker, M. Agosti, H.J. Schek (eds.) Peer-to-Peer, Grid, and Service-Orientation in Digital Library Architectures: 6th Thematic Workshop of the EU Network of Excellence DELOS. Revised Selected Papers, pp. 147–166. Lecture Notes in Computer Science (LNCS) 3664, Springer, Heidelberg, Germany (2005)

11. Agosti, M., Ferro, N.: Annotations as Context for Searching Documents. In: F. Crestani, I. Ruthven (eds.) Proc. 5th International Conference on Conceptions of Library and Information Science – Context: nature, impact and role, pp. 155–170. Lecture Notes in Computer Science (LNCS) 3507, Springer, Heidelberg, Germany (2005)

12. Agosti, M., Ferro, N.: Search Strategies for Finding Annotations and Annotated Documents: the FAST Service. In: H. Legind Larsen, G. Pasi, D. Ortiz-Arroyo, T. Andreasen, H. Christiansen (eds.) Proc. 7th International Conference on Flexible Query Answering Systems (FQAS 2006), pp. 270–281. Lecture Notes in Artificial Intelligence (LNAI) 4027, Springer, Heidelberg, Germany (2006)

13. Agosti, M., Ferro, N.: A Formal Model of Annotations of Digital Content. ACM Transactions on Information Systems (TOIS) **26**(1), 1–55 (2008 (to appear))

14. Agosti, M., Ferro, N., Frommholz, I., Panizzi, E., Putz, W., Thiel, U.: Integration of the DiLAS Annotation Service into Digital Library Infrastructures. In: A. Blandford, J. Gow (eds.) Proc. 1st International Workshop on Digital Libraries in the Context of Users Broader Activities (DL-CUBA 2006), pp. 1–4. http://www.uclic.ucl.ac.uk/events/dl-cuba2006/ [last visited 2007, March 23] (2006)

15. Agosti, M., Ferro, N., Frommholz, I., Thiel, U.: Annotations in Digital Libraries and Collaboratories – Facets, Models and Usage. In: R. Heery, L. Lyon (eds.) Proc. 8th European Conference on Research and Advanced Technology for Digital Libraries (ECDL 2004), pp. 244–255. Lecture Notes in Computer Science (LNCS) 3232, Springer, Heidelberg, Germany (2004)

16. Agosti, M., Ferro, N., Orio, N.: Annotating Illuminated Manuscripts: an Effective Tool for Research and Education. In: M. Marlino, T. Sumner, F. Shipman (eds.) Proc. 5th ACM/IEEE-CS Joint Conference on Digital Libraries (JCDL 2005), pp. 121–130. ACM Press, New York, USA (2005)

17. Agosti, M., Ferro, N., Orio, N.: Graph-based Automatic Suggestion of Relationships among Images of Illuminated Manuscripts. In: H.M. Haddad, K.M. Liebrock, R. Chbeir, M.J. Palakal, S. Ossowski, K. Yetongnoon, R.L. Wainwright, C. Nicolle (eds.) Proc. 21st ACM Symposium on Applied Computing (SAC 2006), pp. 1063–1067. ACM Press, New York, USA (2006)

18. Agosti, M., Ferro, N., Orio, N.: Annotations as a Tool for Disclosing Hidden Relationships between Illuminated Manuscripts. In: Proc. 10th Congress of the Italian Association for Artificial Intelligence. Artificial Intelligence and Human-Oriented Computing (AI*IA 2007). Lecture Notes in Computer Science (LNCS), Springer, Heidelberg, Germany (2007)

19. Agosti, M., Ferro, N., Panizzi, E., Trinchese, R.: Annotation as a Support to User Interaction for Content Enhancement in Digital Libraries. In: A. Celentano, P. Mussio (eds.) Proc. Working Conference on Advanced Visual Interfaces (AVI 2006), pp. 151–154. ACM Press, New York, USA (2006)
20. Agosti, M., Smeaton, A. (eds.): Information Retrieval and Hypertext. Kluwer Academic Publishers, Norwell (MA), USA (1996)
21. Berners-Lee, T.: Universal Resource Identifiers in WWW. RFC 1630 (1994)
22. Berners-Lee, T., Fielding, R., Irvine, U.C., Masinter, L.: Uniform Resource Identifiers (URI): Generic Syntax. RFC 2396 (1998)
23. Bhagwat, D., Chiticariu, L., Tan, W.C., Vijayvargiya, G.: An Annotation Management System for Relational Databases. In: M.A. Nascimento, M.T. Özsu, D. Kossmann, R.J. Miller, J.A. Blakeley, K.B. Schiefer (eds.) Proc. 30th International Conference on Very Large Data Bases (VLDB 2004), pp. 900–911. Morgan Kaufmann (2004)
24. Bottoni, P., Civica, R., Levialdi, S., Orso, L., Panizzi, E., Trinchese, R.: MAD-COW: a Multimedia Digital Annotation System. In: M.F. Costabile (ed.) Proc. Working Conference on Advanced Visual Interfaces (AVI 2004), pp. 55–62. ACM Press, New York, USA (2004)
25. Bottoni, P., Levialdi, S., Rizzo, P.: An Analysis and Case Study of Digital Annotation. In: N. Bianchi-Berthouze (ed.) Proc. 3rd International Workshop on Databases in Networked Information Systems (DNIS 2003), pp. 216–230. Lecture Notes in Computer Science (LNCS) 2822, Springer, Heidelberg, Germany (2003)
26. Buneman, P., Khanna, S., Tajima, K., Tan, W.C.: Archiving Scientific Data. ACM Transactions on Database Systems (TODS) **29**(1), 2–42 (2004)
27. Buneman, P., Khanna, S., Tan, W.C.: Why and Where: A Characterization of Data Provenance. In: J. Van den Bussche, V. Vianu (eds.) Proc. 8th International Conference on Database Theory (ICDT 2001), pp. 316–330. Lecture Notes in Computer Science (LNCS) 1973, Springer, Heidelberg, Germany (2001)
28. Buneman, P., Khanna, S., Tan, W.C.: On Propagation of Deletions and Annotations Through Views. In: S. Abiteboul, P.G. Kolaitis, L. Popa (eds.) Proc. 21st ACM SIGMOD–SIGACT–SIGART Symposium on Principles of Database Systems (PODS 2002), pp. 150–158. ACM Press, New York, USA (2002)
29. Canova, M.G.: La tradizione europea degli erbari miniati e la scuola veneta. In: Di sana pianta. Erbari e taccuini di sanità: le radici storiche della nuova farmacologia, pp. 21–28. Panini, Modena, Italy (1988)
30. Cleverdon, C.W.: The Cranfield Tests on Index Languages Devices. In: K. Spärck Jones, P. Willett (eds.) Readings in Information Retrieval, pp. 47–60. Morgan Kaufmann Publisher, Inc., San Francisco, California, USA (1997)
31. Constantopoulos, P., Doerr, M., Theodoridou, M., Tzobanakis, M.: On Information Organization in Annotation Systems. In: G. Grieser, Y. Tanaka (eds.) Proc. International Workshop on Intuitive Human Interfaces for Organizing and Accessing Intellectual Assets, pp. 189–200. Lecture Notes in Computer Science (LNCS) 3359, Springer, Heidelberg, Germany (2004)
32. Davis, J.R., Huttenlocher, D.P.: Shared Annotation for Cooperative Learning. In: J.L. Schnase, E.L. Cunnius (eds.) Proc. 1st International Conference on Computer Support for Collaborative Learning (CSCL 1995), pp. 84–88. Lawrence Erlbaum Associates Inc., Mahwah (NJ), USA (1995)

33. Ferro, N.: Formal Model and Conceptual Architecture of the Annotation Service for Dynamic Ubiquitous Knowledge Environments. PhD thesis, Department of Information Engineering. University of Padua, Italy (2004)

34. Frommholz, I., Brocks, H., Thiel, U., Neuhold, E., Iannone, L., Semeraro, G., Berardi, M., Ceci, M.: Document-Centered Collaboration for Scholars in the Humanities – The COLLATE System. In: T. Koch, I.T. Sølvberg (eds.) Proc. 7th European Conference on Research and Advanced Technology for Digital Libraries (ECDL 2003), pp. 434–445. Lecture Notes in Computer Science (LNCS) 2769, Springer, Heidelberg, Germany (2003)

35. Frommholz, I., Fuhr, N.: Probabilistic, Object-oriented Logics for Annotation-based Retrieval in Digital Libraries. In: G. Marchionini, M.L. Nelson, C.C. Marshall (eds.) Proc. 6th ACM/IEEE-CS Joint Conference on Digital Libraries (JCDL 2006), pp. 55–64. ACM Press, New York, USA (2006)

36. Giovè Marchioli, N.: Gli strumenti del sapere. I manoscritti padovani tra tipizzazioni generali e peculiarità locali. In: F. Piovan, L. Sitran Rea (eds.) Studenti, Università, città nella storia padovana. Atti del convegno (Padova, 6-8 febbraio 1998), pp. 47–71. Centro per la storia dell'Università di Padova. Contributi, 35, Lint, Trieste, Italia (2001)

37. Golder, S., Huberman, B.A.: Usage Patterns of Collaborative Tagging Systems. Journal of Information Science **32**(2), 198–208 (2006)

38. Golovchinsky, G., Price, M.N., Schilit, B.N.: From Reading to Retrieval: Freeform Ink Annotations as Queries. In: F. Gey, M. Hearst, R. Tong (eds.) Proc. 22nd Annual International ACM SIGIR Conference on Research and Development in Information Retrieval (SIGIR 1999), pp. 19–25. ACM Press, New York, USA (1999)

39. Gonçalves, M.A., Fox, E.A., Watson, L.T., Kipp, N.A.: Streams, Structures, Spaces, Scenarios, Societies (5S): A Formal Model for Digital Libraries. ACM Transactions on Information Systems (TOIS) **22**(2), 270–312 (2004)

40. Groth, D.P., Streefkerk, K.: Provenance and Annotation for Visual Exploration Systems. IEEE Transactions On Visualization And Computer Graphics **12**(6), 1500–1510 (2006)

41. Halasz, F.G.: Reflections on NoteCards: Seven Issues for the Next Generation of Hypermedia Systems. Communications of the ACM (CACM) **31**(7), 836–852 (1988)

42. Halasz, F.G., Moran, T.P., Trigg, R.H.: Notecards in a Nutshell. In: J.M. Carroll, P.P. Tanner (eds.) Proc. Conference on Human Factors in Computing Systems and Graphics Interface (CHI 1987), pp. 45–52. ACM Press, New York, USA (1987)

43. Handschuh, S., Staab, S. (eds.): Annotation for the Semantic Web. IOS Press, Amsterdam, The Netherlands (2003)

44. Hanks, P. (ed.): Collins Dictionary of the English Language. William Collins Sons & Co. Ltd., Glasgow, UK (1979)

45. Hull, D.: Using Statistical Testing in the Evaluation of Retrieval Experiments. In: R. Korfhage, E. Rasmussen, P. Willett (eds.) Proc. 16th Annual International ACM SIGIR Conference on Research and Development in Information Retrieval (SIGIR 1993), pp. 329–338. ACM Press, New York, USA (1993)

46. Hwang, W.Y., Wang, C.Y., Sharples, M.: A study of multimedia annotation of Web-based materials. Computers & Education **48**(4), 680–699 (2007)

47. IEI: Enciclopedia Italiana di scienze, lettere ed arti, Vol. XVII (GIAP–GS). Istituto della Enciclopedia Italiana, Istituto Poligrafico dello Stato, Roma, Italia (1951)
48. IEI: Vocabolario della lingua italiana, Vol. II (D–L). Istituto della Enciclopedia Italiana, Arti Grafiche Ricordi, Monotipia Olivieri, Milano, Italia (1987)
49. Ioannidis, Y., Maier, D., Abiteboul, S., Buneman, P., Davidson, S., Fox, E.A., Halevy, A., Knoblock, C., Rabitti, F., Schek, H.J., Weikum, G.: Digital library information-technology infrastructures. International Journal on Digital Libraries **5**(4), 266–274 (2005)
50. Kahan, J., Koivunen, M.R.: Annotea: an open RDF infrastructure for shared Web annotations. In: V.Y. Shen, N. Saito, M.R. Lyu, M.E. Zurko (eds.) Proc. 10th International Conference on World Wide Web (WWW 2001), pp. 623–632. ACM Press, New York, USA (2001)
51. Marshall, C.C.: Annotation: from Paper Books to the Digital Library. In: R.B. Allen, E. Rasmussen (eds.) Proc. 2nd ACM International Conference on Digital Libraries (DL 1997), pp. 233–240. ACM Press, New York, USA (1997)
52. Marshall, C.C.: Toward an Ecology of Hypertext Annotation. In: R. Akscyn (ed.) Proc. 9th ACM Conference on Hypertext and Hypermedia (HT 1998): links, objects, time and space-structure in hypermedia systems, pp. 40–49. ACM Press, New York, USA (1998)
53. Marshall, C.C., Brush, A.J.B.: From Personal to Shared Annotations. In: L. Terveen, D. Wixon (eds.) Proc. Conference on Human Factors and Computing Systems (CHI 2002) – Extended Abstracts on Human Factors in Computer Systems, pp. 812–813. ACM Press, New York, USA (2002)
54. Marshall, C.C., Brush, A.J.B.: Exploring the Relationship between Personal and Public Annotations. In: H. Chen, H. Wactlar, C.C. Chen, E.P. Lim, M. Christel (eds.) Proc. 4th ACM/IEEE-CS Joint Conference on Digital Libraries (JCDL 2004), pp. 349–357. ACM Press, New York, USA (2004)
55. Nagao, K.: Digital Content Annotation and Transcoding. Artech House, Norwood (MA), USA (2003)
56. Navarro, G., Baeza-Yates, R.: Proximal Nodes: A Model to Query Document Databases by Content and Structure. ACM Transactions on Information Systems (TOIS) **15**(4), 400–435 (1997)
57. NISO: ANSI/NISO Z39.88 - 2004 – The OpenURL Framework for Context-Sensitive Services. National Information Standards Organization (NISO). http://www.niso.org/standards/standard_detail.cfm?std_id=783 [last visited 2007, March 23] (2005)
58. Ovsiannikov, I., Arbib, M.A., Mcneill, T.H.: Annotation Technology. International Journal of Human-Computer Studies **50**, 329–362 (1999)
59. Paskin, N. (ed.): The DOI Handbook – Edition 4.4.1. International DOI Foundation (IDF). http://dx.doi.org/10.1000/186 [last visited 2007, March 23] (2006)
60. Phelps, T.A., Wilensky, R.: Multivalent Annotations. In: C. Peters, C. Thanos (eds.) Proc. 1st European Conference on Research and Advanced Technology for Digital Libraries (ECDL 1997), pp. 287–303. Lecture Notes in Computer Science (LNCS) 1324, Springer, Heidelberg, Germany (1997)
61. van Rijsbergen, C.J.: Information Retrieval, 2nd edn. Butterworths, London, England (1979)
62. Rocci, L.: Vocabolario greco italiano, *34 edizione*. Società Editrice Dante Alighieri, Italia (1989)

63. Salatiele: Ars notariae. In: G. Orlandelli (ed.) Opere dei maestri, Vol. 2. Giuffré, Milano, Italia (1961)
64. Salton, G., McGill, M.J.: Introduction to Modern Information Retrieval. McGraw-Hill, New York, USA (1983)
65. Shipman, F., Price, M.N., Marshall, C.C., Golovchinsky, G.: Identifying Useful Passages in Documents based on Annotation Patterns. In: T. Koch, I.T. Sølvberg (eds.) Proc. 7th European Conference on Research and Advanced Technology for Digital Libraries (ECDL 2003), pp. 101–112. Lecture Notes in Computer Science (LNCS) 2769, Springer, Heidelberg, Germany (2003)
66. Stein, L.D., Eddy, S., Dowell, R.: Distributed Sequence Annotation System (DAS) – Version 1.53. http://www.biodas.org/documents/spec.html [last visited 2007, March 23] (2002)
67. Thiel, U., Brocks, H., Frommholz, I., Dirsch-Weigand, A., Keiper, J., Stein, A., Neuhold, E.J.: COLLATE – A collaboratory supporting research on historic European films. International Journal on Digital Libraries 4(1), 8–12 (2004)
68. W3C: HTML 4.01 Specification – W3C Recommendation 24 December 1999. http://www.w3.org/TR/html4/ [last visited 2007, March 23] (1999)
69. W3C: Annotea Project. http://www.w3.org/2001/Annotea/ [last visited 2007, March 23] (2005)
70. W3C: Semantic Web . http://www.w3.org/2001/sw/ [last visited 2007, March 23] (2007)
71. Xi, W., Zhang, B., Chen, Z., Lu, Y., Yan, S., Ma, W.Y., Fox, E.A.: Link Fusion: A Unified Link Analysis Framework for Multi-Type Interrelated Data Objects. In: S. Feldman, M. Uretsky, M. Najork, C. Wills (eds.) Proc. 13th International Conference on World Wide Web (WWW 2004), pp. 319–327. ACM Press, New York, USA (2004)

Music Indexing and Retrieval for Multimedia Digital Libraries

Nicola Orio

Department of Information Engineering – University of Padua
Via Gradenigo, 6/b – 35131 Padua – Italy
nicola.orio@dei.unipd.it

Abstract. This chapter addresses the problem of the retrieval of music documents from multimedia digital libraries. Some of the peculiarities of the music language are described, showing similarities and differences between indexing and retrieval of textual and music documents. After reviewing the main approaches to music retrieval, a novel methodology is presented, which combines an approximate matching approach with an indexing scheme. The methodology is based on the statistical modeling of musical lexical units with weighted transducers, which are automatically built from the melodic and rhythmic information of lexical units. An experimental evaluation of the methodology is presented, showing encouraging results.

Key words: music retrieval, indexing, approximate matching, weighted transducers

1 Introduction

Users of multimedia digital libraries may have different knowledge and expertise, which are related to the ability to describe their information needs precisely. This is particularly true for music language, where the level of music education may vary remarkably among users, who may range from casual listeners to performers and composers. Untrained users may not be able to use bibliographic values or take advantage of metadata when searching for music. For this reason, the access to music digital libraries should be content-based.

The main idea underlying content-based access and retrieval is that a document can be described by a set of features that are directly computed from its content. This approach is the basis for most of the methodologies for information retrieval, where the content of a textual document – e.g. its set words – is automatically processed and used for indexing and retrieval. Even if multimedia data requires specific methodologies for content extraction, the core information retrieval techniques developed for text may be extended to other media because the underlying models, which are based on statistics and probability theory, are likely to describe fundamental characteristics being shared by different media, languages, and application domains [23]. For the particular case of music language, already in 1996 McLane [30] stated that a challenging research topic would be the application of some standard principles of text information retrieval to music representation.

As is well known, textual information retrieval is based on the concept that *words*, which form a document, can be considered as good content descriptors. Following this idea, documents can be efficiently described using words as index terms, and retrieval can be performed using a measure of similarity between query and documents indexes. If we follow the hypothesis that this principle can be extended to indexing and retrieval of music documents, then ad-hoc algorithms have to be designed to produce musical *lexical units*, like words in textual documents, and compute the *similarity* between such units.

2 Background

Before introducing the approach to music retrieval, some background information needs to be provided. First of all, the limitations of music metadata for a retrieval task are presented to highlight the need for content based approaches. This introduces the main question regarding music, that is, which content is conveyed by a music work. The basic concepts of music retrieval are then introduced by drawing a parallel between the text and the music domains based on the application of well known techniques.

2.1 Music Metadata

Textual metadata have been used for centuries as a tool for the concise and effective description of document content [12]. The extension to other media, such as images and video, proved to be effective as well, because metadata allows for the content of a whole document to be summarized with a small set of keywords. A number of music digital libraries are accessible through the use of metadata, such as Cantate [6] and Musica [36], which allow users access to choral music using metadata and lyrics.

Music metadata describes a number of characteristics of music documents, which can be divided in three main categories:

- *Bibliographic values*, which are shared by almost all media and, in the case of music, also include cataloguing number, the title of a complete work and the titles of its parts (or movements), the names of the authors and of the performers.
- *Information on music form*, which is typical of music, and gives information about genre, time and key signatures, tempo, orchestration, and so on.
- *Additional available information*, such as lyrics for vocal works and, if applicable, links to external documents that create a context for the music work (e.g. a drama, a movie, a poem).

In order to carry out an effective search through music metadata, a user needs to have a good knowledge of the music domain, which may not be the case for casual users of a music digital library. Moreover, music metadata have a number of limitations. For instance, in the case of tonal Western music, it is typical to have titles such as "Fugue in G major" or "Suite", which describe the music form rather than the content. Moreover, the title is often based on some music features for other music genres as well. For instance, a user needs to be aware of the difference between a "jig" and a "reel" in order to effectively use these metadata to retrieve Irish music, and between a "bossa" and a "blues" to retrieve jazz music.

General information is often too generic to be a good discriminator between different music works. For instance, the genre information groups together hundreds of thousands of different works. Moreover, in tonal music there are only 21 major and 21 minor different tonalities, and thousands of compositions can be labeled with the terms "cantata" or "concerto" in classical music, and with the same terms "up tempo" or "slow" in pop and rock. This kind of metadata can be useful to refine the description of a music information need, but it can hardly be used to completely define it. Moreover, a preliminary study on users information needs, presented in [25], showed that users are interested in retrieving songs by their specific content. Additional information in the form of lyrics, when present, can be particularly useful to describe an information need, yet in this case the retrieval of music documents becomes an application of textual information retrieval. Contextual information, such as the movie where a particular soundtrack was used, or the poem that inspired a particular composition, can be very helpful as well to describe a user information need, yet this kind of contextual information applies only to a small percentage of music documents.

What is normally missing in music metadata is a textual description of the document content other than its musical structure, which is a peculiar situation of the music language that is due to the fact that music is not aimed at describing something with a known semantic – like text, images, speech, video, or 3D models. It should be considered that music representation is intrinsically limited because it is aimed at giving directions to performers and not to describe high level characteristics [34]. Finally, it is not clear yet, among music theorists and musicologists, whether music can be considered as a language and whether it describes something other than itself. This is probably the main limitation of the use of metadata for music indexing, and it is the motivation for the increasing number of content-based approaches proposed in recent years.

2.2 The Dimensions of Music

Rhythm, melody, and harmony are different dimensions that capture distinctive features of a music document, thus music has an instrinsic multidimensional nature. These dimensions are conveyed explicitly by music scores and recognized easily by listeners of audio recordings, and are used extensively by music theorists and musicologists as tools to describe, analyze, and study music works. Another perceptually relevant music dimension is timbre, which is related to the quality of sounds and is conveyed only by audio recordings. Yet timbre is a multidimensional feature by itself, and can be described using a set of continuous parameters, such as spectral power energy or Mel-Cepstrum Coefficients, and by perceptually based features such as spectral centroid, roughness, and attack time. As stated in [24], timbre remains a difficult dimension to understand and represent, though studies have been carried out on the perception of timbre similarity [4]. Other dimensions are related to the structure, to the music forms, to the orchestrations. The discussion on content-based music indexing, however, will be limited to the ones that have a symbolic representation, namely rhythm, melody, and harmony – with a special focus on melody. For any chosen dimension, the indexing scheme has to be based on a suitable definition of the particular lexical units of the dimension and their representation. A taxonomy of the characteristics of music and their potential interest for users is reported in [26].

The representation of the melody can build upon traditional score representation, which is based on the drawing of a sequence of notes, each one with a given pitch and a duration relative to the tempo of the piece. This symbolic representation is particularly suitable for indexing, providing that the melodic lexical units are highlighted. This is a more difficult task also for musicians and music scholars; the results of a perceptual study on manual segmentation are presented in a following section. The representation of rhythm can be considered as a variation of melodic representation, where pitch information can be discarded or substituted with the information of the particular percussive instrument that plays each rhythmic element. Similarly, the indexing of the harmonic dimension can be based on common chord representation. In this case there are alternative representations, from figured bass to functional harmony and chord names. An overview of chord representations, aimed at their annotation, is presented in [16]. The segmentation of chords in their lexical units can be based on notions of harmony, including modulations, cadences, and the use of particular chord progressions in different music genres.

The analysis of different dimensions and their representation as building blocks of music documents may be of interest also for musicologists, composers and performers. To this end, it is interesting to cite Humdrum [22], which incorporates retrieval with a number of tools for the manipulation and analysis of music scores.

2.3 Application of Information Retrieval Concepts to Music

Textual information retrieval, which is normally addressed as information retrieval *tout-court*, has a long research tradition and thus is a natural choice for the investigation of how the main concepts underlying the different methodologies can be applied to the music domain. In particular, there are four main steps related to textual document indexing that are relevant to this discussion.

1. Lexical analysis.
2. Stopwords removal.
3. Stemming.
4. Terms weighting.

These steps reflect some considerations on the content-based description of textual documents that have a parallel in the music domain, and are discussed in detail in the following sections. Among the different steps, the last two are the most relevant for the methodology proposed in this chapter.

Lexical Analysis

The basic idea underlying lexical analysis is that *words* are the most relevant content descriptors of a textual document. Thus lexical analysis corresponds to document parsing for highlighting its individual words, which is almost straightforward for many languages, where there is a clear separations between words – blanks, commas, dots, and so on. It can be noted that for some languages, such as Chinese and Japanese, the compounding of ideograms in different words has to be inferred from the context and is a non trivial task.

As regards the parallel of lexical analysis to the music domain the first issue involves the choice of the dimensions to be used as content descriptors. This choice influences the approaches to the lexical analysis. For instance, if rhythm is used to index music documents, the attack time of the different notes has to be automatically detected and filtered, which is an easy task for symbolic documents and can be carried out with good results for documents in audio format too. On the other hand, if harmony is used to compute indexes, lexical analysis has to rely on complex techniques for the automatic extraction of chords from a polyphonic music document, which is still an error prone task especially in the case of audio documents, even though encouraging results have been obtained [15]. For simplicity, it is assumed that a sequence of features is already available, describing some high-level characteristics of a music documents, related to one or more of its dimensions. It is also assumed that the feature extraction may be affected by errors, which should be taken into account during the design of a music retrieval system.

Even after a sequence of features have been automatically extracted, music lexical analysis remains a difficult task. The reason is that music language lacks of explicit separators between candidate index terms for all of its dimensions – like the previous example of documents written in Chinese or Japanese. Melodic phrases, rhythmic patterns and harmonic progressions are not contoured by special signs or sounds that express the presence of a boundary between two lexical units. This is not surprising, because lexical units are not part of the common representation of music documents. Even if there is a wide consensus in considering music as a structured organization of different elements, and not just a pure sequence of acoustic elements, historically there has been no need to represent this aspect directly. Music is printed for musicians, who basically need the information to create a correct performance, and who could infer the presence of basic elements from the context. In order to overcome this problem, different approaches have been proposed in the literature for lexical analysis, considering musical patterns [19], main themes [31], or musical phrases [32].

The consistency between musicians in performing the lexical analysis of some monophonic scores was investigated in a perceptual study [33], showing that all the participants perceived the presence of lexical units, but they were consistent in choosing boundaries only when strong cues were present. The lexical analysis of music documents is still an open problem, both in terms of musicological analysis because alternative theories have been presented, and in terms of indexing and retrieval effectiveness. An experimental evaluation of the effectiveness of different approaches to melodic segmentation was presented in [38]. Figure 1 shows the opening bars of *Psyché* by Jean-Baptiste Lully, which have been segmented using three different segmentation approaches, based on perception, statistical modeling and discontinuity detection, respectively.

Stopwords Removal

The main concept behind stopwords removal is that a subset of the words extracted through lexical analysis may be discarded, eventually affecting efficiency and effectiveness in a positive way. Such words may be either the ones that have only a grammatical function, and thus do not express any semantic, or the ones that are almost uniformly distributed across the documents.

In the case of music, it is difficult to state whether or not a musical lexical unit has a meaning, because it is not clear if music itself is aimed (or even able) to convey any meaning at all. On the other hand, to define how much a

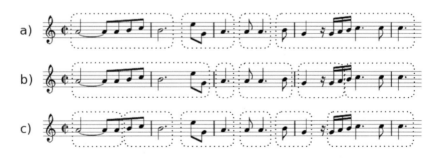

Fig. 1: Example of the results of different segmentation techniques based on: **a)** Gestalt principles, **b)** statistical modeling, **c)** discontinuity detection

particular unit is a good discriminator between different music documents is an easier task. For instance, a lexical unit of two notes, with identical length, that form a major second is likely to be present in almost all works of vocal music, and thus is probably a poor descriptor of music content. Depending on the particular set of features used as content descriptors, the designer of a music retrieval system can make a number of choices about the possible stop-lists of lexical units, which could be driven by both musicological and computational motivations and by the characteristics of the music collection highlighted by a statistical analysis. It should be noted that this approach is not usually exploited in the music information retrieval (MIR) literature, where the term stop-list is seldom used. The common approach is to carefully select the processing parameters to avoid the computation of lexical units that are believed to be uninformative.

Stemming

As described in a previous Chapter, the idea behind stemming is that two index terms may be different but can convey similar meanings. Analogously, two musical lexical units may be slightly different, yet listeners can perceive them as almost identical, or confuse one with the other when recalling them from memory, or consider that they play a similar role in the musical structure. Examples of potential applications of stemming are: identical rhythmic patterns played at a different tempo, melodies that differ only for few intervals that from major turn minor and viceversa, chord progressions where some chords are substituted by others with a similar function.

A way to take into account variants in lexical units is *quantization*. The main motivation of quantization in music processing is probably related to the fact that each feature extraction process is error prone: quantization partially overcomes this problem if erroneous measurements are reported to the same quantized value of the correct one. Moreover, quantization can be useful when the music signal itself may have variations due to expressive performances, such as note durations played with *rubato* or note pitches played with *vibrato*.

Quantization can also be considered a kind of stemming. In fact, it is well known that many works are based on a limited amount of music material, which is varied and developed during the composition [39]. In this case, the conflation of different thematic variations into a single index will improve recall because the user may choose any of these variations to express the same information need. The increase in recall usually corresponds to a lowering in precision, because a quantized lexical unit is usually more generic and less precisely describes a user information need. To this end, the effect on precision due to a coarse quantization can be reduced using long music excerpts as queries [13].

Quantization can be carried out on any music dimension, and at different levels. Table 1 shows possible approaches to the quantization of melodic intervals that have been proposed in the literature.

Table 1: Number of different symbols when quantization is applied to intervals within an octave (only the names of the ascending ones are given)

Quantization level	Symbols
cents $0, 1, \ldots, 1200$	2401
semitones: $0, 1, \ldots, 12$	25
intervals: *unison, second, ..., octave*	15
perceptual intervals: *unison, small, medium, large*	9
direction: *same, up*	3

A similar approach to quantization can be carried out on rhythmic information. It should be noted that score representation itself is a quantized version of possible performances, because playing the exact onset times will result in a "mechanical" performance. In the case of transcriptions of preexisting performances, rhythm quantization is a common practice because the transcriber chooses note onsets as a compromise between the readability of the score and the precision of the reported times. Many approaches to melodic indexing do not take into account note durations, but are based only on pitch information, and they can be considered a limit case where there is only one level of rhythm quantization.

Quantization is a way to deal with musical variants implicitly. In this chapter an approach is proposed which explicitly takes into account differences within melodic phrases by modeling them in a statistical framework. This approach is presented in Sect. 4.

Terms Weighting

As is well known, index terms do not describe the content of a document to the same extent. The importance of a term in describing a document varies along a continuum that ranges from totally irrelevant to completely relevant. For textual information retrieval, it is generally assumed that the frequency at which a word appears in a document is directly proportional to its relevance, while the frequency at which it appears in the collection is inversely proportional to its relevance. These considerations gave birth to a popular weighting scheme, called term frequency - inverse document frequency, in short $tf \cdot idf$, which has been proposed with different variants.

A parallel analysis of units rele. If a musical lexical unit, for any chosen dimension, appears frequently inside a given document, it is very likely that listeners will remember it. Moreover, a frequent lexical unit can be the signature of the style of a composer [8]. Thus, term frequency seems to be a reasonable choice for music documents too. On the other hand, a lexical unit that is very common inside a collection of documents can be related to the style of a thematic collection – the chord progression of blues songs – or can correspond to a simple musical gesture – a major scale – or can be the most used solution for particular passages – the descending bass connecting two chords. Moreover, a user may not use frequent lexical units as parts of his query because it is clear that they will not address any particular document. Thus inverse document frequency seems to be a reasonable choice as well.

However, some care has to be paid to a direct application of a $tf \cdot idf$ weighting scheme to music indexing, at least because users access music documents differently from textual ones. In particular, music documents are accessed many times by users, who may only listen to selected excerpts. Moreover, it is common practice for radio stations to broadcast only the parts of the songs with the sung melody, skipping the intro and the coda. The relative importance by which a lexical unit describes a document should also reflect these aspects, which cannot be inferred by document analysis alone. Moreover, listeners are likely to remember and use in their queries the part of the song where the title or particularly relevant lyrics are sung, which becomes more relevant disregarding its frequency inside the documents and inside the collection. It should be noted that there have been very few studies that investigate the best weighting scheme for music indexing, and in many cases a direct implementation of the $tf \cdot idf$ is used.

The possibility to give different weights to lexical units is a crucial difference between information retrieval and approaches based on approximate string matching techniques. The former allows the documents to be ranked depending on the relevance of their lexical units as content descriptors, while the latter allows the documents to be ranked depending on the degree at which an excerpt of each document matches the query. In other words, a good match with an almost irrelevant excerpt may give a higher rank than a more approximate match with a highly relevant excerpt. A methodology to combine a weighting scheme with approximate matching is presented in Sect. 4.

3 Approaches to Music Retrieval

Searching for a musical work given an approximate description of one or more of its dimensions is the prototype task for a music retrieval system. In principle, retrieval can be carried out on any dimension. For instance, the user could provide an example of the timbre – or of the sound – that he is looking for, or describe the particular structure of a song. However, most of the approaches are based on melody as the main, and often only, content descriptor. This choice depends on the typical interaction paradigm that is used to query a system, called *query by example*, which requires the user to give an example of his information need by singing, humming, or whistling an excerpt of a song.

The research work on melodic retrieval can be grouped depending on the methodologies that have been proposed to compute the similarity between the query and the documents. A classification in three categories is proposed: approaches based on the computation of *index terms*, which play a role similar to words in textual documents, approaches based on *sequence matching* techniques, which consider both the query and the documents as sequences of symbols and model the possible differences between them, and *geometric methods*, which can cope with polyphonic scores and may exploit the properties of continuous distance measures (in particular the triangular inequality) to decrease computational complexity. Of these approaches, the first two are the ones mostly related to the methodology proposed in this paper.

3.1 Melodic Retrieval Based on Index Terms

An example of research work in this group has been presented in [11], where melodies were indexed through the use of N-grams. Experimental results on a collection of folk songs were presented, testing the effects of system parameters such as N-gram length, showing good results in terms of retrieval effectiveness, though the approach did not seem to be robust to decreases in query length. The N-gram approach has been extended in [9] in order to retrieve melodies in a polyphonic score, without prior extraction of the single melodies.

An alternative approach to N-grams has been presented in [32], where indexing was carried out by highlighting musically relevant sequences of notes, called musical phrases. Unlike the previous approaches, the length of indexes was not fixed but depended on the musical context. Phrases could undergo a number of different normalizations, from the complete information on pitch intervals and duration to the simple melodic profile. Segmentation approaches can also be based on recurrent melodic patterns, as proposed in [41] and further developed in [37]. In this latter case, patterns were computed using either only rhythm, or only pitch, or the combined information, and the final retrieval was carried out using a data fusion approach.

An extensive evaluation of segmentation techniques aimed at extracting index terms has been presented in [38]. Experimental results on a collection of about 2300 musical documents in Midi format showed that N-grams are still the best choice for index terms – 0.98 of average precision – and that recurrent patterns were almost comparable to them – 0.96 of average precision. Segmentation approaches based on a priori knowledge of music perception or structure proved to be more sensible to local mismatches between the query and the documents, giving an average precision of about 0.85 in both cases.

3.2 Melodic Retrieval Based on Sequence Matching

The typical application of these approaches is the retrieval of a precise musical work, given an approximate excerpt provided by the user. To this end, a representation of the query is compared with the representations of the documents in the collection each time a new query is submitted to the system. The main positive aspect of these approaches is that they are able to model the possible mismatches between the query and the documents to be retrieved. As is well known from the string processing domain, possible sources of mismatches are insertions and deletions of musical notes. The modification of a note can be considered either as a third source of mismatch or the combination of a deletion and an insertion.

Approximate string matching techniques have been applied to melodic retrieval. One of the first examples was described in [13], where the melodies were represented by three symbols – ascending or descending interval and same note – in order to cope with possible mismatches in pitch between the query and the documents. The work presented in [2] is based on the use of pattern discovery techniques, taken from computational biology, to search for the occurrences of a simplified description of the pitch contour of the query inside the collection of documents. Another approach, reported in [18], applies pattern matching techniques to documents and queries in GUIDO format, exploiting the advantages of this notation in structuring information. Approximate string matching has been used also by [17], adapting the technique to the kind of input provided by the user. The work presented in [20] reports a comparison of different approaches based on a variant of Dynamic Time Warping, with a discussion on computational complexity and scalability of four different techniques. Other examples of sequence matching can be found in [19, 44].

Alternatively to approximate string matching, statistical models have been applied to sequence matching. An application of Markov chains has been proposed in [5] to model a set of themes extracted from musical documents, while an extension to hidden Markov models has been presented in [43] as a tool to model possible errors in sung queries. A mixed methodology has been presented in [21], where the distance function used in a Dynamic Time Warping approach has been computed using a probabilistic model.

Sequence matching techniques are very efficient, with a computational cost for a single comparison that is $\mathbf{O}(m+n)$, where m is the length of the query and n is the size of the document. However, the application of sequence matching may require the sequence representing the query to be compared to all the documents in the collections. Thus the computational cost of a single retrieval is linear with the size of the collection. This clearly implies a low scalability of direct sequence matching. To overcome the problem, pruning techniques have been proposed in the literature. In particular, the approach described in [40] is based on the creation of a tree structure over the collection of documents depending on the melodic similarity between them: comparisons are carried out only along the path, from the root to a leaf, that gives the best sequence matches.

3.3 Melodic Retrieval Based on Geometric Methods

The matching of the query with documents can be computed in a geometric framework. This approach can cope with polyphonic music without requiring prior extraction of the main melody, because the complete score is represented as a set of points, or lines, on a plane: the vertical axis usually corresponds to pitch while the horizontal axis corresponds to time. The same representation applies to queries.

The geometric approach, which has been introduced in [7], is based on the application of a number of translations to the query pattern in order to find the best matches with the geometric representation of each document. Incomplete matches can also be found with a geometric approach, as described in [47] where scores were represented as points on a plane. An extension of the representation of documents is presented in [46], where a polyphonic score is represented as a set of lines on a plane, the position along the time axis and the length of the line are computed from time onset and note duration, respectively. A further improvement has been proposed in [28], where note duration is exploited to create a weight model that penalizes mismatches between long notes.

The computational cost of geometric approaches is $\mathbf{O}(mn \log n)$, where m is the size of the query and n is the size of the score. The increase in computational complexity is compensated by the fact that these approaches can cope with polyphonic scores. As for sequence matching approaches, a retrieval task may require a number of comparisons that is linear with the collection size, if a pruning or indexing technique is not applied.

To this end, an alternative approach for computing the similarity between a bidimensional representation of queries and documents was presented in [45]. The polyphonic scores are represented as weighted points on a plane, where the positions correspond to pitch and onset time of each note, while the weight is computed from note durations. The melodic similarity is computed through two alternative transportation distances, the Earth Mover's Distance and the Proportional Transportation Distance [14]. The Proportional Transportation Distance is a pseudo metric, for which the triangle inequality holds. This property has been exploited to improve retrieval efficiency, because the query is compared only to a reduced set of documents – called *vantage objects* – exploiting the triangular inequality to rule out all the documents that have a distance from the query higher than a given threshold.

4 A Probabilistic Approach to Music Indexing and Retrieval

The methodology presented in this section combines two of the approaches described in Sect. 3, by combining the idea of sequence matching with an indexing scheme. The work is based on two main considerations. On the one hand, indexing techniques are efficient and scalable, but do not take into account the presence of errors in the query, and thus their retrieval effectiveness decreases as the number of errors increases. On the other hand, sequence matching can direct model differences between queries and documents but is characterized by high computational costs, because the complexity is proportional to the collection size. Figure 2 shows an example of common query

Fig. 2: Common pitch errors in users' queries: **a**) original melody, **b**) pitch errors, **c**) tonality errors, **d**) insertion errors, **e**) deletion errors

errors on pitch, where tonality, insertion and deletion errors are also shown. There may also be errors in note durations, both locally – e.g. the user shortens a long note – and globally – e.g. the user sings faster than the original melody.

With the aim of partially overcoming the drawbacks of both techniques, a novel methodology is proposed for describing music documents with *contour models*, which generalize the concept of lexical units. In particular, contour models are computed from melodic N-grams, that is, on sequences of exactly N notes in the melody, and are used as index terms. Retrieval is then carried out by performing an approximate matching between the lexical units extracted from the query and the contour models computed from the collection. The approximate matching is based on an application of Weighted Transducers (WTs) as models for contours. Once the most probable contour models corresponding to a query are computed, retrieval is then carried out using standard techniques. The methodology can be summarized as follows.

At indexing time:

- all the J sequences of N notes in the collection are extracted and used to build WT models M_j, with $j \in J$;
- M_j are indexed using an inverted file, which links each M_j with the music documents it belongs to.

At retrieval time:

- the user's query is transcribed to a sequence of notes, from which all the subsequences Q_i of N notes are computed;
- the probability $p(i, j)$ that Q_i corresponds to model M_j is computed for all i and j;

- the distance between the query and the documents is computed using the Vector Space Model [1], with a variant of the $tf \cdot idf$ weighting scheme that takes into account the probability $p(i, j)$;
- the distance between the query and the documents is used to build a list of potentially relevant documents in descending order of similarity.

This methodology was implemented in a music retrieval prototype, which was tested on a collection of music documents and with a set of audio queries.

4.1 Description of the Model

The approach is based on the application of a probabilistic model [35] that is defined as follows.

Definition 1. A string-to-weight subsequential transducer, or weighted transducer, is an 8-tuple $T = (Q, i, F, \Sigma, \phi, \sigma, \lambda, \rho)$, where:

- Q is the set of N states, each one described by a vector,
- i is the initial state,
- $F \subseteq Q$ is the set of final states,
- Σ is the input alphabet,
- ϕ is the transition density functions mapping $Q \times \Sigma$ to $Q^\star$,
- σ is the output function mapping $Q \times \Sigma$ to $\mathbb{R}_+$,
- $\lambda \in \mathbb{R}_+$ is the initial weight,
- ρ is the final weight function mapping F to $\mathbb{R}_+$.

A string w is accepted by a transducer T if there exists $f \in F$ such that $\phi(i, w) = f$. The output associated with w is: $\lambda + \sigma(i, w) + \rho(f)$.

WTs are similar to Hidden Markov Models (HMMs) [3], with the important difference that the transition density function ϕ is time-varying, because it also depends on the input symbol at time t, and has to be recalculated for each symbol $x(t)$ of the input sequence. The output function σ plays a similar role of the emission probability function of HMMs, that is, the probability of observing a given symbol when in a given state, even if the observation probability is defined as a weight.

The three main problems of HMMs [42] – namely recognition of an unknown sequence, decoding of the most probable state sequence given an observation, and parameters training – can be solved for WTs too. In particular, the problem of recognizing an unknown sequence of observations can be solved by calculating the best weight obtained by a legal state sequence of a model given the input sequence X, and can be computed by equation

$$\sigma(i, f) = \max_{\forall s_k \in Q \,|\, s_1 = i, s_N = f} \sigma(S|X) \tag{1}$$

where S is the sequence of states $s_1, s_2, \ldots, s_N$ and s_k is its generic element.

The recognition of an unknown input sequence is carried out by computing the probability of the most probable path corresponding to the sequence of observations, using the iterative steps:

$$\pi_k(j) = \max_{[s_1 s_2 \ldots s_{k-1}] \subset Q^*} P[s_1 s_2 \ldots s_k = j | T, x_1 x_2 \ldots x_k], \; j \in Q \qquad (2)$$

$$\pi_{k+1}(j) = \left[\max_i \pi_k(i) \phi_{ij}(x_k) \right] \cdot \sigma_j(x_{k+1}), \; 1 \leq k \leq input\, size \qquad (3)$$

The iteration of these two steps over the input sequence X_1^K gives the best state path and the weight of the model conditioned by the input. The weight corresponds to the weight of the last state in the sequence.

4.2 Application of Weighted Transducers to Melody Representation

Once the model and the methods to perform a recognition task have been defined, they can be applied to model melodic contours for a music retrieval task, as described in this section.

The information used to describe a melody is bases on pitch and the duration of events (notes and rests) in the score and in the query. A preprocessing step transforms this initial information in the array [*duration, Δpitch*], where duration is represented in beats and Δpitch$(k) = pitch(k) - pitch(k-1)$, where $pitch(k)$ is the MIDI pitch of note k and hence Δpitch is the difference in semitones between two subsequent notes. Rests are represented with a conventional $\Delta pitch = -50$, which is a value very unlikely to be found in any score.

The input alphabet of the WT is composed by a vector Σ in which the measured duration and the measured Δpitch of the current note in the query are nested.

$$\Sigma = \begin{bmatrix} measured\ duration \\ measured\ \Delta pitch \end{bmatrix} \qquad (4)$$

The variables describing the states are based on the computation, from the score, of the *nominal duration* and *nominal Δpitch*, to which the *variance duration*, conventionally set to $\frac{1}{5}$ of the nominal duration, and *variance Δpitch*, conventionally set to 0.6 semitone, are added. The *variance* are the parameters of independent Gaussian probability distributions, which are centered in *duration* and *Δpitch*, respectively. Finally, a fifth parameter called *distance factor* is added, which is a number that gives a low probability to transitions towards events distant in the score. The distance factor is heuristically set by simply halving the probability each time an event is skipped by a transition.

A generic state Q is then described by the vector.

$$Q = \begin{pmatrix} nominal\ duration \\ nominal\ \Delta pitch \\ variance\ duration \\ variance\ \Delta pitch \\ distance\ factor \end{pmatrix} \qquad (5)$$

where every model state Q corresponds to one contour symbol, that is, to an event in the melody.

Regarding the state topology of the WT, in the proposed application the contour is modeled with only one initial and one final state, giving a trivial definition of functions ρ and λ. The model is automatically built by assigning a different state for each note in the contour, considering that the last note state is also the final state. A non-zero transition probability is assigned between states associated with subsequent notes, while other transitions are placed to admit hops of one or two notes in the original score. Figure 3 depicts a model for a sequence of four notes, where S_0 is the initial state, and states $S_1 \dots S_4$ correspond to the notes in the contour, with S_4 also the only final state.

From each melody in the collection, the system creates a set of reference models. Each model is representative of a contour subsequence of a fixed number of events. Events duration is always normalized to the length of the complete subsequence, to deal with different timings between the documents and the query. Local mismatches are taken into account by the modeling of durations with a Gaussian distribution centered on the nominal duration. The output function σ is given directly by Viterbi decoding, by computing the weights on the best state path. As a consequence, the transition state function ϕ subsumes all the relevant information on the model. As for HMM, ϕ can be given by its transition state matrix $\phi = \{\phi_{ij}(x)\}$, $i, j \in Q$.

The choice of the proposed modeling is motivated by the following characteristics:

- WTs are *stochastic* – it is not known a priori whether the input symbol is a correct note or an error and alternative transitions are taken into account;
- the models are *Markovian* with a *left-to-right* topology – psychological studies [10] showed that melodies are remembered by pitch intervals between successive notes;
- WTs are *time-varying* – the local similarity between the input sequence and the contour may change, depending on previous input, because errors in pitch or duration often affect pitch and duration of subsequent notes.

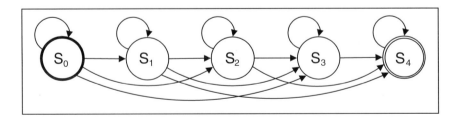

Fig. 3: Weighted Transducer that represents a four notes contour. Arrows are drawn when the transition probability is non zero

It should be noted that this modeling is adequate to manage all query errors shown in Figure 2. For instance, deletion errors of one or two notes are managed by transitions that jump some states in the longest path from i to f, and local errors in pitch and duration are directly modeled by the stochastic nature of the WT. Moreover, insertion errors find a correspondence in autotransitions. Tonality errors and time stretching errors are compensated by adoption of $\Delta pitchs$ and by time relativization on every single contour.

4.3 Computation of the Similarity between a Query and the Documents

Each document in the collection is described by its set of WT models, that are computed from its contours. This representation is the basis for the computation of the similarity between users' query and the documents in the collection.

For each query subsequence s, of the same length of the contours, the weight $v(s,m)$ corresponding to each model m is computed using the Viterbi algorithm described in Sect. 4.1. The output of this step was used to compute a measure of similarity between the query and the documents, using a variant of the $tf \cdot idf$ weighting scheme.

The standard $tf \cdot idf$ computation is based on equation 6 where $freq(m,d)$ is the frequency of model m in document d, N is the number of documents in the collection, n_m is the number of documents that contain contour m.

$$t_{m,d} = \frac{freq(m,d)}{\max_k freq(m,k)} \times \log \frac{N}{n_m} \qquad (6)$$

The $tf \cdot idf$ measure is based on an exact match between query and document terms, this way the value of $t_{m,d}$ can be computed in the same way both for documents and query terms. Given the approximate match due to WTs modeling, the information $v(s,m)$ about the similarity between query sequence and document models has to be added to the model. This is achieved by the following equation:

$$sim(q,d) = \frac{\sum_{s \in q, m \in d} v(s,m) \times occ_q(s) \times t_{m,d}}{\sqrt{\sum_{s \in q}(v(s,m) \times occ_q(s))^2}} \qquad (7)$$

where $occ_q(s)$ is the frequency of sequence s in query q. The denominator is used as a scaling factor to have similarities in the same range. This approach, in its classical version, considers all the models m that match a document term. However, it can be modified to speed up computation time, by considering only the first $Nmax$ models m, ordered by the value of $v(s,m)$.

5 Experiments

The approach was tested using a small collection of 2004 pop songs in MIDI format. The monophonic melody was extracted from each song and used to build the set of WT models. The choice of using monophonic representation depends on the fact that queries are usually monophonic melodies sung by users. In the experiments, contours with a fixed length, from three to seven notes, were used. According to the discussion in Sect. 2, this choice corresponds to using an N-gram approach on the melodic dimension, with different values of N, and considering as stopwords all the sequences with a different length. The choice of this range of N for testing the approach was motivated by the fact that shorter sequences – two or one notes – were considered too generic to be a good content descriptor, while longer sequences – more than seven notes – increased the computational complexity.

Small models are likely to overlap among documents and then the number of new models for each new document is likely to increase sublinearly. In order to reduce the number of models, two contours with the same pitch interval sequence and with durations that differ by of 3% at most were associated with the same model. Figure 4 shows the characteristics of the WT models set depending on the number of note events, one for each row. The first column represents the total number of models for each song, the second the number of new models for each song normalized by the number of models that represent that song, while the last column represents the increase in the number of different models versus the increase in the number of songs.

The most noteowrthing result is given by the last column graphs which shows that for three note models the WT models set size increases sublinearly because of the overlapping of models between documents. The model overlap decreases with the increasing of the model size, down to 1.15 for seven note models. Since this ratio depends on the song number, it is reasonable to assume that the overlap will increase with more complete song collections.

The relationship between the length of the contour and the number of overlapping models is summarized in Table 2.

The queries used in the experiments have been provided by the MAMI team [29], which worked on an experiment on query by singing [27]. In particular, a set of 31 queries were used, for which MAMI experts produced a manual pitch-tracking. The choice of manual transcriptions is due to the fact that the main interest of this work is to model the differences between the melodies in the documents and the melodies provided by the users, while the possible mismatches due to automatic transcriptions are not taken into account. The input of the WTs was extracted from contours of transcribed queries with the same approach described for document contours. Query contours were joined together when the length and the $\Delta pitch$ of each note did not differ over 10% and 0.3 semitones, respectively.

Five tests were carried out, one for each model size from 3 to 7 contour symbols. To this end, the collection was indexed by five WT model sets using

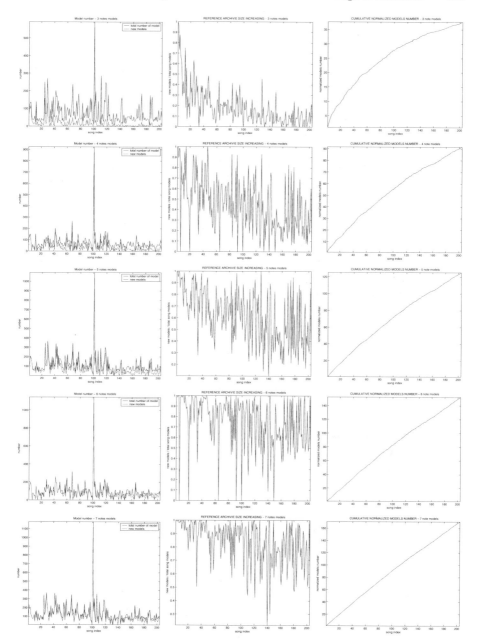

Fig. 4: Number of different models per document (left); number of new models for each new document (middle); number of different models versus number of documents (right) – rows correspond to the increase in the contour length, from 3 to 7 notes

Table 2: Characteristics of the index size depending on the length of the contours

N	models	overlap
3	3485	4.40%
4	7591	1.91%
5	15887	1.45%
6	15911	1.26%
7	23361	1.15%

all the 2004 different music documents, with one index for each model size. The retrieval procedure described in Sect. 4.3 was applied, with different values for $Nmax$. The best retrieval performances were obtained using $Nmax$ in the interval $[3, 5]$. In general a small $Nmax$ value gives a more selected result but reduce the recall.

Results are reported in Table 3, which shows encouraging results obtained with $Nmax = 3$. As expected, models with longer contours improve the average precision because they exploit more information about the melody. The three note model set has a low performance with only 14% average precision which denotes the inadequacy of short models. Increasing the model size, with only four symbol contours the retrieval system produces a substantial performance increase with seven right songs in the first position. The quality of results increase to 50% average presision with seven note models. An unexpected outcome is given by the six note model set, which produces a retrieval precision lower than the five note model set. It is clear that the recall level does not present a variation trend increasing the models size. The number of songs found in the first 50 positions is nearly constant.

These results can be compared with other approaches applied to test collections of similar size. For instance, a HMM-based indexer [43] retrieved the correct song with the highest rank 41.7% of times. In the same paper, a simple string matcher is used as a baseline, giving a value of 16.7% for the same experiment. The approaches based on Dynamic Time Warping [20] gave, in the best case, the relevant document retrieved at top rank 54.0% of times. The results with Markov models [5] showed that in 60.0% of cases the correct song

Table 3: Retrieval performances

N	= 1	≤ 3	≤ 10	≤ 50	precision
3	6.45%	12.90%	35.48%	58.06%	14.3%
4	22.58%	38.71%	51.61%	83.87%	35.0%
5	32.26%	38.71%	64.52%	83.87%	40.4%
6	29.03%	38.71%	54.84%	77.42%	37.4%
7	45.16%	48.39%	58.06%	80.65%	50.0%

was the nearest neighbor of the query. It should be noted that the approaches presented in the literature have a complexity that is linear with the number of documents, while the approach described in this chapter has a complexity that is linear with the number of contour models. All the approaches were tested with real audio queries, while higher precision and recall are expected when symbolic queries are used.

It can be interesting to compare these results with the ones obtained with the same query set, but with a larger test collection [38] using different segmentation techniques combined with a text retrieval approach. When N-grams were used to segment the melodies, the percentage of times the correct song was retrieved at top rank was only 12.6%. A small increase, up to 15.1%, could be obtained using melodic patterns instead of N-grams. This result may show that combining the segmentation with a probabilistic match may considerably improve retrieval effectiveness.

6 Conclusions

This chapter presents an overview of problems and characteristics of music retrieval, and presents a novel methodology based on approximate indexing of music documents. The basic idea is to merge the positive effects of document indexing in terms of efficiency and scalability, with the positive effects of approximate matching in terms of robustness to local mismatches. The methodology was tested on a test collection of music documents, using a set of transcribed audio queries, with encouraging results.

References

1. Baeza-Yates, R., Ribeiro-Neto, B. (eds.): Modern Information Retrieval. ACM Press, New York, NY (1999)
2. Bainbridge, D., Nevill-Manning, C., Witten, I., Smith, L., McNab, R.: Towards a digital library of popular music. In: Proceedings of the ACM Conference on Digital Libraries, pp. 161–169 (1999)
3. Bengio, Y.: Markovian models for sequential data. Neural Computer Surveys **2**, 129–162 (1999)
4. Berenzweig, A., Logan, B., Ellis, D., Whitman, B.: A large-scale evaluation of acoustic and subjective music-similarity measures. Computer Music Journal **28**(2), 63–76 (2004)
5. Birmingham, W., Dannenberg, R., Wakefield, G., Bartsch, M., Bykowski, D., Mazzoni, D., Meek, C., Mellody, M., Rand, W.: MUSART: Music retrieval via aural queries. In: Proceedings of the International Conference on Music Information Retrieval, pp. 73–82 (2001)
6. Cantate: Computer Access to Notation and Text in Music Libraries (July 2007). `http://projects.fnb.nl/cantate/`

7. Clausen, M., Engelbrecht, R., Meyer, D., Schmitz, J.: PROMS: A web-based tool for searching in polyphonic music. In: Proceedings of the International Symposium of Music Information Retrieval (2000)
8. Cope, D.: Pattern matching as an engine for the computer simulation of musical style. In: Proceedings of the International Computer Music Conference, pp. 288–291 (1990)
9. Doraisamy, S., Rüger, S.: A polyphonic music retrieval system using N-grams. In: Proceedings of the International Conference on Music Information Retrieval, pp. 204–209 (2004)
10. Dowling, W.: Scale and contour: Two components of a theory of memory for melodies. Psychological Review $85(4)$, 341–354 (1978)
11. Downie, S., Nelson, M.: Evaluation of a simple and effective music information retrieval method. In: Proceedings of the ACM International Conference on Research and Development in Information Retrieval (SIGIR), pp. 73–80 (2000)
12. Dunn, J., Mayer, C.: VARIATIONS: A Digital Music Library System at Indiana University. In: Proceedings of ACM Conference on Digital Libraries, pp. 12–19 (1999)
13. Ghias, A., Logan, J., Chamberlin, D., Smith, B.: Query by humming: Musical information retrieval in an audio database. In: Proceedings of the ACM Conference on Digital Libraries, pp. 231–236 (1995)
14. Giannopoulos, P., Veltkamp, R.: A pseudo-metric for weighted point sets. In: Proceedings of the European Conference on Computer Vision, pp. 715–730 (2002)
15. Gómez, E., Herrera, P.: Estimating the tonality of polyphonic audio files: Cognitive versus machine learning modelling strategies. In: Proceedings of the International Conference on Music Information Retrieval, pp. 92–95 (2004)
16. Harte, C., Sandler, M., Abdallah, S., Gómez, E.: Symbolic representation of musical chords: a proposed syntax for text annotations. In: Proceedings of the International Conference on Music Information Retrieval, pp. 66–71 (2005)
17. Haus, G., Pollastri, E.: A multimodal framework for music inputs. In: Proceedings of the ACM Multimedia Conference, pp. 282–284 (2000)
18. Hoos, H., Renz, K., Görg, M.: GUIDO/MIR – an experimental musical information retrieval system based on GUIDO music notation. In: Proceedings of the International Symposium on Music Information Retrieval, pp. 41–50 (2001)
19. Hsu, J.L., Liu, C., Chen, A.: Efficient repeating pattern finding in music databases. In: Proceeding of the International Conference on Information and Knowledge Management, pp. 281–288 (1998)
20. Hu, N., Dannenberg, R.: A comparison of melodic database retrieval techniques using sung queries. In: Proceedings of the ACM/IEEE Joint Conference on Digital Libraries, pp. 301–307 (2002)
21. Hu, N., Dannenberg, R., Lewis, A.: A probabilistic model of melodic similarity. In: Proceedings of the International Computer Music Conference, pp. 509–515 (2002)
22. Huron, D.: The Humdrum Toolkit: Reference Manual. Center for Computer Assisted Research in the Humanities, Menlo Park, CA (1995)
23. Jones, K.S., Willett, P.: Readings in Information Retrieval. Morgan Kaufmann, San Francisco, CA (1997)
24. Krumhansl, C.: Why is musical timbre so hard to understand? In: S. Nielsen, O. Olsson (eds.) Structure and Perception Electroacoustic Sound and Music, pp. 45–53. Elsevier, Amsterdam, NL (1989)

25. Lee, J., Downie, J.: Survey of music information needs, uses, and seeking behaviours: Preliminary findings. In: Proceedings of the International Conference on Music Information Retrieval, pp. 441–446 (2004)
26. Lesaffre, M., Leman, M., Tanghe, K., Baets, B.D., Meyer, H.D., Martens, J.P.: User-dependent taxonomy of musical features as a conceptual framework for musical audio-mining technology. In: Proceedings of the Stockholm Music Acoustics Conference, pp. 635–638 (2003)
27. Lesaffre, M., Tanghe, K., Martens, G., Moelants, D., Leman, M., Baets, B.D., Meyer, H.D., Martens, J.P.: The MAMI query-by-voice experiment: Collecting and annotating vocal queries for music information retrieval. In: Proceedings of the International Conference on Music Information Retrieval, pp. 65–71 (2003)
28. Lubiw, A., Tanur, L.: Pattern matching in polyphonic music as a weighted geometric translation problem. In: Proceedings of the International Conference of Music Information Retrieval, pp. 289–296 (2004)
29. MAMI: Musical Audio Mining – "query by humming" (July 2007). http://www.ipem.ugent.be/MAMI/
30. McLane, A.: Music as information. In: M. Williams (ed.) Arist, Vol. 31, chap. 6, pp. 225–262. American Society for Information Science (1996)
31. Meek, C., Birmingham, W.: Automatic thematic extractor. Journal of Intelligent Information Systems 21(1), 9–33 (2003)
32. Melucci, M., Orio, N.: Musical information retrieval using melodic surface. In: Proceedings of the ACM Conference on Digital Libraries, pp. 152–160 (1999)
33. Melucci, M., Orio, N.: A comparison of manual and automatic melody segmentation. In: Proceedings of International Conference on Music Information Retrieval, pp. 7–14 (2002)
34. Middleton, R.: Studying Popular Music. Open University Press, Philadelphia, PA (2002)
35. Mohri, M.: Finite-state transducers in language and speech processing. Computational Linguistics 23(2), 269–311 (1997)
36. Musica: The International Database of Choral Repertoire (July 2007). http://www.musicanet.org/
37. Neve, G., Orio, N.: Indexing and retrieval of music documents through pattern analysis and data fusion techniques. In: Proceedings of the International Conference on Music Information Retrieval, pp. 216–223 (2004)
38. Orio, N., Neve, G.: Experiments on segmentation techniques for music documents indexing. In: Proceedings of the International Conference on Music Information Retrieval, pp. 104–107 (2005)
39. Owen, G.: Using connectionist models to explore complex musical patterns. Computer Music Journal 13(3), 67–75 (1989)
40. Parker, C.: A tree-based method for fast melodic retrieval. In: Proceedings of the ACM/IEEE Joint Conference on Digital Libraries, pp. 254–255 (2004)
41. Pienimäki, A.: Indexing music database using automatic extraction of frequent phrases. In: Proceedings of the International Conference on Music Information Retrieval, pp. 25–30 (2002)
42. Rabiner, L.: A tutorial on hidden Markov models and selected applications. Proceedings of the IEEE 77(2), 257–286 (1989)
43. Shifrin, J., Pardo, B., Meek, C., Birmingham, W.: HMM-based musical query retrieval. In: Proceedings of the ACM/IEEE Joint Conference on Digital Libraries, pp. 295–300 (2002)

44. Tseng, Y.: Content-based retrieval for music collections. In: Proceedings of the ACM International Conference on Research and Development in Information Retrieval (SIGIR), pp. 176–182 (1999)
45. Typke, R., Veltkamp, R., Wiering, F.: Searching notated polyphonic music using transportation distances. In: Proceedings of the ACM International Conference on Multimedia, pp. 128–135 (2004)
46. Ukkonen, E., Lemström, K., Mäkinen, V.: Geometric algorithms for transposition invariant content-based music retrieval. In: Proceedings of the International Conference of Music Information Retrieval, pp. 193–199 (2003)
47. Wiggins, G., Lemström, K., Meredith, D.: SIA(M)ESE: An algorithm for transposition invariant, polyphonic content-based music retrieval. In: Proceedings of the International Conference of Music Information Retrieval, pp. 283–284 (2002)

A Statistical and Graphical Methodology for Comparing Bilingual to Monolingual Cross-Language Information Retrieval

Franco Crivellari, Giorgio Maria Di Nunzio, and Nicola Ferro

Department of Information Engineering – University of Padua
Via Gradenigo, 6/b – 35131 Padua – Italy
{crive, dinunzio, ferro}@dei.unipd.it

Abstract. A new methodology for the evaluation of *MultiLingual Information Access (MLIA)* systems is proposed. This two-fold methodology exploits both statistical analyses and graphical tools in order to provide MLIA researchers guidelines, hints, and directions to drive the design and development of the next generation systems, and to provide a means to interpret and compare experimental results and to present these results to other research communities. An example of the application of this methodology is applied in the real-case study of the monolingual and bilingual tasks of the CLEF 2005 and 2006.

Key words: multilingual information access, experimental evaluation

1 Introduction

The growing interest in *MultiLingual Information Access (MLIA)* is witnessed by the international activities which promote the access, use, and search of digital contents available in multiple languages and in a distributed setting, that is, digital contents held in different places by different organisations. As an example, in the 7th European Community Framework Programme, the i2010 Digital Library Initiative clearly states that the improvement of multilingual and multicultural information access and search is one of the key objectives necessary to *provide access to quality digital content for all* [7, 8]. In addition, the workshop on "New Directions in Multilingual Information Access"[1] has pointed out the need for a stronger knowledge and technology transfer between the MLIA research community and other interested research communities, such as the the digital library community [12].

In this context, the experimental evaluation carried out on MLIA systems takes on a twofold meaning: on the one hand, it should provide guidelines,

---

[1] http://ucdata.berkeley.edu/sigir2006-mlia.htm

hints, and directions to drive the design and development of the next generation MLIA systems; on the other hand, the experimental results should be easily communicated to other research communities and effective tools for interpreting and comparing the experimental result should be made available to those research communities.

In recent years, the evaluation of MLIA systems has been carried out in important international evaluation forums which bring research groups together, provide them with the means for measuring the performances of their systems, and discuss and compare their work. In particular, the *Cross-Language Evaluation Forum (CLEF)*[2] aims at evaluating MLIA systems which operate on European languages in both monolingual and cross-lingual contexts.

We focus our attention on the study of cross-lingual *Information Retrieval System (IRS)* and on a deep analysis of performance comparison between systems which perform monolingual tasks, i.e. querying and finding documents in one language, with respect to those which perform bilingual tasks, i.e. querying in one language and finding documents in another language. Indeed, a common method used to evaluate performances for bilingual retrieval evaluation is to compare results against monolingual baselines. Different performance figures can be adopted to this aim: the *Mean Average Precision (MAP)* is often used as a summary indicator; for example, the recent literature reports figures where the MAP of a bilingual IRS is around 80% of the MAP of a monolingual IRS for the main European languages [5, 6, 9, 14].

The work presented in this paper aims at improving on this way of comparing bilingual and monolingual retrieval and strives to provide better methods and tools for assessing the performances. Another aspect of this work is that it can help the organizers of an evaluation forum during the topic generation process; in particular, the study of the hardness of a topic can be carried out with the goal of refining those topics which have been misinterpreted by systems. Currently, the research challenges described above pose two problems:

1. more sophisticated analysis techniques are needed to assess the performances of MLIA systems in order to effectively support the research for the next generation MLIA systems;
2. since other research communities are involved, we need effective methods and tools for communicating with other communities and to give them the means for easily assessing MLIA systems.

In this context, we propose a twofold methodology which exploits both thorough statistical analyses and graphical tools: the former will provide MLIA researchers with quantitative and more sophisticated analysis techniques, the latter will allow for a more qualitative comparison and an easier presentation of the results. We provide concrete examples about how the proposed methodology can be applied by studying the monolingual and bilingual tasks of the CLEF 2005 and 2006 campaigns. Note that these application

---

[2] http://www.clef-campaign.org/

examples also serve the purpose of validating the proposed methodology in a real setting.

The paper is organized as follows: Sect. 2 introduces the proposed methodology; Sect. 3 describes the experimental setting used for applying the proposed methodology; Sect. 4 provides the application examples and reports the experimental results; finally, Sect. 5 draws some conclusions and provides an outlook for future work.

2 Cross-Lingual Comparison Methodology

The criteria normally adopted to create an experimental collection, consisting of suitable documents, sample topics and relevance judgements, have been adapted to satisfy the particular requirements of the multilingual context, where all language dependent tasks such as topic creation and relevance judgment are performed in a distributed setting by native speakers. In particular, the same set of topics is usually used to query all collections, whatever the task. When a monolingual task is performed, a given set of topics in the same language of the document collection is used (i.e., if a monolingual Portuguese task is performed, a collection of Portuguese documents is used as well as a set of topics in Portuguese); when a bilingual task is performed, the same document collection is used and the topics are the translation of the monolingual ones (i.e., if a bilingual Portuguese task is performed, a collection of Portuguese documents is used and a set of topics in a different language is used) [5, 6].

We exploit this way of constructing the experimental collections to go beyond the simple comparison of the MAP of a bilingual IRS with respect to a monolingual baseline given the same target language (for example, monolingual Portuguese vs. bilingual Portuguese). Indeed, we can perform an analysis on the results obtained on the single topics by monolingual and bilingual systems, because the different topics represent (in various languages) the same information needs, each bilingual topic is the direct translation of the corresponding monolingual one, and the same target test collections are used.

In particular, we propose a comparison methodology consisting of two complementary techniques which are both based on a comparison of results on single topics:

- a deep statistical analysis of both the monolingual and the bilingual tasks, described in Sect. 2.1. This kind of analysis allows us to address the problem of point 1 noted in the previous section;
- a graphical comparison of both the monolingual and the bilingual tasks, described in Sect. 2.2. This kind of comparison allows us to address the problem of point 2 noted in the previous section.

In order to present this methodology, we need to clearly define a measure that has not been used in literature. Given a task, for example monolingual Portuguese, we build a matrix $n \times m$ of n experiments and m topics, and define the following:

	t_1	t_2	$\ldots$	t_m	MAP_e
e_1	AP_{e_1,t_1}	AP_{e_1,t_2}	$\ldots$	AP_{e_1,t_m}	MAP_{e_1}
e_2	AP_{e_2,t_1}	AP_{e_2,t_2}	$\ldots$	AP_{e_2,t_m}	MAP_{e_2}
$\ldots$	$\ldots$	$\ldots$	$\ldots$	$\ldots$	$\ldots$
e_n	AP_{e_n,t_1}	AP_{e_n,t_2}	$\ldots$	AP_{e_n,t_m}	MAP_{e_n}
MAP_t	MAP_{t_1}	MAP_{t_2}	$\ldots$	MAP_{t_m}	

where AP_{e_n,t_m} is the *Average Precision* for the m-th topic of the n-th experiment of the task; MAP_e is the mean of the average precision as known in the literature, that is to say the mean of the average precisions of an experiment across all the topics; MAP_t is the new measure that we introduce which is the mean of the average precisions for a topic across all the experiments of a task. This measure is important since for each topic it gives an indication of the average difficulty of a topic. With this measure, it is possible to compare the average performance between a monolingual task and the corresponding bilingual task (i.e. monolingual Portuguese and bilingual Portuguese) on a particular topic and study whether the translation process brought improvements in the retrieval. However, it is important to stress that the mean is a measure highly influenced by out of range values (or outliers) which, in this case, correspond to average precisions with very high or very low values; for this reason, the value of other statistics, for example the median, can be used together with the mean. The analysis of the difference between the values of the mean and the median can help to spot such cases which are worth a deeper study.

2.1 Statistical Analysis Methodology

As pointed out by [10], a statistical methodology for judging whether measured differences between retrieval methods can be considered statistically significant is needed and, in line with this, CLEF usually performs statistical tests on the collected experiments [1, 5, 6] to assess their performances. On the other hand, these statistical tests are usually aimed at investigating the differences among the experiments within the same task, e.g. the monolingual Portuguese experiments alone or the bilingual Portuguese experiments alone, but they do not perform any kind of cross-task analysis, i.e. some kind of direct comparison between monolingual and bilingual tasks.

Given the average performance for each single topic of the monolingual and bilingual task, we want to study the distribution of these performances and employ different statistical tests to verify the following conditions:

1. the distributions of the performances are normal. This is the first condition to perform the following analyses;
2. the variances of the two distribution are similar. This suggests that even though the passing from one language to another causes a decrease in the performances, nevertheless the effect of the translation does not increase the dispersion of performances, which would add more uncertainty;

3. the mean of the two distributions are different and, in particular, the mean of the monolingual distribution is greater than the mean of the bilingual one. This suggests some loss of performances due to the effect of the translations from one language to another.

Note that we do not aim to demonstrate whether all these conditions simultaneously hold or not. Rather, we want to develop an analysis methodology which allows researchers to gain better insights into these conditions. In fact, the general claim that "the best bilingual MAP_e is around 80% of the best monolingual MAP_e" suggests the idea that monolingual and bilingual systems behave roughly the same but there is some loss in the performances due to the translations. However, we believe that researchers need better tools to face the new challenges in the MLIA field and thus the general claim requires a deeper investigation. Indeed, the above described methodology allows us to have a more precise answer to the questions posed above; in fact, we can assess whether two distributions have comparable shapes, whether they have comparable dispersions, and finally whether they have comparable average measures.

Operatively, we use values of MAP_t calculated from the matrix $n \times m$ of average precisions for a monolingual task and the corresponding bilingual task given the same target language, and we study the conditions stated above on the two distributions, that we name $MAP_{t,mono}$ and $MAP_{t,bili}$.

In order to verify the first condition, we can adopt a normal probability plot, which allows us to compare the distribution of the monolingual experiments and the distribution of the bilingual experiments with respect to a normal distribution. In a normal probability plot, the quantiles of the distribution are increasingly ordered and compared to the quantiles of a normal distribution; if the samples do come from the same distribution, the plot will be linear. The last two conditions, same variance and same mean, are analyzed and studied by means of statistical tests for the equality of two variances and for the equality of two means; the tests that are used in the paper (the F-test and the t-test, respectively) assume that collected data are normally distributed. Therefore, before proceeding, we need verify the normality of the involved distributions by using graphical tools for inspection (i.e. the boxplot, or the normality plot) or normality tests (i.e. the Lilliefors test [2], or the Jarque-Bera test [11]). However, if the normality assumption is violated, a transformation of the data should be performed. The transformation for proportion measures that range from 0 to 1 is the arcsin-root transformation which Tague-Sutcliffe [13] recommends for use with precision/recall measures.

After the check on the normality of data, a test for the equality of variances, the F-test, is carried out to check whether the distributions have the same variance or not, and this step allows us to verify the second condition. Finally, in order to assess whether the mean of the monolingual performances is greater than the bilingual one, a t-test is used. In particular, since we have two paired sets (monolingual and bilingual) of m measured values, where m is the number

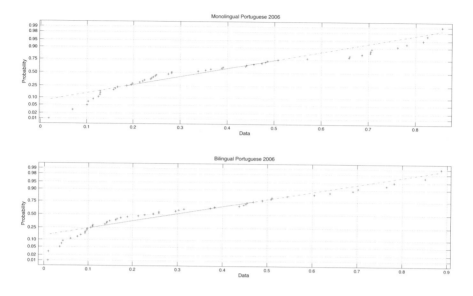

Fig. 1: Normal probability plot for monolingual and bilingual Portuguese 2006

of topics, the paired t-test is used to determine whether they differ from each other in a significant way under the assumptions that the paired differences are independent and identically normally distributed. This step allows us to verify the third condition reported above.

2.2 Graphical Comparison Methodology

In addition to the statistical analyses described in the previous section, we introduce simple and effective graphical tools which allow us to easily compare the performances for each topic of the monolingual and bilingual tasks and to gain a visual explanation of the behavior of the two distributions.

Before introducing specific plots for a topic by topic analysis, we can use standard statistical plots to help understand the type of distributions under consideration. In particular, an example of this a normal probability plot is shown in Fig. 1 for Portuguese monolingual and bilingual tasks. It can be seen that there is almost a perfect match with the straight line that represents the ideal line which indicates the same distribution. In order to understand if the deviation from the straight line is significant or not, statistical tests can be used to verify normality, as suggested in Sect. 2.1.

When a comparison between monolingual and bilingual results is required, a retrieval effectiveness measure to be used as a performance indicator has to first be selected; in our case, we used the average precision. Then, we compute descriptive statistics for the selected measure for each topic; in our studies we used the mean, which is useful when the distributions do not have many outliers, and the median, which is more robust in the case of outliers. We already defined the MAP_t as the mean of average precisions per topic, and the median of average precision per topic will also be useful, here named MEAP_t.

We want to study the performances of specific topics and present data and results with different plots with different goals in mind: on the one hand, we want to give specific hints to the participants about how difficult a topic is, and receive feedback from them in particular for those topics where there is a *visible* difference between the MAP_t and the MEAP_t; on the other hand, we want to study the general results given a monolingual task and bilingual on a particular language and compare the differences, with the aim of analyzing what the most difficult topics in general are (hard topics in monolingual) and the most difficult ones to translate are (hard topics in bilingual, with a significant difference with the respective monolingual result). This graphical analysis should not only help participants in building their Information Retrieval System, but also the organizers of evaluation forums in analyzing deeply what went wrong during the topic creation phase so they can improve the quality of the queries the following year, that is to say by analyzing whether the difficulty of a topic was due to too narrow topics, misspelling errors, or misinterpreted topics.

In a topic by topic analysis, the natural ordering of topics (i.e. the identifier of the topic) can be used to represent the graphs. However, for visualization aspects, it is more convenient to order topics by one of the computed descriptive statistic. Since we are performing a topic-by-topic comparison and we want to compare a monolingual topic with the corresponding bilingual one, topics are ordered according to monolingual results first, and the bilingual topics according to the same order of topics of the monolingual task. Note that ordering of the bilingual topics is usually different from what we would obtain if we increasingly ordered the bilingual topics by the computed descriptive statistic.

Topic by Topic Analysis, Monolingual and Bilingual Separately

Figure 2 summarizes the results for monolingual and bilingual Portuguese 2006; topics are ordered according to the MAP_t, the upper part shows the performances for the monolingual while the bottom part the bilingual ones. For each topic, the average precision of an experiment is plotted with a star; a square represent the MAP_t and a triangle the MEAP_t. At a glance, we can see for each task the average performance of each topic, and if the distance between the square and the triangle is evident we can immediately draw the following conclusions: if the square is above the triangle, it means that the MAP_t was highly influenced by some experiments that performed much better than at least half of the remaining experiments; in the other case, the MAP_t was highly influenced by experiments that performed much worse than at least half of the remaining experiments. Both situations are worth a deeper

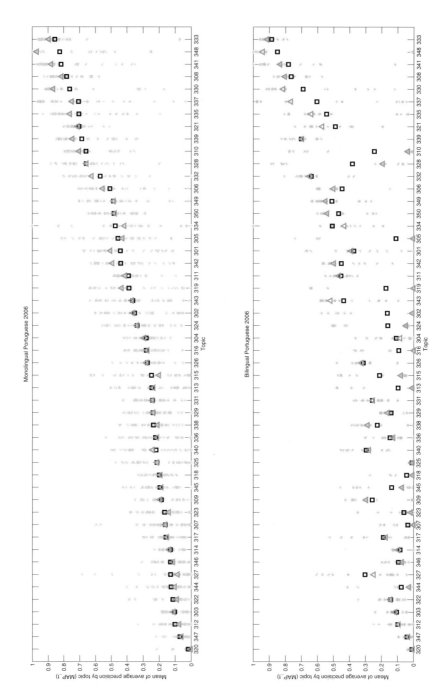

Fig. 2: Example of monolingual vs bilingual Portuguese 2006 comparison plot

study: in the former case, we would be interested in asking the participant who produced the experiment with that performance to study what are the causes of this success (i.e. feedback, query expansion, dictionary, etc.); in the latter case, we would be interested to ask that participant to perform a deeper failure analysis.

With Fig. 2 it is also possible to compare the results of monolingual with bilingual. If we pick a topic in the monolingual part and follow a vertical line, we can read the corresponding performance for the bilingual. For example, topic 327 (left part of the plot) has a MAP_t around 0.1 for monolingual and about 0.3 for the bilingual; this is a case where the process of translation produced a better result. For topic 316 (in the middle), the MAP_t of the monolingual is around 0.3 while the bilingual is about 0.1; this case is interesting for another reason, the $MEAP_t$ of the bilingual is equal to 0.0, which means that at least half of the experiments did not retrieve any relevant document for that topic. However, some experiments did very well (around 0.4), and these are the kinds of experiments that are worth a deeper analysis.

Topic by Topic Analysis, Monolingual and Bilingual Together

Figure 3 shows, for each topic and ordered by monolingual MAP_t, the monolingual MAP_t performances on the x-axis (red circle) plotted against the corresponding bilingual MAP_t performances on the y-axis (blue diamond); a line that highlights the differences between the two values is also shown. If monolingual and bilingual behaved in a similar way, the points would intersect each other and no line would be visible. This representation allows us to directly inspect the differences of the performances in a topic-by-topic fashion and provides us with hints about which topics require a deeper investigation because, for example, performances are too low or differences in the performances are too great. Moreover, this plot also allows us to qualitatively assess the three conditions reported in the previous section: in that case, the bilingual points would have a trend roughly similar to the monolingual ones and they would be below the monolingual ones.

A deeper investigation on performances can be done after a study of Fig. 3: one is about the study of difficult topics; since the left part of this figure shows the topics where the monolingual experiments perform worse, it would be important to study these topics, for example the first quartile of this distribution (topics with lowest MAP_t), and review them together with participants to see if any technological barrier avoided a better performance and with organizers to check and review the topics again to spot any flaws. Both are important because participants would be advised where to improve their systems, and organizers would be advised how to improve the evaluation forum the year after with higher quality topics. Another possible study is to order topics according to the difference in performance between monolingual and bilingual, take the first quartile of this distribution (topics where the difference is negatively higher, or where the line on the plot is longer) and make a deep failure

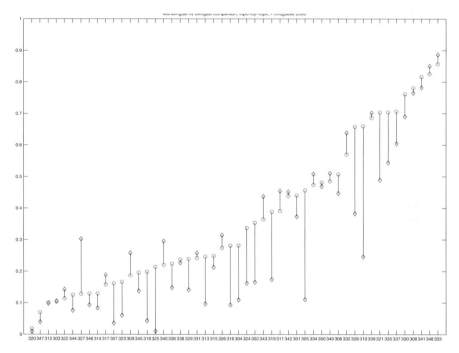

Fig. 3: Example of monolingual vs bilingual Portuguese 2006 comparison plot

analysis in order to understand why the process of translation for this set of topics introduced such a deterioration on the topic.

Monolingual and Bilingual Fitting

We can also use the plot in Fig. 3 as a starting point for a further analysis by interpolating the two series of points in order to compare their trend. In this way, not only do we strengthen the visualization of the behavior of the two distributions and improve their qualitative analysis, but we also bridge the gap between qualitative and quantitative analysis because interpolation techniques provide us with many quantitative indicators about how well an interpolation fits the data.

Figure 4 shows an example of linear fit where, for each topic and ordered by monolingual MAP_t, the monolingual MAP_t performances on the x-axis (red circle) is plotted against the corresponding bilingual MAP_t performances on the y-axis (blue diamond); the least squares fitting lines are drawn for the two tasks, solid for monolingual and dashed for bilingual. If the three conditions introduced in the previous section hold, the two straight lines would have roughly the same slope and the bilingual line would be right shifted with respect to the monolingual one. Two situations are worth a deeper study: the

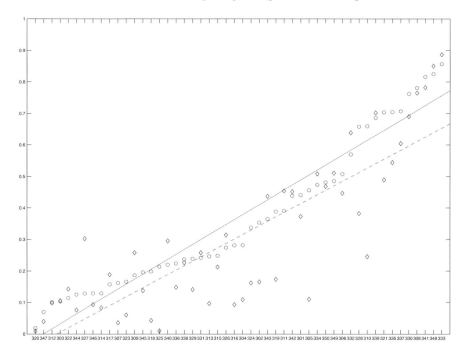

Fig. 4: Example of linear fit of the monolingual and bilingual distribution Portuguese 2006

distance between the two lines and whether the two lines intersect. In the first case, the greater the distance, the greater the difference in performance on average between the monolingual and the bilingual tasks. Figure 4 clearly shows that the monolingual performance is higher with respect to the bilingual one. An example of the second case is shown in Fig. 5 for French 2006; this is a situation where for the most difficult topics (considering monolingual performances) the bilingual task performs better on average, and viceversa for the other topics.

3 Experimental Setting

The experimental collections and experiments used are fully described in [5,6] while in [3,4] the detailed experimental results are reported.

In the CLEF 2005 and 2006 campaigns the languages of the target collection used for the monolingual and bilingual tasks were the same: Bulgarian, English, French, Hungarian, and Portuguese. Since for the bilingual task an experiment may use as the source language one of a set of possible choices (for example, English to French, or German to Portuguese) the performance of a

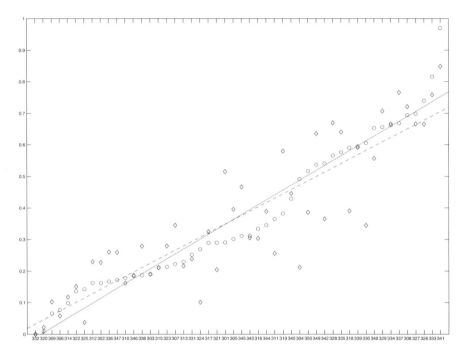

Fig. 5: Example of linear fit of the monolingual and bilingual distribution French 2006

bilingual task can be biased by languages that are particularly difficult, although interesting to study for *Information Retrieval (IR)* research goals (for example, languages such Hindi, Indonesian, or Amharic). In order to make the comparison between monolingual and bilingual performances as flawless as possible we decided to take only those experiments of a bilingual task that have English as the source language. Moreover, since we needed a sufficient number of experiments for each task to have reliable statistical analyses, we selected the tasks with the most experiments, as reported in Table 1. Remember that each one of these tasks has 50 topics.

Table 1: Number of experiments per tasks

Track	# Runs	
	CLEF 2005	CLEF 2006
Monolingual French	38	27
Monolingual Portuguese	32	37
Bilingual English to French	12	8
Bilingual English to Portuguese	19	18

For each task, we built a matrix $n \times m$ of n experiments and m topics:

$$
\begin{array}{c|cccc}
 & t_1 & t_2 & \cdots & t_m \\
\hline
e_1 & AP_{e_1,t_1} & AP_{e_1,t_2} & \cdots & AP_{e_1,t_m} \\
e_2 & AP_{e_n,t_1} & AP_{e_n,t_2} & \cdots & AP_{e_n,t_m} \\
\cdots & \cdots & \cdots & \cdots & \cdots \\
e_n & AP_{e_n,t_1} & AP_{e_n,t_2} & \cdots & AP_{e_n,t_m}
\end{array}
$$

where at position (i,j), with $1 \leq i \leq n$ and $1 \leq j \leq m$, we have the average precision (AP) of experiment e_1 on topic t_j.

Then, we took the mean of the transformed performances by columns, that is, we took the average performances for each topic. As a result we had a vector for each task, like:

$$
v_{task}^T = [MAP_{t_1} \; MAP_{t_2} \; \cdots \; MAP_{t_m}] \, ,
$$

where MAP_{t_1} is the mean calculated for the first column, that is, the first topic of the task.

The aim of the experimental analysis is to study the distribution of the mean of both the monolingual and bilingual tasks and compare them.

4 Application Example and Experimental Results

The results presented are divided into years (2005 and 2006) and language (French and Portuguese). First the result of the normality test is presented, then the results of the analysis of variance are shown, and finally the analysis of the mean is discussed.

Each calculation was carried out using MATLAB (version 7.2 R2006a) and MATLAB Statistics Toolbox (version 5.2 R2006a).

4.1 Statistical Analysis Methodology

Since the data proved normal after a normality test, no arcsin-root transformation was adopted. In all the analyses, an alpha level of 5% was used.

CLEF 2005

The first analysis examines the variances of the data of the monolingual and the bilingual tasks. In Table 2, the results for the monolingual French versus bilingual French and the monolingual Portuguese vs bilingual Portuguese are presented. All the hypotheses are shown, starting from the most important one: the variances of the monolingual, σ_{mono}^2, and the bilingual, σ_{bili}^2, are equal. The other two hypotheses are important because the outcome shows that it is better not to reject them instead of accepting the alternative hypothesis which is, in those cases, σ_{mono}^2 is either greater or less than σ_{bili}^2.

Table 2: Variance tests (F-tests) on CLEF 2005 data

		$H_0 : \sigma^2_{mono} = \sigma^2_{bili}$	$H_0 : \sigma^2_{mono} <= \sigma^2_{bili}$	$H_0 : \sigma^2_{mono} => \sigma^2_{bili}$
French	p–value	0.8281	0.5859	0.4141
	outcome	not reject	not reject	not reject
Portuguese	p–value	0.9661	0.4831	0.5169
	outcome	not reject	not reject	not reject

The second analysis considers the means of the monolingual, μ_{mono}, and bilingual, μ_{bili}, performances. Even though the hypothesis stated in Sect. 2.1, that is, the mean of the monolingual performances are better than the bilingual ones, is the main one, we believe it is important to consider all the aspects of the analysis. For this reason, we have presented the results for all the hypotheses in Table 3. It is interesting to see the differences between the French tests that result all in favor of the null hypothesis, that is to say it is preferable never to accept the alternative hypotheses that μ_{mono} is either greater or less than μ_{bili}. On the other hand, the analysis of Portuguese tasks shows that with the combination of all the hypotheses there is strong evidence that the mean of the performance of the monolingual Portuguese is greater than the bilingual one.

CLEF 2006

The analyses of the variances of the data of the monolingual and the bilingual tasks are shown in Table 4 for both the monolingual French vs bilingual French and the monolingual Portuguese vs bilingual Portuguese. All the tests confirm the hypothesis that the variances of the monolingual and bilingual tasks are equal.

The two-samples paired t-test on the mean of the performances, shown in Table 5, confirms the outcome of the CLEF 2005: the tests on the French tasks are all in favor of the null hypothesis, that is to say the means are equal; the tests on the Portuguese tasks confirm that there is strong evidence that the mean of the performance of the monolingual Portuguese is greater than the bilingual one.

Table 3: Two-samples Paired t-test on CLEF 2005 data

		$H_0 : \mu_{mono} = \mu_{bili}$	$H_0 : \mu_{mono} <= \mu_{bili}$	$H_0 : \mu_{mono} => \mu_{bili}$
French	p–value	0.8532	0.4266	0.5734
	outcome	not reject	not reject	not reject
Portuguese	p–value	0.0000	0.0000	1.0000
	outcome	**reject**	**reject**	not reject

Table 4: Variance tests (F-tests) on CLEF 2006 data

		$H_0 : \sigma^2_{mono} = \sigma^2_{bili}$	$H_0 : \sigma^2_{mono} <= \sigma^2_{bili}$	$H_0 : \sigma^2_{mono} => \sigma^2_{bili}$
French	p–value	0.8019	0.4009	0.5991
	outcome	not reject	not reject	not reject
Portuguese	p–value	0.4270	0.7865	0.2135
	outcome	not reject	not reject	not reject

4.2 Graphical Comparison Methodology

In addition to the statistical analyses, we also present an effective graphical tool that gives a visual explanation of the behavior of the distributions of the monolingual and bilingual performances. Figures and plots were already shown in Sect. 2.2 and we cannot report the complete set of plots here for space reasons. On the other hand, we want to comment on those plots in the light of the statistical analyses carried out in the previous section.

First, testing whether two distributions have similar shape and testing the normality of data can be done by means of standard tools such as the quantile-quantile plot and the normal probability plot. Quantile-quantile plots show that any monolingual-bilingual pair, both for French and Portuguese, has a regular linear trend, that is to say the shapes of the distributions are similar. The normal probability plot also shows the same regularity, which is sometimes violated along the tails of the distributions.

Figure 2 focuses on the difference in performance of the single topic for Portuguese 2006 tasks; a line that connects two points highlights the difference between the monolingual and bilingual performances. This plot shows at a glance an immediate snapshot of what the hardest topics are.

In addition, Fig. 4 and Fig. 5 show a further analysis of the same data by interpolating the two series of points in order to extrapolate and compare their trend. In Fig. 5, a linear interpolation of the French 2006 tasks is performed. The two lines are very close and cross themselves; this figure clearly shows that even the linear interpolation of the monolingual and bilingual French data gives a positive response to the question that, in this case, the monolingual and bilingual performances are equal. Notice that we also have an indication

Table 5: Two-samples Paired t-test on CLEF 2006 data

		$H_0 : \mu_{mono} = \mu_{bili}$	$H_0 : \mu_{mono} <= \mu_{bili}$	$H_0 : \mu_{mono} => \mu_{bili}$
French	p–value	0.6860	0.3430	0.6570
	outcome	not reject	not reject	not reject
Portuguese	p–value	0.0001	0.0001	0.9999
	outcome	**reject**	**reject**	not reject

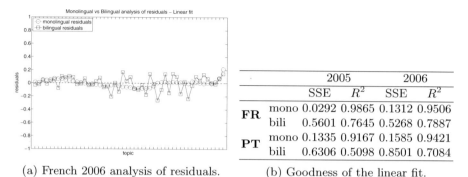

·	2005		2006	
	SSE	R^2	SSE	R^2
FR mono	0.0292	0.9865	0.1312	0.9506
bili	0.5601	0.7645	0.5268	0.7887
PT mono	0.1335	0.9167	0.1585	0.9421
bili	0.6306	0.5098	0.8501	0.7084

(a) French 2006 analysis of residuals.   (b) Goodness of the linear fit.

Fig. 6: Analysis of residuals of linear fitting (monolingual vs bilingual French 2006) and goodness-of-fit measures for all tasks of French (FR) and Portuguese (PT)

of when the monolingual performance is better or worse than the bilingual; for example, for low performances bilingual performs better than monolingual while for high performances monolingual performs better. In Fig. 4 the inter-polation is done on the Portuguese 2006 data. In this case, the interpolating line of the bilingual is clearly below the monolingual one, confirming the test done on the analysis of the means, the output of which was that the mean of the monolingual task was greater than the bilingual one.

Usually, when a linear interpolation is performed, it is important to assess how well the line fits the actual data. This analysis can be done by means of a graphical inspection of the plot of residuals or by means of some measures. In Fig. 6a the analysis of residuals plot is shown for French 2006 data. It is interesting to note how the ordered monolingual performance fits almost perfectly while the bilingual one is evenly distributed around the line. In general, we also noted that the tails of the residuals are usually far from the best fitting line. In Fig. 6b the sum of squares error (SSE) and the squared correlation coefficient (R^2) are shown. The SSE is close to zero both for the monolingual interpolation and the bilingual interpolation, which means a good interpolation. The R^2 is above 0.90 in many cases, which confirms that when the performances are ordered from the worst to the best, the shape of the scatterplot produced is very close to a linear one.

5 Conclusions

In this paper, we proposed a methodology which exploits both statistical anal-yses and graphical tools for the evaluation of MLIA systems. The statistical analysis provides MLIA researchers guidelines to drive the design and devel-opment of the next generation MLIA systems; the graphical tool provides a means to interpret experimental results and to present the results to other research communities easily. We provided concrete examples about how the proposed methodology can be applied by the analysis of the monolingual and bilingual tasks of the CLEF 2005 and 2006 campaigns.

A definition of a more general framework for the statistical analyses of results is one of the points of future work. In particular, we would not like to limit analysis to the situation where there are only two levels of independent variables, but to generalize it with techniques of the analysis of variance. However, this generalization requires a careful study of the not–so–easy situation of having together sets of repeated (an experiment tested on different topics) and paired (monolingual topic vs bilingual topic) measures. When the general framework is clearly defined, we will be able not only to answer questions such as whether monolingual is better than bilingual, but also to study the variability of the performances due to the differences among topics, the variability of performances due to the differences among experiments, as well as the variability of the interaction between these two factors.

References

1. Braschler, M., Di Nunzio, G.M., Ferro, N., Peters, C.: CLEF 2004: Ad Hoc Track Overview and Results Analysis. In: C. Peters, P. Clough, J. Gonzalo, G.J.F. Jones, M. Kluck, B. Magnini (eds.) Multilingual Information Access for Text, Speech and Images: Fifth Workshop of the Cross–Language Evaluation Forum (CLEF 2004) Revised Selected Papers, pp. 10–26. Lecture Notes in Computer Science (LNCS) 3491, Springer, Heidelberg, Germany (2005)
2. Conover, W.J.: Practical Nonparametric Statistics, 1st edn. John Wiley and Sons, New York, USA (1971)
3. Di Nunzio, G.M., Ferro, N.: Appendix A. Results of the Core Tracks and Domain-Specific Tracks. In: C. Peters, V. Quochi (eds.) Working Notes for the CLEF 2005 Workshop. http://www.clef-campaign.org/2005/working_notes/workingnotes2005/appendix_a.pdf [last visited 2007, March 23] (2005)
4. Di Nunzio, G.M., Ferro, N.: Appendix A: Results of the Ad-hoc Bilingual and Monolingual Tasks. In: A. Nardi, C. Peters, J.L. Vicedo (eds.) Working Notes for the CLEF 2006 Workshop. http://www.clef-campaign.org/2006/working_notes/workingnotes2006/Appendix_Ad-Hoc.pdf [last visited 2007, March 23] (2006)
5. Di Nunzio, G.M., Ferro, N., Jones, G.J.F., Peters, C.: CLEF 2005: Ad Hoc Track Overview. In: C. Peters, F.C. Gey, J. Gonzalo, G.J.F. Jones, M. Kluck, B. Magnini, H. Müller, M. de Rijke (eds.) Accessing Multilingual Information Repositories: Sixth Workshop of the Cross–Language Evaluation Forum (CLEF 2005). Revised Selected Papers, pp. 11–36. Lecture Notes in Computer Science (LNCS) 4022, Springer, Heidelberg, Germany (2006)
6. Di Nunzio, G.M., Ferro, N., Mandl, T., Peters, C.: CLEF 2006: Ad Hoc Track Overview. In: A. Nardi, C. Peters, J.L. Vicedo (eds.) Working Notes for the CLEF 2006 Workshop. http://www.clef-campaign.org/2006/working_notes/workingnotes2006/dinunzioOCLEF2006.pdf [last visited 2007, March 23] (2006)

7. European Commission: Commission Recommendation of 24 August 2006 on the digitisation and online accessibility of cultural material and digital preservation. Official Journal of the European Union, OJ L 236, 31.8.2006 **49**, 28–30 (2006)
8. European Commission Information Society and Media: i2010: Digital Libraries. `http://europa.eu.int/information_society/activities/digital_libraries/doc/brochures/dl_brochure_2006.pdf` [last visited 2007, March 23] (2006)
9. Gonzalo, J., Peters, C.: The Impact of Evaluation on Multilingual Text Retrieval. In: R. Baeza-Yates, N. Ziviani, G. Marchionini, A. Moffat, J. Tait (eds.) Proc. 28th Annual International ACM SIGIR Conference on Research and Development in Information Retrieval (SIGIR 2005), pp. 603–604. ACM Press, New York, USA (2005)
10. Hull, D.: Using Statistical Testing in the Evaluation of Retrieval Experiments. In: R. Korfhage, E. Rasmussen, P. Willett (eds.) Proc. 16th Annual International ACM SIGIR Conference on Research and Development in Information Retrieval (SIGIR 1993), pp. 329–338. ACM Press, New York, USA (1993)
11. Judge, G.G., Hill, R.C., Griffiths, W.E., Lütkepohl, H., Lee, T.C.: Introduction to the Theory and Practice of Econometrics, 2nd edn. John Wiley and Sons, New York, USA (1988)
12. Peters, C.: Multilingual Information Access for Digital Libraries: The Impact of Evaluation on System Development. In: C. Thanos (ed.) DELOS Research Activities 2006, pp. 105–107. ISTI-CNR at Gruppo ALI, Pisa, Italy (2006)
13. Tague-Sutcliffe, J.: The Pragmatics of Information Retrieval Experimentation, Revisited. In: K. Spack Jones, P. Willett (eds.) Readings in Information Retrieval, pp. 205–216. Morgan Kaufmann Publisher, Inc., San Francisco, California, USA (1997)
14. Wang, J., Oard, D.W.: Combining Bidirectional Translation and Synonymy for Cross-Language Information Retrieval. In: E.N. Efthimiadis, S. Dumais, D. Hawking, K. Järvelin (eds.) Proc. 29th Annual International ACM SIGIR Conference on Research and Development in Information Retrieval (SIGIR 2006), pp. 202–209. ACM Press, New York, USA (2006)

Index

2DPM, 76

abstract of document, 3
ADMV project, 9
algorithm
  Expectation-Maximization, 67
  Focused Angular Region, 87
  Hyper-linked Induced Topic Search,
    64
annotated object, 125, 126
annotation, 113, 115
  access, 115
  collaborative application, 113
  content enrichment, 113
  data curation, 113
  formal model, 124, 125, 128
  gloss, 117
  historical viewpoint, 117
  learning application, 113
  metadata, 119, 122
  search, 115
  social network, 113
  system viewpoint, 119
  temporal dimension, 129
  user viewpoint, 115
annotation management system, 114,
    119, 121
  FAST, 122
annotation service, 115
  DiLAS, 122
  FAST, 122
annotation viewpoint, 115
associative information retrieval, 5

ATC, 76
Automated Text Categorization, 76
automatic indexing, 7, 13
automatic indexing process, 7
automatic text categorizer, 76
automaton
  finite-state automaton, 65
  stochastic finite-state automaton, 66
auxiliary data, 16
average precision, 34, 72, 174

basis, 44, 46, 49
  basis vector, 44, 48
  representation of a context, 44
Bayes' theorem, 30, 44, 62
Bayesian classifier, 78
benchmark collection, 89
  Reuters, 89
bibliographic document, 3
BIODAS, 121
browsing, 6, 14, 15, 23, 126

catalogue document, 3
categorization
  accuracy, 76
  binary, 77
  multi–label, 77
  one-vs-all, 77
  parameter tuning, 76
  probabilistic model, 76
  single–label, 77
categorization status value, 77
categorization system, 76
categorizer, 77

The Information Retrieval Series